Angular Services

Design state-of-the-art applications with customized Angular services

Sohail Salehi

BIRMINGHAM - MUMBAI

Angular Services

First published: February 2017

Production reference: 1200217

Published by Packt Publishing Ltd.

Livery Place
35 Livery Street
Birmingham
B3 2PB, UK.
ISBN 978-1-78588-261-6

www.packtpub.com

Credits

Author

Sohail Salehi

Reviewer

Phodal Huang

Commissioning Editor

Amarabha Banerjee

Acquisition Editor

Larissa Pinto

Content Development Editor

Samantha Gonsalves

Technical Editor

Anushree Arun Tendulkar

Copy Editor

Safis Editing

Project Coordinator

Devanshi Doshi

Proofreader

Safis Editing

Indexer

Mariammal Chettiyar

Graphics

Jason Monteiro

Production Coordinator

Shraddha Falebhai

About the Author

Sohail Salehi is a veteran developer who recently decided to become a data scientist. He believes when you look at a programming challenge from a data scientist perspective, things started to change slightly and what used to be the ultimate solution, somehow morphs into a stepping stone for what really matters--data.

He won't lay down some tests and codes as soon as a programming challenge is handed to him, rather he has started to think WHY do we need to gather data, WHAT potential value is hidden inside this data and HOW to convert this potential into value that will make business thrive.

Although he has written a couple of other programming books before, *The Sherlock Project* is his first attempt to look at the programming challenge from a different perspective. This story is about discovering hidden values inside data and it is the project that he discusses in this book, *Angular Services*. In the past decade, he worked on some interesting projects with teams of bright developers. But challenges such as handling the traffic for a national newspaper website (*NZ Herald*) or creating a new game for Lotto (*Lotto - 2nd Chance*) are not attractive to him anymore. After he got his first certificate in Machine Learning from University of Washington, he decided to combine his development skills with new concepts that he is discovering in his new professional life and provide creative solutions for daily data-related challenges.

Technical concepts are not his only passion. He is an avid traveler and an adventurous surfer. Currently he lives in Bali, where the big waves are roaring most of the year, and he benefits from the rich Balinese culture and stunning tropical nature, which brings out the best of himself.

I would like to thank the Packt Publishing team for supporting me and giving me the opportunity to write and publish another book. My special thanks to Samantha Gonsalves, who helped me all the way and patiently directed me to the path and the goals we set for this book whenever I was off track.

About the Reviewer

Phodal Huang is a developer, creator, and author. He works for *ThoughtWorks* as a consultant. He currently focuses on IoT and frontend development. He is the author of *Design Internet of Things* and *Growth: Thinking in Full Stack* (in publishing) in Chinese.

He is an open source enthusiast, and has created a series of projects in GitHub. After daily work, he likes to reinvent some wheels for fun. He created the application Growth with Ionic 2 and Angular 2, which is about coaching newbies about programming. You can find out more wheels on his GitHub page, `http://github.com/phodal`.

He loves designing, writing, hacking, traveling, you can also find out more about him on his personal website at `http://www.phodal.com`.

He has reviewed *Learning Internet of Things* and *Design IoT Projects*.

www.PacktPub.com

For support files and downloads related to your book, please visit `www.PacktPub.com`.

Did you know that Packt offers eBook versions of every book published, with PDF and ePub files available? You can upgrade to the eBook version at `www.PacktPub.com` and as a print book customer, you are entitled to a discount on the eBook copy. Get in touch with us at `service@packtpub.com` for more details.

At `www.PacktPub.com`, you can also read a collection of free technical articles, sign up for a range of free newsletters and receive exclusive discounts and offers on Packt books and eBooks.

`https://www.packtpub.com/mapt`

Get the most in-demand software skills with Mapt. Mapt gives you full access to all Packt books and video courses, as well as industry-leading tools to help you plan your personal development and advance your career.

Why subscribe?

- Fully searchable across every book published by Packt
- Copy and paste, print, and bookmark content
- On demand and accessible via a web browser

Customer Feedback

Thanks for purchasing this Packt book. At Packt, quality is at the heart of our editorial process. To help us improve, please leave us an honest review on this book's Amazon page at `https://www.amazon.com/Angular-Services/dp/1785882619`.

If you'd like to join our team of regular reviewers, you can email us at `customerreviews@packtpub.com`. We award our regular reviewers with free eBooks and videos in exchange for their valuable feedback. Help us be relentless in improving our products!

Table of Contents

Preface

I always had a thing for the less traveled roads and it reflects itself in this book, *Angular Services*, as well. When it is about showing the power of front-end frameworks, there are tons of tutorials and contents on how to build To-Do list applications, or time trackers, or any other use cases and path ways which has been explored, explained and exhausted excessively.

What I've aimed for in this book is slightly different. Yes, the subject still Angular Services and we learn about all Angular framework features along the way, but the vehicle is a Machine Learning flavored application called 'The Sherlock Project' which explores:

- Reactive eXtension (rx.js) and observable objects
- The importance of a good Model
- The HTTP requests and how Angular Http module or third party libraries handle it
- The 3 way data-binding offered by the modern noSQL database: Firebase Realtime Database
- Data visualization provided by VizJS

What makes this book different is the use of Regression algorithm to explore major news agency outlets and other online resources, in order to get some insight about a news item. Basically we are using Angular Services as a host to several tools and concepts, so they work together and deliver four main tasks:

- collect data
- analyse and organize keywords
- generate reports for items we are interested in
- and finally evaluate the accuracy of the generated reports

Perhaps that is the main reason that unlike other books, we didn't invest much efforts on how pretty our application looks, rather we focused on what it does and how unique it is. The code is open source and you are most welcome to take it to the next level by adding missing bits and pieces and decorating it with all the pretty bells and whistles that a front-end application deserves.

What this book covers

Chapter 1, Setting Up the Environment, tells you about what you need to get a basic Angular project up and running. The WebStorm IDE (offered by JetBrains) is free for non-commercial use and open source project. The official seed project (offered by Angular team) introduced in this chapter contains all the dependencies (Angular, TypeScript, WebPack and so on) plus the basic components to render a simple page.

Chapter 2, Introducing Wire-Frames, demonstrates the road map we are going to explore for the rest of the book. It explains the components we are going to implement for this project and briefly introduces the services we are going to create to deliver the task of each remaining chapters.

Chapter 3, The Collector Service - Using Controllers to Collect Data, describes the basic Angular concepts like Components, data-binding, decorators and so on during implementation an HTTP service for hitting on RSS outputs and gathering some news. This is where Firebase Realtime Database will be introduced as well and we will see how to use it to record JSON objects as database entries.

Chapter 4, The Rating Service - Data Management, introduces the pipes for the first time and implements a sorting pipe for ordering data in a particular way. In this chapter, we will see how to use TypeScript classes not only to implement Components and Services, but also for creating business logic for models as well.

Chapter 5, The Notifier Service - Creating Cron Jobs in Angular, creates the logic for automated tasks. It will demonstrate a data flow which utilizes the services created in the previous chapters for collecting, rating, and storing qualified news in a list ready to be fetched and notified by the application or later via email. We will see how to implement the helper functions for calculating dates, finding out dated items, and keeping the database clean on each automated job cycle, as well.

Chapter 6, The Evidence Tree Builder Service - Implementing the Business Logic, presents the idea of gathering evidence which supports investigation for the article of our interest. We will study the ways we evaluate an article and how to measure, weigh down, and lift up the value of certain words in any article. We'll learn how to see an article as a bag of words and how to use this concept to calculate. Thus chapter also introduces two major libraries Google Custom Search Engine (CSE) and VisJS for data visualization.

Chapter 7, The Report Generator Service - Creating Controllers to Set Report Template, exposes the possible ways for implementing parent child interaction mechanisms where the child gets data models provided by the parent and fires back requests to the parent. We will learn how to implement components to read the result of previously saved data objects, parse them, and assemble new objects that can be used as building blocks of a report.

Chapter 8, The Accuracy Manager Service - Putting It All Together, implements the cure and prevention codes inside the application and save the programming resources by halting undesired situations. We will learn how to use global variables exported from the application module in order to store local variables and analyze their contents on demand.

What you need for this book

A usual front-end development machine with basic hardware configuration, plus latest stable versions of NodeJS, WebStorm and official Angular seed project is all you need to follow along and implement the concepts introduced in each chapter. The seed project in chapter one, contains all you need to get started. Later in the following chapters, you will need a cloud account (Google account) to benefit from CSE (Custom Search Engine) and Firebase.

Who this book is for

If you are a JavaScript developer who is moving on to Angular and have some experience in developing applications, then this book is for you. You need not have any knowledge of on Angular or its services.

Conventions

In this book, you will find a number of text styles that distinguish between different kinds of information. Here are some examples of these styles and an explanation of their meaning.

Code words in text, database table names, folder names, filenames, file extensions, path names, dummy URLs, user input, and Twitter handles are shown as follows: "The next lines of code read the link and assign it to the to the `BeautifulSoup` function."

A block of code is set as follows:

```
#import packages into the project
from bs4 import BeautifulSoup
from urllib.request import urlopen
import pandas as pd
```

When we wish to draw your attention to a particular part of a code block, the relevant lines or items are set in bold:

```
<head>
<script src="d3.js" charset="utf-8"></script>
  <meta charset="utf-8">
  <meta name="viewport" content="width=device-width">
  <title>JS Bin</title>
</head>
```

When we wish to draw your attention to a particular part of a code block, the relevant lines or items are set in bold: [default] exten => s,1,Dial(Zap/1|30) exten => s,2,Voicemail(u100) exten => s,102,Voicemail(b100) exten => i,1,Voicemail(s0) Any command-line input or output is written as follows:

```
C:\Python34\Scripts> pip install -upgrade pip
C:\Python34\Scripts> pip install pandas
```

New terms and **important words** are shown in bold. Words that you see on the screen, for example, in menus or dialog boxes, appear in the text like this: "In order to download new modules, we will go to **Files | Settings | Project Name | Project Interpreter**."

Warnings or important notes appear in a box like this.

Tips and tricks appear like this.

Reader feedback

Feedback from our readers is always welcome. Let us know what you think about this book-what you liked or disliked. Reader feedback is important for us as it helps us develop titles that you will really get the most out of. To send us general feedback, simply e-mail feedback@packtpub.com, and mention the book's title in the subject of your message. If there is a topic that you have expertise in and you are interested in either writing or contributing to a book, see our author guide at www.packtpub.com/authors.

Customer support

Now that you are the proud owner of a Packt book, we have a number of things to help you to get the most from your purchase.

Downloading the example code

You can download the example code files for this book from your account at `http://www.packtpub.com`. If you purchased this book elsewhere, you can visit `http://www.packtpub.com/support`and register to have the files e-mailed directly to you.

You can download the code files by following these steps:

1. Log in or register to our website using your e-mail address and password.
2. Hover the mouse pointer on the **SUPPORT** tab at the top.
3. Click on **Code Downloads & Errata**.
4. Enter the name of the book in the **Search** box.
5. Select the book for which you're looking to download the code files.
6. Choose from the drop-down menu where you purchased this book from.
7. Click on **Code Download**.

Once the file is downloaded, please make sure that you unzip or extract the folder using the latest version of:

- WinRAR / 7-Zip for Windows
- Zipeg / iZip / UnRarX for Mac
- 7-Zip / PeaZip for Linux

The code bundle for the book is also hosted on GitHub at `https://github.com/PacktPublishing/Angular-Services`. We also have other code bundles from our rich catalog of books and videos available at `https://github.com/PacktPublishing/`. Check them out!

Downloading the color images of this book

We also provide you with a PDF file that has color images of the screenshots/diagrams used in this book. The color images will help you better understand the changes in the output. You can download this file from `https://www.packtpub.com/sites/default/files/downloads/AngularServices_ColorImages.pdf`.

Errata

Although we have taken every care to ensure the accuracy of our content, mistakes do happen. If you find a mistake in one of our books-maybe a mistake in the text or the code-we would be grateful if you could report this to us. By doing so, you can save other readers from frustration and help us improve subsequent versions of this book. If you find any errata, please report them by visiting `http://www.packtpub.com/submit-errata`, selecting your book, clicking on the **Errata Submission Form** link, and entering the details of your errata. Once your errata are verified, your submission will be accepted and the errata will be uploaded to our website or added to any list of existing errata under the Errata section of that title.

To view the previously submitted errata, go to `https://www.packtpub.com/books/content/support`and enter the name of the book in the search field. The required information will appear under the **Errata** section.

Piracy

Piracy of copyrighted material on the Internet is an ongoing problem across all media. At Packt, we take the protection of our copyright and licenses very seriously. If you come across any illegal copies of our works in any form on the Internet, please provide us with the location address or website name immediately so that we can pursue a remedy.

Please contact us at `copyright@packtpub.com` with a link to the suspected pirated material.

We appreciate your help in protecting our authors and our ability to bring you valuable content.

Questions

If you have a problem with any aspect of this book, you can contact us at `questions@packtpub.com`, and we will do our best to address the problem.

1
Setting Up the Environment

The two fundamental questions that one can ask when a new development tool is announced or launched are: how different is the new tool from other competitor tools and how enhanced is it when compared to its own previous versions? If we are going to invest our time in learning a new framework, common sense says we need to ensure that we get a good return on our investment. There are so many good articles out there about the pros and cons of each framework. To me, choosing Angular boils down to the following three aspects:

- **The foundation**: Angular is introduced and supported by **Google** and targeted at *evergreen* modern browsers. This means that we, as developers, don't need to look out for hacky solutions in each browser upgrade anymore. The browser will always be updated to the latest version available, letting Angular worry about the new changes and leaving us out of it. This way, we can focus more on our development tasks.
- **The community**: Think about the community as an asset; the bigger the community, the wider the range of solutions to a particular problem. Looking at the statistics, the Angular community is still way ahead of others, and the good news is that this community is leaning toward being more involved and contributing more on all levels.

- **The solution**: If you look at the previous JS frameworks, you will see most of them focus on solving a problem for a browser first, and then for mobile devices. The argument for that could be simple–JS wasn't meant to be a language for mobile development. However, things have changed to a great extent over recent years and people now use mobile devices more than before. I personally believe that a complex native mobile application, which is implemented in Java or C, is more performant compared to its equivalent implemented in JS, but the thing here is that not every mobile application needs to be complex. So, business owners have started asking questions like *"Why do I need a machine gun to kill a fly?"*

With that question in mind, Angular chose a different approach. It solves the performance challenges faced by mobile devices first. In other words, if your Angular application is fast enough on mobile environments, then it is lightning fast in the *evergreen* browsers.

So, that is what we will do in this chapter:

- First, we will learn about Angular and the main problem it solves
- Then, we will talk a little bit about JavaScript history and the differences between Angular and AngularJS 1
- Next we will introduce *The Sherlock Project*
- Finally, we will install the tools and libraries we need to implement this project.

Introducing Angular

The previous JS frameworks we used had a fluid and easy workflow toward building web applications rapidly. However, as developers, what we are struggling with is technical debt.

In simple words, we could quickly build a web application with an impressive UI, but as the product kept growing and the change requests started kicking in, we had to deal with all maintenance nightmares that forced a long list of maintenance tasks and heavy costs to the business. Basically, the framework that used to be an amazing asset turned into a hairy liability (or technical debt if you like).

One of the major revamps in Angular is the removal of a lot of modules resulting in a lighter and faster core. For example, if you are coming from an Angular 1.x background and don't see `$scope` or `$log` in the new version, don't panic, they are still available to you via other means. There is no need to add overhead to the loading time if we are not going to use all the modules, so taking the modules out of the core results in a better performance.

So, to answer the question, one of the main issues Angular addresses is the *performance issue*. This is done through a lot of structural changes that we will get into over the course of the subsequent chapters.

There is no backward compatibility

To answer this heading, no, we don't have backward compatibility. If you have some Angular projects implemented with the previous version, depending on the complexity of the project, I wouldn't recommend migrating to the new version. Most likely, you will end up hammering a lot of changes into your migrated Angular project and in the end, you will realize it was more cost effective to just create a new project based on Angular from scratch.

Please keep in mind that the previous versions of Angular and Angular share a name, but they have huge differences in their nature and that is the price we pay for a better performance.

Previous knowledge of AngularJS 1.x is not necessary

You might be wondering if you need to know AngularJS 1.x before diving into Angular. Absolutely not. To be more specific, it might be even better if you don't have any experience using Angular at all. This is because your mind wouldn't be preoccupied with obsolete rules and syntax. For example, we will see a lot of annotations in Angular that might make you uncomfortable if you come from an Angular 1 background. Also, there are different types of dependency injections and child injectors, which are totally new concepts introduced in Angular. Moreover, there are new features for templating and data binding, which help to improve loading time by asynchronous processing.

The relationship between ECMAScript, AtScript, and TypeScript

The current edition of **ECMAScript** (**ES5**) is the one that is widely accepted among all well-known browsers. You can think of it as the traditional JavaScript; whatever code is written in ES5 can be executed directly in the browsers.

The problem is that most modern JavaScript frameworks contain features that require more than the traditional JavaScript capabilities. That is the reason ES6 was introduced. With this edition, and any future ECMAScript editions, we will be able to empower JavaScript with the features we need.

Now, the challenge is in running the new code in the current browsers. Most browsers nowadays recognize standard JavaScript codes only. So, we need a mediator to transform ES6 to ES5. That mediator is called a **transpiler** and the technical term for transformations is **transpiling**. There are many good transpilers out there and you are free to choose whatever you feel comfortable with.

Apart from TypeScript, you might want to consider **Babel** (`babeljs.io`) as your main transpiler.

Google originally planned to use **AtScript** to implement Angular; later they joined forces with Microsoft and introduced **TypeScript** as the official transpiler for Angular.

The following figure summarizes the relationship between various editions of ECMAScript, AtScript, and TypeScript.

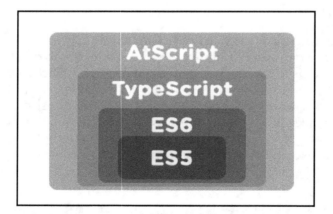

For more details about JavaScript, ECMAScript, and how they evolved during the past decade, visit `https://en.wikipedia.org/wiki/ECMAScript`.

Setting up tools and getting started!

It is important to get the foundation right before installing anything else. Depending on your operating system, install **Node.js** and its package manager, **npm**. You can find a detailed installation manual on the Node.js official website, at `https://nodejs.org/en/`.

 Ensure that both Node.js and npm are installed globally (they are accessible system wide) and have the right permissions.

At the time of writing this book, npm comes with Node.js out-of-the-box. However, in case their policy changes in the future, you can always download the npm and follow the installation process from `https://npmjs.com`.

The next stop would be the IDE; feel free to choose anything that you are comfortable with. Even a simple text editor will do. In this book, I will use WebStorm because of its embedded TypeScript syntax support and Angular features, which speeds up the development process. Moreover, it is lightweight enough to handle the project we are about to develop. You can download it from `https://jetbrains.com/webstorm/download`.

During the first few chapters, we will use simple objects and arrays as placeholders for the data. However, at some stage, we will need to persist the data in our application. This means we need a database. In this book we are going to use Firebase Realtime Database. It is a free NoSQL cloud database provided by Google which come with whatever we need from a real-time and secure database.

For now, just leave the database subject. You don't need to create any connections or database objects for the first few chapters. We will revisit this later in `Chapter 4`, *The Rating Service – Data Management*.

Setting up the seed project

The final requirement to get started would be an Angular seed project to shape the initial structure of our project. If you look at the public source code repositories, you can find several versions of these seeds. I prefer the official one for the following two reasons:

- Custom-made seeds usually come with a personal twist depending on the developers taste. Although sometimes it might be a great help, since we are going to build everything from scratch and learn the fundamental concepts, they are not favorable to our project.

- The official seeds are usually minimal. They are very slim and don't contain an overwhelming amount of 3rd party packages and environmental configurations.

Speaking about packages, you might be wondering what happened to the other JavaScript packages we needed for this application; we didn't install anything other than Node and npm. The next section will answer this question.

Setting up an Angular project in WebStorm

Assuming that you installed WebStorm, fire the IDE and check out a new project from a Git repository.

Now, set the repository URL to `https://github.com/angular/angular2-seed.git` and save the project in a folder called `the sherlock project`, as shown:

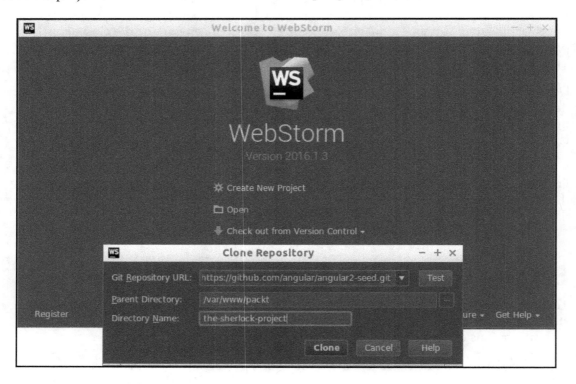

Click on the **Clone** button and open the project in WebStorm. Next, click on the `packages.json` file and observe the dependencies. As you can see, this is a very lean seed with minimal configurations. It contains the Angular release candidate 2, plus the required modules to get the project up and running.

As you see in the following screenshot, apart from main Angular modules, we have the `rxjs` library, which is the *Reactive eXtension for JS* and we will use it for transforming, composing, and querying streams of data.

```
File  Edit  View  Navigate  Code  Refactor  Run  Tools  VCS  Window  Help
the-sherlock-project    package.json
Project                          package.json
the-sherlock-project  /var/www/
  src
    .editorconfig             30      "dependencies": {
    .gitignore                31        "@angular/http": "2.0.0-rc.1",
    LICENSE                   32        "@angular/common": "2.0.0-rc.1",
    package.json              33        "@angular/compiler": "2.0.0-rc.1",
    README.md                 34        "@angular/core": "2.0.0-rc.1",
    tsconfig.json             35        "@angular/platform-browser": "2.0.0-rc.1",
    typings.json              36        "@angular/platform-browser-dynamic": "2.0.0-rc.1",
    webpack.config.js         37        "@angular/platform-server": "2.0.0-rc.1",
  External Libraries          38        "@angular/router": "2.0.0-rc.1",
                              39        "core-js": "^2.2.0",
                              40        "rxjs": "5.0.0-beta.6",
                              41        "zone.js": "~0.6.12"
                              42      },
```

The first thing we need to do is install all the required dependencies defined inside the `package.json` file. Right-click on the file and select the `run npm install` option.

> Please note installing packages using right-click and choosing the installation command is valid inside the IDE only. If you prefer to use the command line, simply use the following command:
> `$ npm install`

Installing the packages for the first time will take a while. In the meantime, explore the `devDependencies` section of `package.json` in the editor. As you see, we have all the required bells and whistles to run the project, including TypeScript and web server to start the development:

```
"devDependencies": {
    "awesome-typescript-loader": "~0.16.2",
    "es6-promise": "3.0.2",
    "es6-shim": "0.35.0",
    "reflect-metadata": "0.1.2",
    "source-map-loader": "^0.1.5",
    "typescript": "~1.8.9",
```

```
    "typings": "~1.0.3",
    "webpack": "^1.12.9",
    "webpack-dev-server": "^1.14.0",
    "webpack-merge": "^0.8.4"
},
```

We also have some nifty scripts defined inside `package.json` that automate useful processes. For example, to start a web server and see the seed in action, we can simply execute the following command in a terminal. (These scripts are shipped with the seed project and they are located inside the `package.json` file, under the `script` property. There is nothing special about them, they are just simple npm commands and you are more than welcome to add your commands if you like):

```
$ npm run server
```

Alternatively, we can right-click on the `package.json` file and select **Show npm Scripts**. This will open another side tab in WebStorm and show all the available scripts inside the current file:

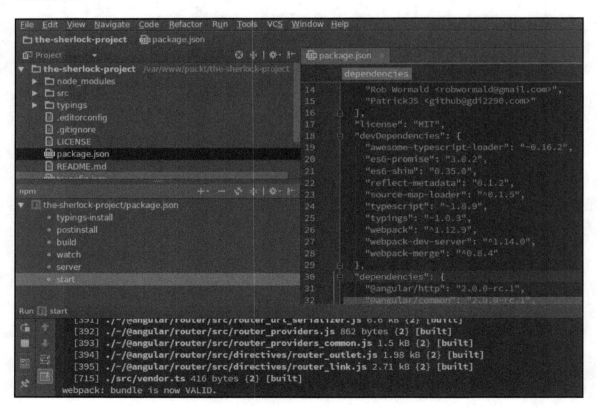

Double-click on the start script and it will run the web server and load the seed application on port `3000`. This means that if you visit `http://localhost:3000`, you will see the seed application in your browser, as illustrated:

> If you are wondering where the port number comes from, look into the `package.json` file and examine the server key under the `scripts` section:
> `"server": "webpack-dev-server --inline --colors --progress --display-error-details --display-cached --port 3000 --content-base src"`

There is one more thing before we move on to the next topic. If you open any `.ts` file, WebStorm will ask you if you want it to transpile the code to JavaScript. If you say `no` once, it will never show up again.

In the following screenshot, below the tabs we can see the question (**Compile TypeScript to JavaScript?**) and possible answers (**OK**, **No**, **Configure**):

```
json package.json  ×   TS app.ts  ×
Compile TypeScript to JavaScript?                                    OK No Configure
1   import {LocationStrategy, HashLocationStrategy} from '@angular/common';
2   import {bootstrap} from '@angular/platform-browser-dynamic';
3   import {provide, enableProdMode} from '@angular/core';
4   import {HTTP_PROVIDERS} from '@angular/http';
5   import {ROUTER_PROVIDERS} from '@angular/router';
```

Choose **No** because we don't need WebStorm to transpile for us because the start script already contains a transpiler that takes care of all the transformations for us.

Frontend developers versus backend developers

Recently, I had an interesting conversation with a couple of colleagues of mine, which is worth sharing here in this chapter. One of them is an avid frontend developer and the other is a seasoned backend developer. You guessed what I'm going to talk about–the debate between backend/frontend developers and who is better. We saw these kind of debates between backend and frontend people in development communities long enough.

However, the interesting thing, which, in my opinion, will show up more often in the next few months (years), is a fading border between the ends (frontend/backend).

It feels like the reason that some traditional frontend developers are holding up their guard against new changes in Angular is not just because the syntax has changed, thus causing a steep learning curve, but mostly because they now have to deal with concepts that have existed natively in backend development for many years. Hence, the reason that backend developers are becoming more open to the changes introduced in Angular is that these changes seem natural to them.

Annotations or child dependency injections, for example, is not a big deal to backenders as much as it bothers the frontenders. I won't be surprised to see a noticeable shift in both the camps in the years to come. Probably, we will see more backenders who are willing to use Angular as a good candidate for some, if not all, of their backend projects and probably we will see more frontenders taking object-oriented concepts and best practices more seriously. Given that JavaScript was originally a functional scripting language, they will probably try to catch up with the other camp as fast as they can.

There is no comparison here and I am not saying which camp has an advantage over the other one. My point is, before modern frontend frameworks, JavaScript was open to be used in a quick and dirty inline script to solve problems quickly.

While this is a very convenient approach, it causes serious problems when you want to scale a web application. Imagine the time and effort you might have to make finding all of those dependent codes and refactoring them to reflect the required changes.

When it comes to scalability, we need a full separation between layers and that requires developers to move away from traditional JavaScript and embrace more OOP best practices in their day-to-day development tasks.

That's what has been practiced in all modern frontend frameworks and Angular takes it to the next level by completely restructuring the **model-view-*** concept and opening doors to the future features, which will eventually be a native part of any web browser.

Introducing The Sherlock Project

During the course of this journey, we will dive into all new Angular concepts by implementing a semi-AI project, called *The Sherlock Project*.

This project will basically be about collecting facts, evaluating and ranking them, and making a decision about how truthful they are.

To achieve this goal, we will implement a couple of services and inject them to the project wherever they are needed. Each chapter will discuss one aspect of the project and will focus on one related service. At the end, all services will come together to act as one big project.

Summary

This chapter covered a brief introduction to Angular. We saw where Angular comes from, what problems it will solve, and how we can benefit from it.

We talked about the project that we will be creating with Angular. We also saw which other tools are needed for our project and how to install and configure them. Finally, we cloned an Angular seed project, installed all its dependencies, and started a web server to examine the application output in a browser.

In the next chapter, we will create all the required wireframes for this project and use them as a base structure for the rest of the book.

2

Introducing Wire-Frames

In this chapter, we are going to create all wire-frames for this project. Each wire-frame here is a simple component and a template with minimum code. We are not going to create major business logic here. There are just blueprints to clarify the road map for this project. So wire-frames are the very basic foundations for the business logic that we are going to create and the layout that we are going to show to the user.

As we discuss the wire-frames and later implement them in the chapters to come, we will walk through the eight fundamental concepts in Angular in this chapter. These concepts are:

- Modules
- Components
- Templates
- Metadata
- Data Binding
- Directive
- Services
- Dependency Injection

What is a module?

The short answer is: every class you create in Angular is a module. The contents of a module could be anything. It could be a component, a service, a simple piece of data, and even they could be a library of other modules. They might look different, but they share one purpose: modules bring (export) one piece of functionality to the Angular projects.

Creating Angular projects in a modular fashion makes the testing and maintenance tasks easy and helps the scalability in the future. However, you are not limited to an Angular modular approach and you can use your own style.

Later in this chapter, we will see that there is an export keyword in front of each class keyword:

```
export class MyClassName{}
```

This is how Angular shares the logic inside that module (class) with the rest of the project. To use this module in other parts of a project, we just need to import it. Imagine the preceding code is saved inside a file named: `myclassname.ts`. To use that module in another module we will import it at top of the code as follows:

```
import './myclassname';
```

Please note that we don't need to mention the file format (`.ts`) while importing them.

Components – the reusable objects

Components in Angular 2 are building blocks that address and provide solutions for different concerns in a web app. If we can solve one problem in one component, it means we can use that same component later in other parts of the current project or other projects. They are usually used to handle a part of a view (an HTML template). So if we create a component for a progress bar, we can use it later anywhere in the project where we need it. We can use components in other projects as well. For example, a component for a navigation bar that is created in one project, can be imported and be used in other projects in the future.

Components are basically nothing more than a class, with a bunch of methods, properties, and other usual codes. Inside the seed project that we set up in the previous chapter, open the `src/app/about/about.ts` file, and observe the code:

```
// src/app/about/about.ts
import {Component} from '@angular/core';
@Component({
  selector: 'about',

  styleUrls: ['./about.css'],
```

```
    templateUrl: './about.html'
})
export class About {

}
```

Looking at this file, we can immediately notice two things:

- In this project, all classes (modules) are written in TypeScript (.ts files)
- Inside a component we have the required code to deal with the template (about.html and html.css), the data, and how the view should behave based on the provided logic

A component is a TypeScript class, which handles views via a provided template, data, and the logic. We will see how to build the component from scratch in the next section. For now, go ahead and delete everything inside the app/ folder. Yes, all the contents of the about/, home/ and github/ folders. Don't worry; we will be recreating them soon.

The root component

In this book, we will have a couple of components and services that will work together to achieve a goal. But we need a root component to act as a communication center between all these players. This root component will control the application flow. Let's start by creating this component:

1. Inside the WebStorm IDE, open the app.ts file, and notice the export line:

   ```
   export class AppComponent {}
   ```

2. As we saw before, the export keyword simply indicates that we are willing to share this class with every other player in the project. In other words, if anyone needs this class, they just need to import it in their own body.
3. The plan is to make the AppComponent class as the root component for our project, that is why we have the Component function imported from the Angular2 core module:

   ```
   import {Component} from 'angular2/core';
   export class Sherlock {}
   ```

4. This code should be self explanatory. Normally each import command has two main parameters. First we need to mention the name of the function we are interested in – Component – and then we should indicate the module we want to grab it from – angular2/core.

 If you just mention the module name without any specific function, everything in that class will be imported.

6. Importing a module is not enough and it doesn't turn our AppComponent class into a component. We need to use a decorator to declare the app.ts file as a component. A decorator contains some meta-data that defines the nature of a class and how it is going to do it.

7. In this example, we are using the Component function, which we imported earlier. This function accepts an object that defines how things will be done inside the app component:

```
// src/app/app.ts
import {Component} from 'angular2/core';
@Component({
  selector: 'app',
  templateUrl: './app.html'
})
```

8. The first property inside the @Component decorator is a selector. Basically, it is a CSS selector, which means whatever is assigned to this property will become a valid HTML tag later. In other words, it is perfectly fine to have a custom tag like <app></app> in your HTML template. The templateUrl property contains the path and the file for this Component's template.

9. Having these properties in place, let's have a look at the app.html file:

```
# src/app/app.html
<h3>
  Angular 2 Seed
</h3>
<nav>
  <a [routerLink]="['/']">Home</a>
  <a [routerLink]="['/about']">About</a>
  <a [routerLink]="['/github','angular']">Github Repos</a>
</nav>
<main>
  <router-outlet></router-outlet>
</main>
```

10. This file is the place where we define all basic structure for our application. Since we removed all previous folders, we can replace the header and the navigation tags with the following:

```
<h1>The Sherlock Project</h1>
```

Updating the Bootstrap file

Now before checking the results in the browser, there are a few updates that we need to do. First, open the `app.modules.ts` file inside the `src/app` folder and notice the import lines. The red color for the imported class means it does not exist:

```
import {About} from './about/about';
```

That is right, because we removed all previous definitions in the seed project, so remove all troubled lines. That includes the following imports:

```
import {About} from './about/about';
import {Home} from './home/home';
import {RepoBrowser} from './github/repo-browser/repo-browser';
import {RepoList} from './github/repo-list/repo-list';
import {RepoDetail} from './github/repo-detail/repo-detail';
```

 Please notice that we don't need to mention the extension (`.ts`) for the file we are importing.

When you do so, the 'Declarations' start to complain. So remove all missing elements from that line, too. After all of these changes, the `app.modules.ts` should look as follows:

```
// src/app/app.module.ts
import {NgModule} from '@angular/core'
import {RouterModule} from "@angular/router";
import {rootRouterConfig} from "./app.routes";
import {AppComponent} from "./app";
import {FormsModule} from "@angular/forms";
import {BrowserModule} from "@angular/platform-browser";
import {HttpModule} from "@angular/http";
import {LocationStrategy, HashLocationStrategy}
    from '@angular/common';

@NgModule({
  declarations: [AppComponent],
  imports     : [BrowserModule, FormsModule, HttpModule,
```

```
        RouterModule.forRoot(rootRouterConfig)],

    providers    : [{provide: LocationStrategy,
        useClass: HashLocationStrategy}],

    bootstrap    : [AppComponent]
})
export class AppModule {

}
```

Now let's take a step back and look into the `NgModule()` function. As you can see, we imported this function from the core module, and as its name suggests, we use it to define modules. You might ask since a Component and a Module both are TypeScript classes, what is the difference between these two? You can consider Modules as a container to organize other building blocks in Angular 2. So it is safe to say a Module is bigger than a Component and it has more sophisticated functions and decorators to serve specific purposes. Perhaps the most significant feature of a module is the mechanism that it uses to bootstrap an application.

Look at the bootstrap key inside the `@NgModule()` function. This is where we define the entry point to our application. We will talk about it in more details in the following section.

Next, open the `index.html` at the root of the project and notice the `<app>` tag in it:

```
<app>
  Loading...
</app>
```

In Angular vocabulary, this tag is called a directive and it is the same selector property that we have defined inside our App component. It is like a place holder for the template assigned to the App component.

The last file that we need to update is the `app.routes.ts`, which contains all the routes for the previous menu system. Since we removed home, about, and GitHub components any reference to them will cause errors. So remove all references, and at the end of the file it should look as follows:

```
// src/app/app.routes.ts
import {Routes} from '@angular/router';
export const rootRouterConfig: Routes = [];
```

Running the web server

To see these updates in the browser, first run the web server in the background. Open a new terminal window – or use the embedded terminal in WebStorm IDE – and run the following command:

```
$ npm run server
```

It will take a few moments to build the app in the background and run the web server. Once the web server is up and running, open a browser window and visit the `http://localhost:3000`.

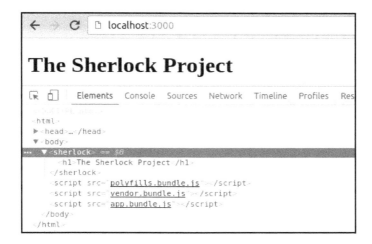

Now if you inspect the code inside the browser, you will notice the new `<app>` tag in the page

Bootstrapping versus root component

You might ask why we need a bootstrap file to load the root component? Couldn't we have the root component in charge of loading everything itself? The answer is yes, we could. But, the good thing about having a bootstrap is better isolation, and as a result, better separation of concerns. Look at all those JavaScript files included in the `index.html` and compare it to the contents of `app.html`:

```
# index.html
<!DOCTYPE html>
<html>
```

```
<head>
  <!-- head contents -->
</head>
<body>
  <app>
    Loading...
  </app>
  <script src="polyfills.bundle.js"></script>
  <script src="vendor.bundle.js"></script>
  <script src="app.bundle.js"></script>
</body>
</html>

# app/app.html
<h1>The Sherlock Project</h1>
```

Having a bootstrap in a project gives us more flexibility on the environmental and the browser settings and leaves the actual project code lean and clean. For example, if we need a routing system in our application, it will be better to load it inside the bootstrap rather than adding it manually to each component.

The big picture

Now that we have the root component in place, we can add all wire-frames for this project:

```
The Sherlock Project
|- Collector
|- Rating
|- Notifier
|- Evidence
|- AI
|- Report
|- Autopilot
'- Accuracy
```

Each wire-frame introduced here represents one of the chapters for the remainder of this book. They will have different functionality, UI, inputs and outputs, but they will have one thing in common. The root Component – AppComponent – connects them all together and will be in charge of loading and navigating through the appropriate page.

Please keep in mind that what we will create here is just a simple blueprint for coming chapters, that's why we call them wire-frame. As we go through each chapter, we will take each of these wire-frames and enhance them by adding proper services, data, templates, and so on.

The navigation system

Before continuing to implement wire-frames, let's put the navigation system in place. For now we are going to create a navigation bar with options for Chapters 3 to 10. However, you might have noticed that Chapter 5, *The Notifier Service – Creating Cron Jobs in Angular*, needs a different type of UI and putting it inside a menu item doesn't make sense. That makes perfect sense, but for now we tend to keep things as simple as possible. The objective for assigning each chapter to a menu item is for easier demonstration only. Once we have all components, services, and their functionality in place, we can review the whole UI and modify it to a better one.

The Angular router module

All routing features in Angular 2 are available inside the angular2/router module. So if we load it inside the bootstrap-er we can access all of those features through any component in this project. The Angular 2 seed project has already provided the required configurations and we don't need to do anything. But to see how it is done, let's checkout the index.html file and follow the references over there. Open the index.html and notice the JavaScript files included there:

```
# index.html
    <script src="polyfills.bundle.js"></script>
    <script src="vendor.bundle.js"></script>
    <script src="app.bundle.js"></script>
```

The files we are interested in are vendor.bundle.js and app.bundle.js. It seems that they should be at the same place where index.html exists, but there is no sign of them.

We talked about what is happening here in Chapter 1, *Setting Up the Environment*. As a reminder, please keep in mind that .ts files should be TRANSPILED into .js files before a browser can recognize and execute them, because TypeScript is the JavaScript from the future.

We have already seen what is inside the app.modules.ts and we know it is a bootstrap-er for our project. Have a look inside the vendor.browser.ts file:

```
// Angular 2
import '@angular/platform-browser-dynamic';
import '@angular/platform-browser';
import '@angular/core';
import '@angular/http';
import '@angular/router';
```

As you can see, the real magic happens here. All required modules to make Angular dance to our project demands are imported here, and of course the last line indicates that we are willing to use routing features in our application. So having all Angular bells and whistles bootstrapped, let's see how we can use them.

Routing configuration

The first step to use routing in any component is importing the required functions. We know the required modules have been bootstrapped already, so open the `app.routes.ts` file and notice the Routes function:

```
// app/app.routes.ts
import {Routes} from '@angular/router';

export const rootRouterConfig: Routes = [];
```

This is where we can define an array of route objects for our project. We will come to this later and will fill it up with proper configuration data after we have created a few components for our wire-frames.

The navigation bar template

To simplify the theming process, we will use CSS files from the Twitter Bootstrap framework. So head to: `http://getbootstrap.com/getting-started/` and from the CDN grab the bootstrap css files only. We don't need optional themes or JavaScript files.

Bootstrap CDN

The folks over at MaxCDN graciously provide CDN support for Bootstrap's CSS and JavaScript. Just use these Bootstrap CDN links.

```
<!-- Latest compiled and minified CSS -->
<link rel="stylesheet" href="https://maxcdn.bootstrapcdn.com/bootstrap/3.3.6/css/bootstrap.min.css" integrity="sha384-1q8mTJOASx8j1Au+a5WDVnPi21lkFfwwEAa8hDDdjZlpLegxhjVME1fgjWPGmkzs7" crossorigin="anonymous">

<!-- Optional theme -->
<link rel="stylesheet" href="https://maxcdn.bootstrapcdn.com/bootstrap/3.3.6/css/bootstrap-theme.min.css" integrity="sha384-fLW2N01lMqjakBkx3l/M9EahuwpSfeNvV63J5ezn3uZzapT0u7EYsXMjQV+0En5r" crossorigin="anonymous">

<!-- Latest compiled and minified JavaScript -->
<script src="https://maxcdn.bootstrapcdn.com/bootstrap/3.3.6/js/bootstrap.min.js" integrity="sha384-0mSbJDEHialfmuBBQP6A4Qrprq5OVfW37PRR3j5ELqxss1yVqOtnepnHVP9aJ7xS" crossorigin="anonymous"></script>
```

Copy

Open the `index.html` and reference the CSS file over there:

```
#index.html
#...
    <!-- Latest compiled and minified CSS -->
    <link rel="stylesheet" href=
"https://maxcdn.bootstrapcdn.com/bootstrap/3.3.6/css/bootstrap.min.css"
crossorigin="anonymous">
```

Having the styles in place now we can use them to create the menu. We can hard-code the navigation template into `app/app.html` and set a menu item for each chapter. But since we know how components work, let's create a component for it.

 If you look at the package.json, you will see bootstrap has been already defined as part of this project's dependencies and if you check the node_moduules/bootstrap folder at the root of the project, you will see the bootstrap contents over there. But I highly recommend using CDNs at any chance you get. It improves the performance in your projects.

The navigation component

Start by creating the required folder and TypeScript class for the navigation component:

1. Right-click on the app folder and choose the new TypeScript file and enter this path and filename over there: `app/navigation/navigation.component.ts`.

2. Add the following contents in this class:

```
// app/navigation/navigation.component.ts
import {Component} from '@angular/core';

@Component({
  selector: 'sh-nav',
  templateUrl: './navigation.html'
})
export class NavigationComponent {}
```

3. Now create the template for navigation and add the following menu items to it:

```
# app/navigation/navigation.html
<ul class="nav nav-pills">
  <li role="presentation"><a href="#">Collector</a></li>
  <li role="presentation"><a href="#">Rating</a></li>
  <li role="presentation"><a href="#">Notifier</a></li>
  <li role="presentation"><a href="#">Evidence</a></li>
```

```
    <li role="presentation"><a href="#">AI</a></li>
    <li role="presentation"><a href="#">Report</a></li>
    <li role="presentation"><a href="#">Auto Pilot</a></li>
    <li role="presentation"><a href="#">Accuracy</a></li>
</ul>
```

The basic navigation component is ready. Let's see how we can use it in the root component.

Importing and using the navigation component

To use the navigation component, first we need to inform the root component about its existence:

1. Open `app/app.ts` and first import the `nav` component and then add a new directive for navigation inside the `@Component` decorator:

```
// app/app.ts
import {Component} from '@angular/core';
import {Routes} from '@angular/router';
import {NavigationComponent} from
"./navigation/navigation.component";

@Component({
  selector: 'app',
  templateUrl: './app/app.html',
  directives: [NavigationComponent]
})

export class AppComponent {
}
```

Directives and components are two different building blocks (refer to the beginning of this chapter to see all eight building blocks in Angular). So the important question here is why are we using directives property to import a component?

The fact is in Angular projects, both directives and components are serving the same purpose. They are both created to modify DOM elements and add new features to them. The only difference is a component has a template, but a directive doesn't.

For that reason, inside a `@Component()` decorator we can use directives: property to import both components and directives.

1. Next we need to declare this new component in our bootstrapper. So open the app.modules.ts file and add the new `NavigationComponent` under the declare key as follows:

```
// src/app/app.modue.ts
import {NavigationComponent} from
"./navigation/navigation.component";
//...
@NgModule({
  declarations: [AppComponent, NavigationComponent],
  //...
})
export class AppModule {
}
```

2. Now we have access to the selector defined in the navigation component. So open app.`html` and add the following line to it:

```
<h1>The Sherlock Project</h1>
<sh-nav></sh-nav>
```

We don't need to worry about the look for now as it will be replaced by proper UI items as we complete each chapter.

Those navigation bar items are plain HTML tags that do nothing. Let's create a few components for each item and assign it to them.

The collector wire-frame

This application is about investigating articles and news and finding the truth about them. So as the very first step we need to find them. The Collector's task is to fetch original news or articles from the given sources and organize them based on our desired format. The news/articles source could be anything. It could be a plain URL, an XML file, or simply a keyword which we can search to find related news. That means the user interface for the Collector will contain a couple of input boxes to enter a URL, RSS feeds or trending keywords, and a submit button.

Depending on the entry, we need a logic (we will see it will be a service) which processes the request, fetches the contents, figures out the title, body, the news source and the URL for each content, and saves them into a database table for future usage. The following diagram describes the work-flow in the Collector:

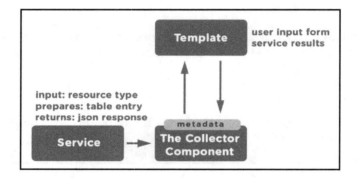

The collector component

Looking at the preceding diagram, it indicates that we need a component to provide a view and call a service upon user input:

1. So right-click on the /app folder and create a new TypeScript file.

Mentioning the folder name in front of the TypeScript file will create that folder as well.

2. As we know, this TypeScript file is going to be a component. So import the required module and add metadata properties as follows:

```
// app/collector/collector.component.ts
import {Component} from '@angular/core';
@Component({
  selector: 'sh-collector',
  templateUrl: 'app/collector/collector.html'
})
export class CollectorComponent {}
```

The sh-collector (sh as in sherlock) is the HTML element that we can refer to anywhere we need this component. In other words, anywhere we use the `<sh-collector></sh-collector>` tag the contents of the Collector template will be inserted there. But currently we don't have any templates.

3. So create the `collector/collector.html` file and add the following contents to it:

```
<h4>Collector's placeholder</h4>
```

Instead of `templateUrl`, we can use the template property and put the template directly inside the following component:

```
@Component({
  selector: 'sh-collector',
  templateUrl: '<h4>Collector's placeholder</h4>'
})
```

But as the template grows, the component class loses its readability. So it is better to have separate template files for big projects.

So now we have a new `CollectorComponent` with a valid template. Let's put it into a test and checkout the result inside the browser.

Accessing a component via root

In order to use the collector component inside the root component (`app.ts`) we need to inform the root about it. So declare the CollectorComponent inside the app.modules.ts.

 Notice that as soon as you add the `CollectorComponent` in the declarations array, WebStorm IDE imports the related class automatically.

If you are not using WebStorm, you need to manually import the `collector.component.ts` into the root otherwise you will get an error later:

```
// src/app/app.ts
//...
import {CollectorComponent}from "./collector/collector.component";
//...
```

Also don't forget to declare the new component in the module file:

```
// src/app/app.modue.ts
import {CollectorComponent} from "./collector/collector.component";
//...
@NgModule({
  declarations: [AppComponent, NavigationComponent, CollectorComponent],
  //...
})
export class AppModule {
}
```

Now that we have the Collector component imported, we have access to its selector. To prove that, edit the app.html as follows and check the result in the browser:

```
# src/app/app.html
<h1>The Sherlock Project</h1>
<sh-nav></sh-nav>
<sh-collector></sh-collector>
```

What is happening here is, Angular loads the root template (`app.html`) and looks into the available selectors. Because the `<sh-collecotr>` tag belongs to the Collector component, it looks into the templates and as a result, loads the contents from `collector.html`.

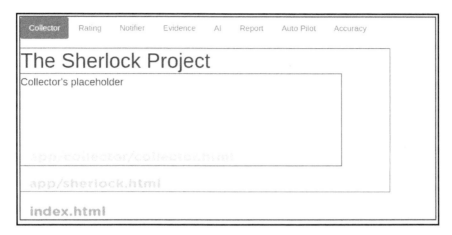

We have a functioning Collector component and a blue print for developing business logic behind it. Don't worry about the service and implementing the collecting/organizing mechanism. We will spend a whole chapter on that. Let's move on to the next wire-frame.

The other concern is hard coding the new component into the root component. Probably we don't want to do that. What would best suit us is loading the component's template dynamically, based on the selected menu item. We will get to that soon after adding a few more components.

The rating wire-frame

Collecting articles and news is not enough and we want to know which entry has the highest score for investigation. The question is how do we rate them and what measures and factors should we use in our rating mechanism.

Initially, we can come up with some basic rules. For example, if the source of the news or article is a well known news agency, we should give them a different rank compared to the articles coming from a personal web log. Or if the news title has some trending keywords – which we can find from Google Trends, for example – then we should give them a higher rank compared to general and bland titles.

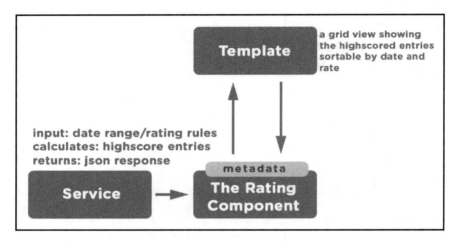

Also the date of the entry matters, too. We don't want to waste our resources on investigating old news. So everything about an entry counts.

Once again, we will spend a whole chapter on dealing with all of these business rules. For now let's just create the Rating component and modify the root component so it can recognize it.

The rating component

Like before, create a new TypeScript class in app/rating/rating.component.ts and add the following contents to it:

```
// app/rating/rating.component.ts
import {Component} from '@angular/core';

@Component({
  selector: 'sh-rating',
  templateUrl: './app/rating/rating.html'
})
export class RatingComponent {}
```

The naming convention for TypeScript classes is simple. It follows `filename.type.ts`, where type reveals the nature of the file. For example, for components and services we use `filename.component.ts` and `filename.service.ts`, respectively.

You can add place holder contents in the `rating.html` file and import and test the new component in the root like before.

The notifier wire-frame

The Notifier is a little bit more sophisticated. It will use the Collector service to collect and the rating service to rate the collected items, and it does this job automatically in specific hours. It is like implementing a Linux cron job inside Angular.

Please note we don't need the Collector and the Rating components for this wire-frame. Rather we need the mechanism that does the collecting and rating tasks. This situation should explain the difference between directives and components and the importance of each concept better. In `Chapter 5`, *The Notifier Service- Creating Cron Jobs in Angular* where we implement the service for this business logic – we will deal with the details of this requirement. There we will also discuss the dependency injection and child injectors in more details.

Let's say we want to be informed twice a day about all news which has a minimum rank of 8/10. Moreover, let's assume we want to be notified via e-mail and also we want to see a daily/weekly/monthly graph that demonstrates alerting keywords and news.

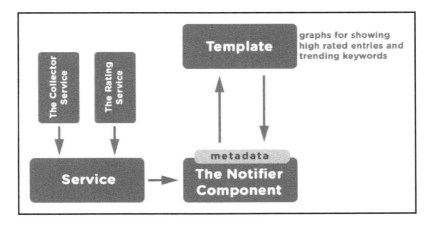

The notifier component

There is nothing special about creating this component. As usual, create the folder and the TypeScript and the HTML files and fill them up with the basic contents. However, let's discuss another Angular concept here and see how we can implement it in this component.

As we will see in the coming chapters, sometimes we need to send data from a component to the template, or from a template to a component, or even in both directions simultaneously. This is called data binding and Angular provides 1-way and 2-way data binding.

Let's start with the simplest form of data binding. Imagine in our Notifier component – via a service – we get some information from Collector and Rating services and save them in some private variables. Now we need a mechanism to pass the contents of those variables into the Notifier template. First create the private variables in the `NotifierComponent` class and initialize them with some strings. We don't need to worry about calling actual services to initialize them for now:

```
// app/notifier/notifier.component.ts
import {Component} from '@angular/core';

@Component({
  selector: 'sh-notifier',
  templateUrl: './app/notifier/notifier.html'
})

export class NotifierComponent {
  data = {
    collector: "collecting data",
    rating: "rating data"
  };
}
```

Now create the template with the following contents:

```
# app/notifier/notifier.html
<div class="container">
  <h5>{{data.collector}}</h5>
  <h5>{{data.rating}}</h5>
</div>
```

 Double curly braces means interpolation. In other words, {{data.collector}} means: look into the NotifierComponent class and find the data object and whatever is saved in its collector property and show it here.

You can check the result by adding the `<sh-notifier></sh-notifier>` selector to `sherlock.html` and visiting the page in the browser.

Passing data from a component to the template in this way is called property binding. Later we will replace hard coded values in each property with the returned values from actual child services

Updating the navigation system

So far we have created one root component, three components for the wire-frames, and one component for navigation system. Now it is the right time to take hard coded values out of the root template and replace them with actual routes. We are going to put the Android router module in charge of updating the view based on the selected menu item.

Before changing anything, click on any link in the navigation bar and notice the "loading…" message. The current `<a href="#">` in each menu item, refreshes the whole page and completely reloads `index.html` every time. This is not ideal. The goal is to update a specific area of the index page with the view of a component associated with the menu item.

 Applications that update only a specific part of a screen are called SPA (Single Page Application) and they are very efficient in terms of reducing loading time. All page contents will be loaded and cached once and later requesting any page will be done in the background asynchronously.

Single Page Application

The idea behind creating SPA was to provide a better user experience by reducing the number of un-necessary requests to some page elements. Take Gmail, for example. Imagine how annoying it would be if, by clicking on each e-mail, the whole page would go blank and all the headers sidebars, and footers would reload again. Instead, when we click on an e-mail only the content section of the page will be replaced by the contents of the selected e-mail.

It is safe to say, SPA is a good solution for highly responsive applications. It is fast, clean, and gives the users exactly what they are looking for. Having said that, we should be very cautious about the loop wholes shipped with this solution. Back to the Gmail example, have you experienced working with Gmail on slow connections? It automatically offers the 'basic html' e-mail (in some rare occasions it freezes). The reason is SPA usually grows to an optimal size and when it hits that threshold it causes long delays. The details on cons and pros of this solution is beyond the scope of this book, but we can mention issues such as security measures, forcing the client to have JavaScript enabled, memory leaks, and so on. Yet we cannot deny the convenience that Single Page Applications provide.

The moral of the story is this: if you have an application idea that is not going to bombard servers with tons of background requests and doesn't need some sort of unusual security measures then go for an SPA solution.

Switching to SPA

To turn this application into an SPA, follow these steps:

1. Open app.routes.ts, import all components, and then define routes for each component as follows:

```
// src/app/app.routes.ts
import {Routes} from '@angular/router';
import {CollectorComponent} from "./collector/collector.component";
import {RatingComponent} from "./rating/rating.component";
import {NotifierComponent} from "./notifier/notifier.component";

export const rootRouterConfig: Routes = [
  {path: '', redirectTo: 'collector', pathMatch: 'full'},
  {path: 'collector', component: CollectorComponent},
  {path: 'rating', component: RatingComponent},
  {path: 'notifier', component: NotifierComponent}
];
```

Now notice the array of objects that were passed to the Routes variable. The first property is path: and it is indicating the URL that will be displayed in the browser address bar. The second property is the component and it associates the template of the current component to the current URL.

2. Now remove all hard coded directives from app.html and update it as follows:

```
<h1>The Sherlock Project</h1>
<sh-nav></sh-nav>
<router-outlet></router-outlet>
```

If you wonder where this <router-outlet> comes from, look into the 'imports' definition inside the `app.modules.ts` file. The RouterOutlet's job is simple. It shows the template associated with each link inside the `<router-outlet>` directive.

However, if you click on any menu item, nothing happens. We need to do one more step and BIND the content of each component's view to the DOM element. Remember, as we mentioned before, one of the ways that we can talk to DOM is via property binding.

3. Open the `navigation.html` template and replace all anchor tags with the following properties:

```
<ul class="nav nav-pills">
    <li role="presentation"><a
[routerLink]="['/collector']">Collector</a></li>
    <li role="presentation"><a
[routerLink]="['/rating']">Rating</a></li>
    <li role="presentation"><a
[routerLink]="['/notifier']">Notifier</a></li>
    <li role="presentation"><a
[routerLink]="['/evidence']">Evidence</a></li>
    <li role="presentation"><a [routerLink]="['/ai']">AI</a></li>
    <li role="presentation"><a
[routerLink]="['/report']">Report</a></li>
    <li role="presentation"><a [routerLink]="['/autopilot']">Auto
Pilot</a></li>
    <li role="presentation"><a
[routerLink]="['/accuracy']">Accuracy</a></li>
</ul>
```

Here we are binding the templates assigned to each path to the Angular router. Now if you click on any link, the related template will be displayed inside the <router-outlet> directive.

Now that the navigation system is in place, let's finish the rest of the wire-frames for our project.

The Evidence Tree Builder Wire-frame

As part of investigation, we need to collect the evidence related to the article of our interest. The tricky part is how much evidence are we willing to collect?

Search any keywords in Google and you will get zillions of results. Obviously we don't want to include all of them. We need a business rule to filter out the irrelevant results and choose – let's say – up to 10 relevant evidences for each main node and five evidences for each branch. It is totally up to us how deep we want that tree to be. But let's start simple and add more complexity to it as we proceed.

We need to persist the nodes and branches to the database, and before that we need to create a specific document that can handle all relevant evidence. These will all be defined as child services for this component.

The other important factor here is showing the results in an interactive way. All inspectors used to have an investigation board that they pinned the related photos, papers, and so on and connected them via threads. In Chapter 6, *The Evidence Tree Builder Service – Implementing the Business Logic*, we will implement a service to create a mindmap with interactive nodes from the collected evidence. We will use the new Angular Animation framework for visual effects.

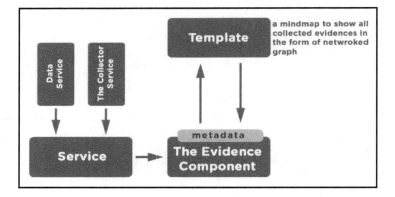

The Evidence component

The Evidence component shell doesn't have anything significant. Go ahead and follow the same pattern to create the folder, the .ts file, and .html file for this component:

```
// app/evidence/evidence.component.ts
import {Component} from '@angular/core';
@Component({
  selector: 'sh-collector',
  templateUrl: './app/evidence/evidence.html'
})
export class EvidenceComponent {}
```

Don't forget to update the root component (sherlock.ts). Import the Evidence component, and then update the directives and routes as well:

```
// app/sherlock.ts
//...
import {EvidenceComponent} from "./evidence/evidence.component";

@Component({
  selector: 'sherlock-app',
  templateUrl: './app/sherlock.html',
  directives: [
    //...
      EvidenceComponent
  ]
})
@Routes([
  //...
  {path: '/evidence', component: EvidenceComponent},
])
export class Sherlock {}
```

The AI Wire-frame

This is the brain of our application. After all of the collecting, rating, and so on, it is time for decision making. We need an Artificial Intelligence mechanism to observe the inputs and find the answer to a question or simply make a statement for the provided news or article.

To find the answer, we can look into the evidence tree, and depending on the tree's depth, ask a couple of yes/no questions. Again, we need to define some business rules for our questions, and then weight the value of their answers.

To expand it a little more, imagine we have some news and we ask a fundamental question about it. Then we build an evidence tree with a three level depth. The number of evidence for the main node is 10 so we need to find out if each piece of evidence supports our question? (the answer is yes) Is it against our evidence? (which means the answer is no). Or is it neutral? Then we add the value of the answers (each yes has the value of +1, no = -1, and neutral answers are 0). If the total sum is a positive number then the answer to the question at that level is yes, if it is negative the answer is no, and if it is zero, the answer is NA.

Then we repeat the same process for the evidences at the next level in the tree. Depending on the depth of our tree and the strength of the answer we get at each level, we can make a decision and answer the fundamental questions asked about the selected news.

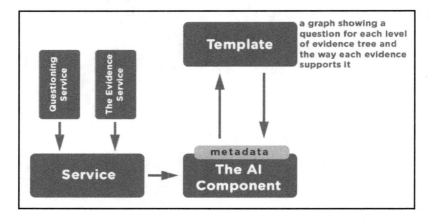

The AI Component

I believe by following the same pattern we have seen before, you can create the component and its template for AI. So to save some space, for the remaining components I won't include the code. You can refer to the code repository for this project and see the complete code for this chapter here:
https://github.com/Soolan/the-sherlock-project

The Report Generator Wire-frame

It is nice to have a report page showing all statistics about the news of our interest. A page with strong visuals that contains charts showing a number of evidence, answers, AI results, and so on.

This wire-frame would be a good place to introduce some third-party Angular modules and how to benefit from them for implementing a better user experienc

The Auto-pilot Wire-frame

After creating all required components and services, it is good to have a component that automates the whole process. In other words, we just need to create a configuration file that defines how each component should behave and feed it to the auto-pilot. Then by pushing a single button, it will collect, rate, notify, build an evidence tree, and make decisions about the selected news.

The auto-pilot will integrate all previous services in one big workflow. So we need a special template for it. That template should contain two progress bar components: one for overall progress and the other for the progress in the current step.

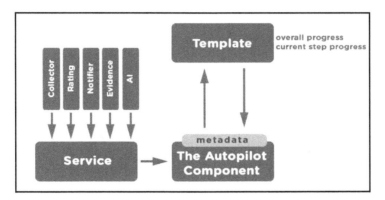

The Accuracy Manager Wire-frame

We can not solidly rely on our AI component only. It is good to have a feedback mechanism to evaluate the result of our AI mechanism after a specific time-frame. When we get fresh news to investigate and find the answer to a fundamental question for that news, normally we need to wait for a couple of days (or week's maybe) for the truth to be revealed.

Then we can compare our AI results with the truth and find out how accurate our application is. After collecting the feedback, later we can decide what to do with it. We can tweak our current business log to achieve better results, for example, or we can add new pieces of logic and new mechanisms to catch all the missing parts and improve the quality of our application.

So the wire-frame for the Accuracy Manager is very simple: it looks for the same news for the given keywords after a specific time frame. If the new version of that news exists it notifies us and fetches a fresh copy of it. Then we can compare the result and mark the investigation as a success or failure.

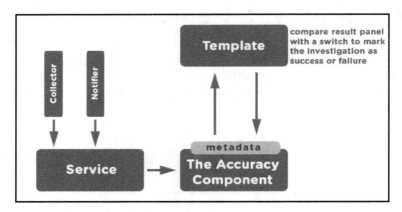

Summary

This chapter was about understanding different parts of our project and how they work together as a whole to investigate selected news and articles.

We saw how to bootstrap our project, how to define a root component, and how to put it in charge of controlling other components including the navigation component. We then saw how to use the Angular router module to set up a dynamic navigation system for a SPA – Single Page Application. Later, we learned about the difference between directives and components and we saw how to implement property binding to pass data from the component to DOM.

In the next chapter, we will start implementing the required business logic and services for the Collector component.

3

The Collector Service - Using Controllers to Collect Data

In this chapter, we are going to take the Collector component to the next level and add some business logic to it. As we saw earlier in the preceding chapter, components are simple TypeScript classes with properties and methods. Each component has a view and can communicate with that view in any directions:

- From component to template
- From template to component
- Or simultaneously in both directions

The properties in a component class are basically data holders for a view and the methods implement what views intend to do (the behavior of the view). These methods are mostly triggered by the template events. However, there are scenarios where a story happens outside of the component/template relationship. Lets find out more about it.

The main topics of this chapter are:

- Services and how they are beneficial to our project
- Dependency injection framework
- Various types of bindings in Angular
- Firebase Realtime database

What is a service and why do we need them?

Sometimes implementing business logic in a web application requires fetching some data from other resources. In other words, we don't need any template; we are only interested in specific data.

For example, the Collector component is in charge of collecting news from various sources. To implement this business logic, we can add a few methods inside the component class and directly feed the results to the component template. But this solution is not ideal. First, the number of lines in the component class will grow unnecessarily. That will violate modularity rules and Angular best practices – keeping classes small. As a result, it will force higher maintenance costs in the future.

Moreover, when we need the same logic in another part of the application (or in a totally different application) we can't use it because it is coupled to a specific component class itself.

The better approach is to implement that business logic in another class – called a service – and import it to our Collector component or other components when it is needed. Figure (A) and (B) demonstrate the wrong and the right way of implementing business logic, respectively.

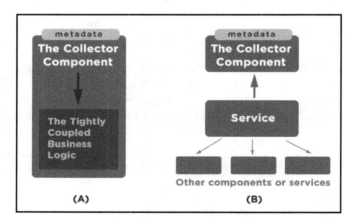

This way we only implement that piece of business logic once so we can test, refactor, debug, and maintain it efficiently.

Updating the collector component

To see a service in action, first let's update our previous wire-frame and modify the template. Let's say we need to see a list of news headlines which we can select among them and (later in `Chapter 4`, *The Rating Service – Data Management*) decide which ones have the higher value (rate) for investigation.

Showing a list of news headlines means we have to implement a mechanism which loops through the available items and displays them. Open the Collector component first and create new properties as follows:

```
// app/collector/collector.component.ts
import {Component} from '@angular/core';
@Component({
  selector: 'sh-collector',
  templateUrl: './collector.html'
})

export class CollectorComponent {
  caption = "Some news worth investigating";
  headlines  = [
    "Lorem ipsum dolor sit amet",
    "consectetuer adipiscing elit",
    "Integer tincidunt Cras dapibus",
    "Quia dolori non voluptas "
  ];
}
```

For now just use the hard-coded data. We will replace it with real data by the end of this chapter. Now head to the template and bind these properties to the proper DOM elements as follows:

```
# app/collector/collector.html
<div class="container">
  <div class="row">
    <h4>{{caption}}</h4>
  </div>
  <div class="row">
    <ul class="list-unstyled">
      <li *ngFor="let headline of headlines; let i=index">
        <input type="checkbox">{{i+1}} - {{headline}}
      </li>
    </ul>
  </div>
</div>
```

The first thing to notice here is the way loops are implemented in Angular. The `*ngFor` is a directive that create loops inside the template. We can define local variables in the view with the `let` keyword. `headlines` is the array property that we have created and initialized in our component's class.

So each element of that array will be stored in the `headline` local variable, which will be displayed in the template later via a pair of curly braces (interpolation).

Printing the value of a property via `{{property}}`, or a local variable as in `{{headline}}` is called **interpolation**.

The `*ngFor` directive comes with a couple of handy variables such as index, first, last, even, and odd, which can be used in a template as they were needed. In this example, we used the index variable as a counter for each headline.

The index variable indicates the current iterator repetition and it starts from zero. That's why we had to add 1 to it in order to see the proper headline number.

Later, we will see how to use conditional templates and even/odd variables to create a striped style list.

The collector service

We can create a service to return those hard-coded values inside the heading property. To do so, create a new TypeScript class named `collector.service.ts` and add the following contents to it:

```
// app/collector/collector.service.ts
export class CollectorService {
  getHeadlines(): string[] {
    return [
      "Lorem ipsum dolor sit amet",
      "consectetuer adipiscing elit",
      "Integer tincidunt Cras dapibus",
      "Quia dolori non voluptas "
    ];
  }
}
```

Nothing special is happening here. This is an ordinary class with a simple method, which returns an array of strings. This is the simplest form of creating a class for our collector service. You may have noticed we didn't import any other modules or add any decoration to this class. We will improve it as we continue.

The Dependency Injection

Having a service in place, now we can delegate the news assignment task to it. To do so, first import the `service` class into the `component` class:

```
// app/collector/collector.component.ts
import {Component} from '@angular/core';
import {CollectorService} from './collector.service';
//...
```

Now we need to create that service and pass it to this component. Technically, we don't need to do it ourselves. There is a framework called Dependency Injection and it is in charge of instantiating that service for us.

The Dependency Injection framework looks for all dependencies for a particular class and automatically initializes–injects–them all. All the Dependency Injection framework needs to know is where that service lives. In other words, it needs the name of the service provider.

We can inform the Dependency Injection framework about the service(s) we are interested in via `providers` metadata as follows:

```
// app/collector/collector.component.ts
//...
@Component({
  selector: 'sh-collector',
  templateUrl: './collector.html',
  providers: [CollectorService]
})
//...
```

Now that we have the service available to our component, we can reference and use it via a constructor:

```
// app/collector/collector.component.ts
//...
export class CollectorComponent {
  caption = "Some news worth investigating";
  headlines;
  constructor (collectorService: CollectorService) {
```

```
    this.headlines = collectorService.getHeadlines()
  }
}
```

To recap, this is how the Dependency Injection framework acts:

1. First it looks into the constructor and realizes there is a dependency to `CollectorService`.
2. Next it checks the meta-data available inside the `@Component` decorator and finds out that there is a class called `CollectorService` inside the providers array.
3. Finally, it finds that class in the code – it has been imported already at the beginning of the code – and injects it to our component.

Now the news assignment task is done outside of the component, which makes our classes easier to maintain. If you visit the application in your browser, you will see the collector component calls its service, to list a couple of hard-coded items:

Property binding

We saw the easiest form of property binding through interpolation before. But it is better to use interpolation if you want to show a message *between* HTML tags. In order to edit the properties of a DOM element, we use different syntax as follows:

```
[property]="expression"
```

For example, in the following DOM element:

```
<input type="email" [placeholder]="emailPlaceHolder" >
```

The square brackets indicate that we are binding the `<input>` placeholder property to the `emailPlaceHolder` property defined somewhere in a component class:

```
// some component class
export class EmailComponent {
  emailPlaceHolder = "please enter your email";
}
```

We can apply similar syntax to bind to a CSS class or even a CSS style.

Class binding

Other types of property binding includes, class binding–where you bind a specific CSS class to a DOM element based on a given expression. For example, we can define a new `isContainer` property in our class as follows:

```
// app/collector/collector.component.ts
//...
export class CollectorComponent {
  //...
  isContainer = "true";
 //...
}
```

Then modify the template to add a CSS class based on the property defined inside the component:

```
# app/collector/collector.html
<div [class.container]="isContainer">
  #...
</div>
```

If you inspect the code in your browser, you will see it has the same effect as before, except now we create it via property binding.

Let's take the current template one step further and use style binding to apply different styles to each headline. We are going to create a stripped style for headlines.

Style binding

Let's see how we can use style binding to set different background colors for even/odd rows in the headline. As we saw before, the *ngFor directive provides other variables such as "even" and "odd", which we can benefit from them here.

Please keep in mind you can always use CSS3 n[th]-child to achieve the same effect.

To achieve this stripped effect, simply modify the template as follows:

```
# app/collector/collector.html
<div [class.container]="isContainer">
  <div class="row">
    <h4>{{caption}}</h4>
  </div>
  <div class="row">
    <ul class="list-unstyled">
      <li *ngFor="let headline of headlines; let i=index; let o=odd;">
        <div class="row" [style.backgroundColor]="o ? 'Khaki':'ivory'">
        <input type="checkbox">{{i+1}} - {{headline}}
        </div>
      </li>
    </ul>
  </div>
</div>
```

First we defined a local variable o and assigned it to the odd variable of the ngFor directive. Now based on the value of this variable we can set the background color for each row:

```
<div class="row" [style.backgroundColor]="o ? 'Khaki':'ivory'">
```

In other words, the [style.backgroundColor] property does the binding for us. If we are in an odd row, that means the value of 'o' will be evaluated as 'true' and the khaki color will be set for the background, and otherwise the color will be set to ivory.

Please keep in mind that the *ngFor loop starts from index 0.

Check out the result in your browser:

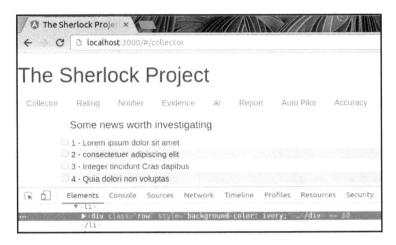

Event binding

Sometimes we need to direct the data flow from the template to the component. In other words, we need to listen for an event in a DOM element and act upon it inside the Component class. That means we need to bind a method to an event–that is why it is called event binding.

The event binding syntax is very easy. On the left side, we mention the name of the event we are interested in, and on the right side we write the method name–in the component class–which this event will be bound to:

```
(event) = "onEvent(parameters)"
```

To see how it works, let's listen for checked headlines and show them in the console. Later in this chapter, we will see how to persist the selected headlines in a database for future reference. But for now logging them in the browser's console will be enough.

1. First we need to listen for change events on the checkbox elements, so modify the `<input>` tag as follows:

```
# app/collector/collector.html
# ...
<li *ngFor="let headline of headlines; let i=index; let o=odd;">
  <div class="row" [style.backgroundColor]="o ? 'Khaki':'ivory'" >
    <input type="checkbox" #cb
           (change)="onChange(headline, cb.checked)">
    {{i+1}} - {{headline}}
  </div>
</li>
# ...
```

2. As you can see, we are interested in change events for the check-boxes and it is assigned to the `onChange()` method, which we will implement in a minute. But before moving on, let's examine a few things in the template. There is a new local variable called `cb` and it is defined differently.

> Using the # symbol is another way to define local variables in a template. In other words, `#cb` has the same effect as `let cb`.

2. We need those local variables because we want to be able to check the status on each news item independently. Now that we have a local variable for checkboxes, we can access their checked property and send it to the – soon to be implemented – `onChecked()` method.

3. We are sending two parameters to that method:

    - The headline content
        - The checked/unchecked status

        Now open the component class and implement the following method over there:

```
// app/collector/collector.component.ts
//...
export class CollectorComponent {
```

```
//...
onChange(item, status){
  console.log(item, status);
}
}
```

4. Nothing impressive is happening here. We get the same two parameters from the template and log them inside the chrome console. If you look in the console, every time you check/uncheck a news item a message will be logged over there.

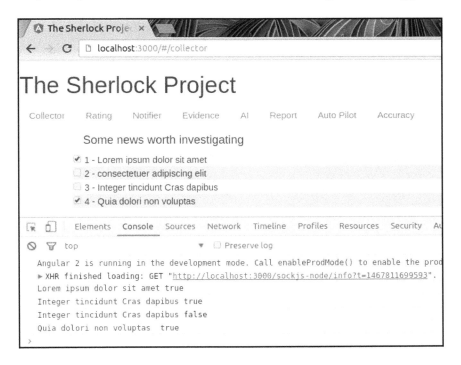

Getting the real news

So far we have used a hard-coded array inside our service as the source of news. Now it is the time to fetch the real headlines from news agency servers. The Angular HTTP service is in charge of communicating with servers over HTTP protocols.

It sends HTTP requests from the application to the server and receives some responses from them. Then it is our job to do something with those responses inside our app. For example, we can find CNN top stories in the following URL: http://rss.cnn.com/rss/edition.rss

Let's hit that URL and get the headlines and replace them with the hard-coded array in our service. To renovate the current Collector service, open the file and make the following changes to it:

```
// app/collector/collector.service.ts
import {Http} from '@angular/http';
import {Injectable} from "@angular/core";

@Injectable()
export class CollectorService {
  private url =
'https://query.yahooapis.com/v1/public/yql?q=select%20title%2Clink%2Cdescri
ption%20from%20rss%20where%20url%3D%22http%3A%2F%2Frss.cnn.com%2Frss%2Fedit
ion.rss%3Fformat%3Dxml%22&format=json&diagnostics=true&callback=';
  private http;

  constructor(http:Http) {
    this.http = http;
  }

  getHeadlines() {
    return this.http.get(this.url)
      .map(res => res.json())
      .map(data => data.query.results.item);
  }
}
```

The first obvious step is importing the http module from Angular. As you can see further down the track, we are constructing the http object and using its methods.

 If you are wondering where and when this service has been provided to our project, check the bootstrapper again. If you can remember, the reason we are using bootstrap is booting and maintaining project requirements from one place:

```
// src/app.module.ts
//...
import {NgModule, CUSTOM_ELEMENTS_SCHEMA} from '@angular/core'
@NgModule({
  //...
  bootstrap   : [AppComponent]
})
//...
```

The next important thing is importing and using the `@Injectable` decorator in this class. We are going to inject this service in the `Collector` component later, so we need to make sure that it is injectable.

The next step is preparing the news RSS. The RSS resources on their own are not beneficial to our application. We need to convert their content into JSON strings. In this example, we are using Yahoo APIs, which provide selective JSON properties in the response.

> Any feed reader which produces JSON output can be used as the source. You can use feed handler from the Google APIs, for example: `https://ajax.googleapis.com/ajax/services/feed/load?v=1.0&q=http://rss.cnn.com/rss/edition.rss`

Now we use the `http` object inside the `getHeadlines()` method:

```
getHeadlines() {
  return this.http.get(this.url)
    .map(res => res.json())
    .map(data => data.query.results.item);
}
```

It makes a GET request and maps the JSON response to data property.

Before moving on to the next section, there is one more thing that is worth noticing. In the Yahoo API, we are using YQL to query an RSS link and extract the properties we are interested in. You can read more about it on the Yahoo website. You can find the YQL documentation here: `https://developer.yahoo.com/yql/guide/`.

Just keep in mind that YQL queries look very much like SQL.

For example, in the previous link we selected title, link, and description properties. If you try that link in your browser you will notice those properties in the output. If you want to get all available keys, simply change the previous query to the following:

```
https://query.yahooapis.com/v1/public/yql?q=select * from rss where
url="http://rss.cnn.com/rss/edition.rss?format=xml"&format=json&diagnostics
=true
```

Angular and observable objects

If you look at the browser, you will find that the Collector page is empty and there are a bunch of errors in the console. That is because we are trying to work with Observable objects without including the related library into our project. In our Angular 2 seed project, there is a place for vendor packages:

```
src/vendor.browser.ts
```

Open this file and simply uncomment the line that imports the RxJS library:

```
// src/vendor.browser.ts
// ...
// RxJS 5
import 'rxjs/Rx';
//...
```

Now we can investigate how Observable objects work here. Checking the `http` object, the task of the `get()` method is obvious. It is a simple HTTP GET request and returns a response. But what about those `map()` functions? Where do they come from and what do they do? To answer that question, hold the *Ctrl* key (or *command* key if you are using Mac) in your IDE and click on the Http object inside the `collector.service.ts`. This will take you directly to the definition of the `get()` method inside the `http.d.ts` file.

> If you have trouble with your IDE, you can find this file under the following path:
> node_modules/@angular/http/src/http.d.ts

As you can see, the return type for all HTTP requests is Observable:

```
// node_modules/@angular/http/src/http.d.ts
//...
/**
 * Performs a request with `get` http method.
 */
get(url: string, options?: RequestOptionsArgs): Observable<Response>;
//...
```

The Observable data type is used for asynchronous data that will show up over time. In a GET request, for example, all we can do is make the request. We don't know when the response will show up. Depending on so many factors (including internet speed, server setup, and so on), the response could be immediate, or it could take a couple of seconds.

Angular uses **Reactive Extensions** (**RxJS library**) in its core modules. So when we use an HTTP module, for example, observable is part of the deal by default. We will learn about them and what they can do as we continue. For now just be aware that the return type of HTTP requests in Angular is Observable so we can subscribe to it and do so many amazing things. In our service, for example, we can use reactive operators on the returned values and fine tune the output:

```
// app/collector/collector.service.ts
//...
    getHeadlines() {
      return this.http.get(this.url)
        .map(res => res.json())
        .map(data => data.query.results.item);
    }
//...
```

In other words, we mapped (converted) the response object to a JSON response and then we mapped (focused) the data part of the response body to the {query:{results:{items[]}}} property. To clarify the second map() function, open the request URL in the browser and notice the JSON response properties in the browser:

```
{
- query: {
    count: 49,
    created: "2016-07-06T01:39:09Z",
    lang: "en-US",
  - diagnostics: {
      publiclyCallable: "true",
    - url: {
        execution-start-time: "1",
        execution-stop-time: "313",
        execution-time: "312",
        content: "http://rss.cnn.com/rss/edition.rss?format=xml"
      },
      user-time: "319",
      service-time: "312",
      build-version: "0.2.28"
    },
  - results: {
    - item: [
      - {
          title: "Clinton 'extremely careless' but no charges recommended ",
          link: "http://www.cnn.com/2016/07/05/politics/fbi-director-doesnt-reco
        },
```

parsing JSON file

If you want to learn more about Reactive Extensions, visit their website and check out their documentations: http://reactivex.io

Updating the collector component

Now we have an observable object that gives us a JSON string that contains news items. The best way to collect these news items from the Collector service is by subscribing to the observable object and then passing the news array to the template.

Using the `subscribe()` function, we fetch the 'data' array and push it into our private property – headlines – for later access:

```
// app/collector/collector.component.ts
//...
export class CollectorComponent {
  //....
  constructor (collectorService: CollectorService) {
    collectorService.getHeadlines()
      .subscribe(
        data => {
          this.headlines = data;
        }
      );
  }
  //...
}
```

As we saw inside the service, the data is already mapped to an array of the news. So when we assign it to the `headlines` property, what we get in the template is an array of objects with various properties including link, title, and description:

```
item: [
  {
    title:"Clinton 'extremely careless' but no charges recommended ",
    link:
"http://www.cnn.com/2016/07/05/politics/fbi-director-doesnt-recommend-charg
es-against-hillary-clinton/index.html"
  },
  {
    link:
"http://www.cnn.com/2016/07/05/politics/obama-clinton-campaign-charlotte/in
dex.html",
    title: "Obama joins Clinton on campaign trail",
    description: "President Barack Obama makes his campaign trail debut
with Hillary Clinton Tuesday, his own legacy at stake as he works to elect
a Democratic successor."
  },
  ...
]
```

That means we can use these properties in the template through interpolation and add links for each headline as follows:

```
# app/collector/collector.html
#...
   <ul class="list-unstyled">
      <li *ngFor="let headline of headlines; let i=index; let o=odd;">
         <div class="row" [style.backgroundColor]="o ? 'Khaki':'ivory'" >
            <input type="checkbox" #cb (change)="onChange(headline,
cb.checked)">
            {{i+1}} - {{headline.title}}
            <a href="{{headline.link}}">(read more)</a>
         </div>
      </li>
   </ul>
```

Now check out the result in the browser and you will see a better result from our improved service:

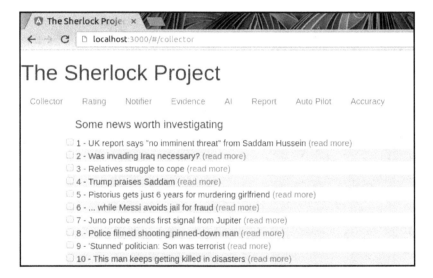

The access control problem

If you couldn't fetch the news from CNN, probably your browser's security policy prevents the HTTP request to be processed as expected.

Some older versions of `webpack-dev-server` might give you a major headache when requesting RSS feeds on your local machine. In other words, you might see the following error while requesting a resource from localhost:

```
⊗ XMLHttpRequest cannot load                                    :3000/#/collector:1
  https://ajax.googleapis.com/ajax/services/feed/load?
  v=1.0&q=http://rss.cnn.com/rss/edition.rss. No 'Access-Control-Allow-Origin'
  header is present on the requested resource. Origin 'http://localhost:3000'
  is therefore not allowed access.
```

In that case, the easiest way to work around it is by starting the browser from the command line without web security:

```
$ google-chrome-stable --disable-web-security –user-data-dir
```

The other – *but not recommended* – solution would be adding a new header to the HTTP request, which explicitly indicates that we want to access to the server from localhost. But this is not a good idea because at some stage we are going to deploy the application on the production server, which has its own settings and configurations. However, as a temporary solution, you can add the `Headers` object and modify the `Collector` service as follows:

```
// app/collector/collector.service.ts
import {Http, Headers} from '@angular/http';

export class CollectorService {
  //...
  constructor(http:Http, headers:Headers) {
    this.http = http;
    this.headers = headers;
    this.headers.append("Access-Control-Allow-Origin", "*");
  }
  //...
}
```

If you have to modify the headers manually, probably the better option would be editing the `webpack.config.js` file at the root of your project and adding a header key to it as follows:

```
// Webpack Config
var webpackConfig = {
  headers: {
    "Access-Control-Allow-Origin": "*",
    "Access-Control-Allow-Credentials": "true",
    "Access-Control-Allow-Headers": "Content-Type,Authorization",
    "Access-Control-Allow-Methods": "GET,POST,PUT,DELETE,OPTIONS"
  },
  //...
```

```
}
```

All previous solutions are hacky and they might not work based on your system or server configurations. The neat solution is provided in the latest Webpack version using the new proxy key in the `webpack.config.js` file. They use `http-proxy-middleware` to optionally proxy requests to a separate, possibly external, backend server.

Just open the `webpack.config.js` file and add the proxy key as follows:

```
// webpack.config.js
//...
  devServer: {
    //...
    proxy: {
      '/collector': {
        target: 'https://query.yahooapis.com/v1/public/yql',
        secure: false
      }
    }
  },
//...
```

Saving objects in a database

When it is about database related Angular apps, traditionally MEAN stack (MangoDB, Express, Angular, and Node) comes to mind. It is still a great choice, but there has been way better options provided by Google recently.

In this book, we are going to use Firebase. Firebase is a cloud platform for implementing web and mobile applications, which is packed with all you might need to develop, grow, and monetize applications.

What we are going to use in this chapter is the Firebase Realtime Database. It is realtime because it is a NoSQL database, where the moment you push a new JSON object to it, the new object will show up in the database and the moment you make any changes on the database itself, the change will be appear on the application instantly.

It is like the two-way data binding that we talked about earlier in this chapter, but way better. Some developers believe it is a three-way data binding, because Firebase is like a glue between Angular and DOM. Let's start exploring this platform by configuring a new project in it.

Setting up The Sherlock Project on Firebase

Firebase is a cloud platform, so we don't need to install anything locally on our machine. To use Firebase tools and features in our project, all we need to do is create a new project there and get the required credentials:

1. Head to `https://console.firebase.google.com`, click the **CREATE NEW PROJECT** button, and enter the name of the project there:

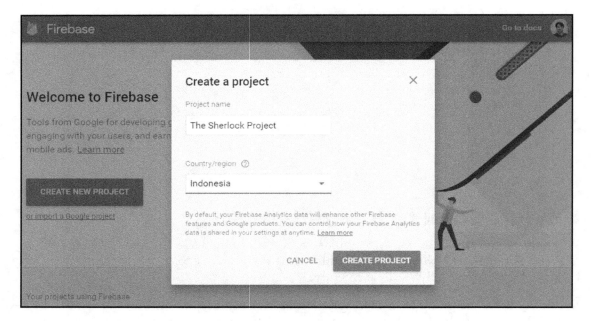

2. In the next page just copy all the credentials lines. We don't need to copy the whole script because we are not going to use JavaScript for using Firebase.

 We will use AngularFire to import and use Firebase. Using AngularFire makes the project and the development process consistent. Because as we will see, it comes with its own set of classes and methods, which we can use directly inside our Angular components and services.

2. You can head to `https://angularfire2.com/api/` and follow the installation steps over there to get Firebase up and running. But since we are using a seed project, there are a few minor changes in the configuration files as follows:

3. Install AngularFire2 and Firebase libraries as follows:

```
npm install angularfire2 firebase –save
```

4. Install Firebase typings as follows:

```
typings install file:node_modules/angularfire2/firebase3.d.ts --save --global && typings install
```

5. Add AngularFire2 to the bootstrap as follows:

```
// src/app/app.modules.ts
//...


import { AngularFireModule } from 'angularfire2';

export const firebaseConfig = {
  apiKey: "AIzauhkjSyA8wZ9r-5BsMC9a73-6_rC9a7kHpk",
  authDomain: "the-sherlock-project.firebaseapp.com",
  databaseURL: "https://the-sherlock-project.firebaseio.com",
```

```
        storageBucket: "the-sherlock-project.appspot.com"
    }

    @NgModule({
      //...
      imports     : [//...
AngularFireModule.initializeApp(firebaseConfig),],
      //...
    })
    //...
```

6. If the webpack is still running, shut it down and start it again from the command line:

   npm start

7. Although we are running the webpack in watch mode, on very rare occasions webpack does not recognize new libraries. Restarting the webpack will rebuild the project with the new Firebase libraries and make them available to inject in our components.

8. Alternatively, in WebStorm IDE you can use the *Ctrl+F5* shortcut keys to restart the webserver.

Saving objects to the database

Now we can test the Firebase Realtime Database in our project. Let's modify the onChange() method in CollectorComponent and save a new object in the database every time a news items is checked. To do that, first we need to create a parent object in Firebase Realtime Database:

1. In the Firebase console, select the Sherlock Project and click on **Database** in the sidebar:

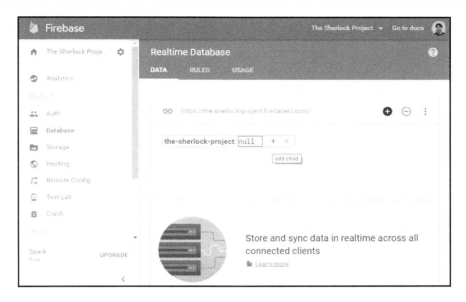

2. If you move the mouse over the project name, a plus sign appears with *add child* as tooltip. Click on the plus sign and enter `Collector` for the **Name** field. Leave the **Value** field empty and instead click on the plus sign for the `Collector` key and add the following values to it. Click the **Add** button when it is done:

3. Click the **Add** button when it is done.
4. Now open the Collector component, import the AngularFire module, and construct a new AngularFire object as follows:

```
// src/app/collector/collector.component.ts
//...
import {AngularFire, FirebaseObjectObservable} from
"angularfire2/angularfire2";
```

```
//...
export class CollectorComponent {
  //...
  private items: FirebaseObjectObservable<any>;

  constructor (collectorService: CollectorService, af: AngularFire)
{
    //...
    this.items = af.database.object('/Collector');
  }
  //...
}
```

Please note the type for the items class. Firebase inherits the same Observable object provided by ReactJS.

5. The `database.object('/Collector')` method grabs the `Collector` key that we have created earlier in the database and assigns it to the private variable 'items' defined in this class.

6. Now that we have access to the `Collector` key we can add child objects to it. We don't want to see the result only in the console anymore, rather we want to save them in the database. So go to the `onChange()` method and replace all the `log()` commands with the following:

```
// src/app/collector/collector.component.ts
//...
export class CollectorComponent {
  //...
  onChange(item){
    this.items.set({news:item});
  }
}
```

The `set()` method creates a new child object for a given parent. If the child has been created already, then it will overwrite it. Select any news inside your application, and check out the database and you will see the news is saved over there:

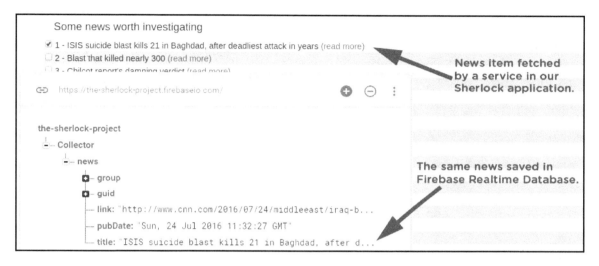

Can you spot the problem here?

1. Select another item and check the database.
2. Now uncheck the first news and look at the database again.

Basically, every time the status of an item changes (check/unchecked) it will be overwritten on the same entry in the database.

This is not what we want. We simply want to add new entries to the database, when the user clicks on an item in the app–without losing previous entries. Let's see how we can fix it.

Working with data via lists

You might think, we can re-factor the `onChange()` method, so it can differentiate between checked and un-checked items and save only selected news. That might solve a part of the issue, but the main problem (objects being overwritten) still exists.

The solution relies on another AngularFire object called `FirebaseListObservable`. With the list objects we can push entries without losing the previous objects. In our previous example, we updated the code and replaced the `object.set()` method with the `list.push()` method as follows:

```
// src/app/collector/collector.component.ts
//...
import {AngularFire, FirebaseListObservable} from
"angularfire2/angularfire2";
//...
export class CollectorComponent {
  //...
  constructor (collectorService: CollectorService, af: AngularFire) {
    //...
    this.items = af.database.list('/Collector');
  }

  onChange(item){
    this.items.push(item);
  }
}
```

Now inside the collector page, select a few news entries from the collected news and check out the database:

It seems we have a unique key for each entry, which is generated automatically. This could be very helpful when we need to query specific items. We will learn more about it in the next chapter.

So far the overwritten object issue is solved now we need to fix the `onChange()` method to make sure only checked items are persisted to the database. Right now if we check and then uncheck an item, it will be recorded in the database twice under two different keys. The ideal solution would be removing the unchecked item from the database.

But the big challenge here is we don't have access to the key property of selected items. Remember, we fetch the news via another Observable object, which has nothing to do with the Firebase Observable object.

So the simple solution here is to hide the selected news items. That way we won't let the user push duplicate items to the db. In the next chapter, we will talk about how to do more sophisticated queries and update and delete items based on their keys.

For now, open `collector.html` and add a hidden property to the `<div>` tag as follows:

```
# src/app/collector/collector.html
<div [class.container]="isContainer">
  #...
  <div class="row">
    <ul class="list-unstyled">
      <li *ngFor="let headline of headlines; let i=index; let o=odd;">
        <div [hidden]="cb.checked" class="row" [style.backgroundColor]="o ?
'Khaki':'ivory'">
          <input type="checkbox" #cb
                 (change)="onChange(headline, cb.checked)">
          {{i+1}} - {{headline.title}}
          <a href="{{headline.link}}">(read more)</a>
        </div>
      </li>
    </ul>
  </div>
</div>
```

As you can see, the condition for hiding the news depends on the value of the checkboxes:

```
<div [hidden]="cb.checked">
```

If it was checked, the value of the property binding evaluates to true and it will be hidden. Check the result and you will find out that every selected piece of news will disappear from the list while it is being pushed to the database.

Summary

In this chapter, we took the Collector component to the next level by adding a service to it. We saw how to delegate data handling tasks to services. We learned about the Dependency Injection framework and how it handles all required dependencies for a class. We used the Angular HTTP module for communicating with news servers and saw how to subscribe to observable objects to get the information that we are interested in.

We learned about the Firebase and its Realtime Database and used it to save news entries as objects.

In the next chapter, we will see how to evaluate a news headline and find out if it is worthy of spending time for further investigations.

4
The Rating Service - Data Management

So far we have collected news headlines from CNN and saved them to the Firebase Realtime Database successfully. In this chapter, we are going to implement a service that has three main responsibilities:

- Create and save a rating logic
- Query the recorded news
- Calculate the rank and sort the collected items based on their rank

While doing these steps we will learn about how to query Firebase objects and extract the piece of data that we are looking for. But before we continue, please be advised that the purpose of the Ranking Service in our project is to help us to find which headline is worth investigation.

So basically it is just a helper and at the end of the day, you are the one who will decide which headline you should chose. In other words, in this chapter we will use the Rating service just to get some insight and find a direction. However, in the chapters to come – especially when we set everything in auto pilot mode – we will see how we can delegate decision making tasks completely to the service we will create in this chapter.

The other important things worth noticing are the factors we choose for our ranking logic. In this chapter, we use date and trendy keywords as a measure for ranking. However, please note that you can choose as many ranking factors as you want and organize them the way it suits your needs. As you will see in the code, we will have a good separation of concerns (SoC), which gives you freedom to customize the ranking logic based on your own business requirements.

> *In computer science, separation of concerns (SoC) is a design principle for separating a computer program into distinct sections, such that each section addresses a separate concern.*

> *– Wikipedia*

Setting the ranking parameters

If we are going to choose two simple factors to rate the headlines, I would say lets do it based on the freshness of the news and the important keywords available in each headline. We don't want to investigate yesterday's news, so let's say if the news belongs to a timestamp within 24 hours from now, we give them a score of 1 and any news older than that won't score any points.

Keywords are important as well. A headline with important keywords deserves to receive a higher rate compared to bland and uninteresting topics. But how can we decide which keywords are important?

We can define a dictionary of keywords and save it into our Firebase db. That might be a good – temporary – solution, but in the long term it won't be practical or reliable. First, as the dictionary grows, analyzing the headlines and looking for keywords takes longer time. Secondly, how can we be certain that the keywords we have selected are trending globally and have a good rate in well-known search engines?

For these reasons, it seems we need a limited list of keywords – say 20 keywords – which have the highest searching ranks and will be replaced – or re-ranked – on a daily, or even hourly basis. Lucky for us we can benefit from Google Trends to find today's hot keywords.

The Google Trends service

We can use Google Trends to gain some insight regarding which search keywords are trending in a particular region within a specific time span. This service that is packed with loads of visualized data provides you with valuable information about almost any keyword you choose.

Head to `https://www.google.com/trends` page and see the default page for these services:

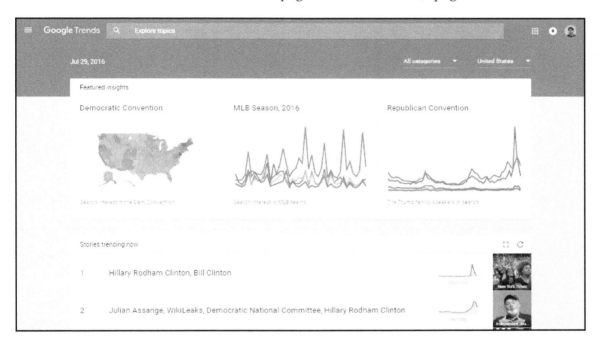

Beneath the graphs there are an infinite loop of trending keywords, their related stories, and a snapshot of their trending graph over the past 10 years. This service does not limit you to the trending keywords of the moment and if you want to look for your OWN specific keywords and want to compare them to each other you can try the following query parameters (here we are comparing Clinton, Sanders, and Trump as an example):

```
https://www.google.com/trends/explore?date=all&q=Clinton,Sanders,Trump&hl=en-US
```

This will draw a couple of charts showing the result of those comparisons in multiple ways:

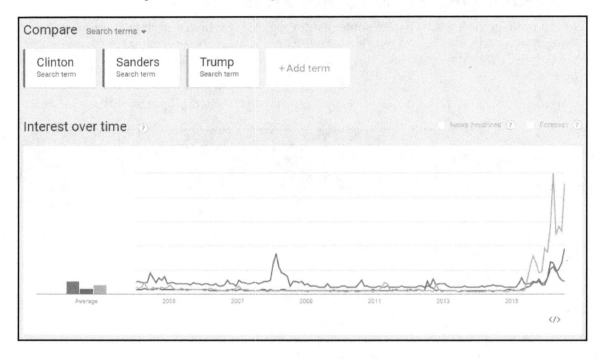

As I mentioned before, it can give us a better clue on selecting a headline among a bunch of high rated items.

Obtaining the Trending Keywords

The URLs provided in the previous topic seems very rich and they are packed with a lot of unnecessary information. But we are looking for the keywords only so we need to simplify the output and narrow it down to keywords. A solution like this might be helpful:

```
https://www.google.com/trends/hottrends/atom/hourly
```

```
What are people searching for on Google today? http://www.google.com/trends/hottrends/atom/hourly.2007-
08 2016-07-30T00:00:00Z 2016-07-30T00:00:00Z
```

- Buffalo Wild Wings
- San Diego
- Zika virus
- DJ Khaled
- Captain Fantastic
- Cheesecake Factory
- Café Society
- Antonio Armstrong
- Alligator gar
- Bill Clinton Balloons
- Tyler Posey
- Ichiro
- Mikaela Kellner
- Gigi Hadid
- Jimmy Buffett
- Hillary Clinton
- North Korea
- Jason Bourne
- PGA Championship
- Katy Perry

]]>

It looks much better, but it would be more practical if we could get that list in some sort of JSON formatted response. We did it before and we can use Google API services here to format the output the way that we like:

```
https://developers.google.com/speed/libraries/
```

Although the output is formatted nicely, it has a fall back to responding with redundant data. Besides it seems like we have to take too many extra steps to get a crowded output like this:

```
entries: [
  {
    title: "Buffalo Wild Wings",
    link:
"http://www.google.com/trends/hottrends?pn=p1#a=20160729-Buffalo+Wild+Wings
",
    author: "",
    publishedDate: "Fri, 29 Jul 2016 10:00:00 -0700",
    contentSnippet: "National Chicken Wing Day ",
    content: "National Chicken Wing Day, National Wing Day",
  },
  ...
]
```

After trying several avenues, I found that the following solution is very direct and neat:

```
http://hawttrends.appspot.com/api/terms/
```

It simply provides a list of 20 keywords – which have been trending in the past 60 minutes – in a very clean JSON format:

```
1:  [
      "Buffalo Wild Wings",
      "San Diego",
      "Zika virus",
      "DJ Khaled",
      "Captain Fantastic",
      ...
    ]
```

All we need to do is to fetch the first property and use it as a list of recently updated keywords in our service.

 If you wonder why we prefer appspot.com over Google, it is because even Google relies on that service. It might sound weird because why should Google – the number one search engine in the world – fetch the trending keywords from a – not very famous – domain like appspot.com? But believe it or not, this is where Google Trends originally come from. If you check the "who is" information for that domain, you will see the owner is Google, but there are rumors which say the Trends idea came from the appspot guys first and later Google bought it. Regardless of the origins, now Google owns it and we are going to benefit from it in this project.

But we can't simply use the last link. We will have the same CORS issue and this time setting the right headers for HTTP requests won't solve our problem either. So we can try another approach for getting the resources from another domain.

CORS versus JSONP

Some servers don't accept CORS requests, but they might have an older solution called JSONP (JSON with Padding). For example, if you send the following request to Wikipedia:

```
https://en.wikipedia.org/w/api.php?action=opensearch&search=bali&format=json
```

It will send back a normal JSON response. But you can demand a JSONP response by adding another parameter to the URL as follows:

```
https://en.wikipedia.org/w/api.php?callback=JSONP_CALLBACK&action=opensearch&search=bali&format=json
```

This time the previous JSON response will be wrapped into a function as follows:

```
/**/JSONP_CALLBACK(
[
  "bali",
  [
    "Bali",
    "Bali Nine",
    "Bali Communiqué"
  ],
  ...
)
```

Angular gets that `JSONP_CALLBACK` part and makes it recognizable to its Http module by converting it to the `ng_jsonp` directive. From that point onwards, the response is available to the Angular application and we can use it inside our components.

But life is not always that easy. If you check the Web you will find almost everyone takes the Wikipedia APIs as an example, but no one tries to fetch Google trends via this link:

```
http://hawttrends.appspot.com/api/terms
```

Try the preceding link and you will get an "unexpected token:" error in your console and there is NO way to get rid of it.

So what is the solution? The fact is WebPack should be in charge of handling CORS headers in HTTP requests, but as we know there are always unexpected issues in some versions. At the time of reading this chapter, if you have a functioning WebPack package, then you don't need to take any extra steps to process your URL and make it behave properly.

However, if you have any problems with your responses, simply pass the URL to a third-party API (such as Google API or Yahoo API) and unify the response to a proper JSON stream. We will see how to do that in the next section.

The rating service structure

To make the development clear and easy, let's create the service class with empty methods and implement them as we proceed.

Head to the `/rating` folder inside your source code and create a new class as follows:

```
// src/app/rating/rating.service.ts
import {Injectable} from "@angular/core";

@Injectable()
export class RatingService {
  //ToDo: construct the service object
  constructor() {}
  //ToDo: get the collected news from Firebase db
  getNews() {}

  //ToDo: get the latest trends to show them inside the template
  getTrends() {}
  //ToDo: rate the news based on constructed rules
  rateNews(){}
}
```

The first thing that we need to take care of is the business logic that we are going to use for rating. As we discussed before, the news date and number of important keywords are what we are going to begin with. This business logic will live in its own class (Separation of Concerns). That means if it was required to change or add more rating items to it in the future, it can be done easily without disturbing other parts of the code.

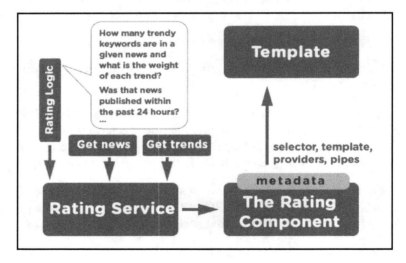

The rating logic structure

The initial rating logic will have three methods:

- `getTrends()`: To fetch the latest trends from a URL
- `rateTrends()`: To rate a particular news entry based on the trend
- `rateDate()`: To rate a particular news entry based on its published date

First we need to fetch a list of keywords, which have been trending for the past hour. Then we need to investigate the news items and find out if any of the current trends are available in them. If the answer is yes we need to add the rank of each trend to the news. In other words, not all items in Google Trends have the same value and they are sorted by their popularity. Finally, we need to give an extra point to the news that was published in the last 24 hours. Based on this logic, create a new class named `rating.logic.ts` and add the initial code as follows:

```
// src/app/rating/rating.logic.ts
export class RatingLogic {
  //ToDo: construct the service object
  constructor() {}

  //ToDo: Fetch the latest trends from the given URL
  getTrends () {}

  //ToDo: Rate a given news item based on the trends
  rateTrends() {}

  //ToDo: Rate a given news item based on the published date
  rateDate() {}
}
```

Having the blueprints in place, it is time to implement the code for the rating logic, and later the rating service.

Implementing the rating logic

We know that the logic we are creating here is going to be injected somewhere else later and we also know that we are going to make a GET request here. So the first obvious steps are importing the required modules and constructing the logic object as follows:

```
// src/app/rating/rating.logic.ts
import {Injectable} from '@angular/core';
import {Http} from "@angular/http";
```

```
@Injectable()
export class RatingLogic {
  private url =
'https://query.yahooapis.com/v1/public/yql?q=select%20*%20%20from%20json%20
where%20url%3D%22http%3A%2F%2Fhawttrends.appspot.com%2Fapi%2Fterms%2F%22&fo
rmat=json&diagnostics=true&callback=';
  private http;
  private trends;

  constructor(http: Http) {
    this.http = http;
  }
//...
}
```

 Please pay attention to the url variable. We passed the appspot.com link to the Yahoo APIs to get a flawless JSON response.

Next let's fetch some trends and store them in the trends private variable:

```
// src/app/rating/rating.logic.ts
//...
export class RatingLogic {
  //...
  getTrends (count) {
    var trends = [];
    this.http.get(this.url)
      .toPromise()
      .then(res => res.json())
      .then(data => data.query.results.json._)
      .then(function(data) {
        for (var i=0; i<count; i++)
          trends.push({'keyword':data[i], 'rank': count-i});
      });
    this.trends = trends;
    return trends;
  }
  //...
}
```

We can hard code the number of trends in this class, but it is better if we give the service the power to make a decision about it. That is why we have created a 'count' parameter in this method which will receive a value from a calling service later.

The important thing in this code snippet is what we do with the keywords after fetching them. Inside the for loop, we assemble an object with two values: {keyword, rank} and we use the 'count' parameter as a means to set the rank for each given keyword. In other words, as the number of iterations increases, the rank of each keyword decreases. That way the most popular keywords receive higher ranks, which is what we are looking for. At the end, each object is saved into arrays waiting for the later calls.

Next we need to rate the available trends for a given news item:

```
// src/app/rating/rating.logic.ts
//...
export class RatingLogic {
  //...
  rateTrends(newsItem) {
    var trendsRank = 0;
    this.trends.forEach(
      function (trend) {
        if(newsItem.indexOf(trend.keyword)>0){
          trendsRank += trend.rank;
        }
      });
    return trendsRank;
  }
  //...
}
```

We have an array of trends from the previous method, so all we need to do is loop through them and see if they occur in the given news (string). If the answer is yes, the RANK of the current trend will be added to the rank of the news (initially it was set to zero) and the final news rank will be returned at the end.

The last method in this class finds out if the news was published recently:

```
// src/app/rating/rating.logic.ts
//...
export class RatingLogic {
  //...
  rateDate(newsDate) {
    var last24Hours = 86400000; // 24*60*60*1000
    var now = new Date().getTime();
    var then= new Date(newsDate).getTime();
    if((now - then) < last24Hours)
      return 1;
    return 0;
  }
  //...
}
```

This method gets the published date as a string, converts it to milliseconds, and in case it was within the last 24 hours, returns 1. The returned value from this function will be considered as an extra point for the final news rank.

Implementing the rating service

The business logic for the rating is in place. Now we can use it inside our service. Let's start by constructing the service object and initializing some private variables:

```
// src/app/rating/rating.service.ts
import {Injectable} from "@angular/core";
import {
  FirebaseListObservable, AngularFire
} from "angularfire2/angularfire2";
import {RatingLogic} from "./rating.logic";

@Injectable()
export class RatingService {
  private news: FirebaseListObservable<any>;
  private rl;
  private trends;
  protected numberOfTrends = 20;

  constructor(af: AngularFire, rl: RatingLogic) {
    this.news = af.database.list('/Collector');
    this.rl   = rl;
    this.trends =rl.getTrends(this.numberOfTrends)
  }

  getNews() {
    return this.news;
  }

  getTrends() {
    return this.trends;
  }
  //...
}
```

In the previous chapter, we saw how to fetch items stored in Firebase Realtime Database. Here we use the same approach to get stored news items. In the service class, we can set the number of trends and call the rating logic' getTrends() to get the latest trends. The getNews() and getTrends() methods in this class will be called later inside the component to pass the related data to the template.

Now we need to implement the main concept of this chapter. The rating mechanism is about applying some rating logic to available data and passing the result to the component. That means the core concept of the rating service emerges inside the `rateNews()` method.

The first challenge is accessing the individual properties of each entry. We got all stored news by a simple `list()` method call. Now we need to find the key for each entry and from there drill down to individual properties. In AngularFire, we can use the $key identifier to access the key. Consider the following code snippet, for example:

```
this.news
  .subscribe(
    snapshots => { snapshots.forEach(
      function(snapshot) {
        console.log(snapshot.$key);
      });
  });
```

Now check out the console in your browser and compare it to your Firebase console:

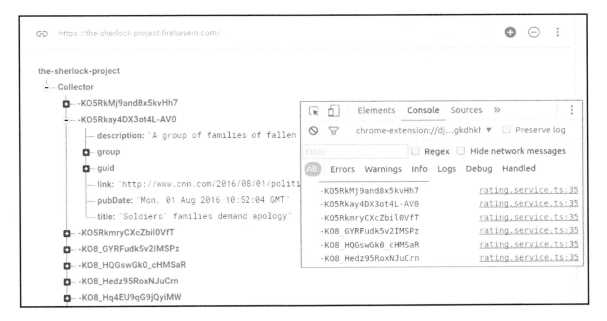

It seems we managed to get the keys successfully, but it doesn't help us to go any further. There is another identifier called $value, which can get the value of any selected key, ONLY IF it is a primitive value (number, string, or Boolean values). Looking at the Firebase console, we see that the value for each news item is another object with a bunch of properties. So the preceding code snippet is not the right choice.

The right answer for our problem is getting a reference to the value part (the object, if you like) of each key. With that reference access we will be able to fetch the value of each property individually. The following code demonstrates how to do that:

```
// src/app/rating/rating.service.ts
//...
export class RatingService {
  //...
  rateNews() {
    var news = [];
    var self = this;
    // first get a reference to the value part of news object
    this.news._ref.once("value")
      // then loop through each news item
      .then(snapshots => { snapshots.forEach(
        function(snapshot) {
          var newsRank;
          // save individual news components in a set of variables
          var title = snapshot.child("title").val();
          var desc = snapshot.child("description").val();
          var date = snapshot.child("pubDate").val();
          var link = snapshot.child("link").val();
          // calculate the news rank
          newsRank =
            self.rl.rateTrends(title+' '+desc) + self.rl.rateDate(date);
          // push the ranked news into an array of news objects
          news.push({
            'title':title,
            'descrition': desc,
            'rank': newsRank,
            'link': link
          });
        })});
    return news;
  }
}
```

After accessing the values of each property, we can call methods in the `RatingLogic` class to evaluate the value of each rating parameter and add them up into one variable:

```
newsRank = self.rl.rateTrends(title+desc)+self.rl.rateDate(date);
```

You might wonder why we combined the news title and news description and passed the result to the rateTrends() method for evaluation. There are two reasons behind it. First of all, in some news items fetched from the RSS link the title or description part might be empty. That could happen for many reasons, including the technical issues in the third-party RSS reader. Check the news stored in your Firebase Database and see it for yourself. The other reason is more precise rating results. Sometimes the trends we are looking for are hidden inside the description, not the title of a news item. We don't want to lose the true value of trends just because it is either in the title or in the description.

After accessing the properties and evaluating the trend and date rank, the final step would be saving the the final object into an array and returning it to the component for future use.

The rating component

Now that we have all players in place, it is time to update our component to glue everything together. Open the component file and update it as follows:

```
// src/app/rating/rating.component.ts
import {Component} from '@angular/core';
import {RatingLogic} from './rating.logic';
import {RatingService} from './rating.service';

@Component({
  selector: 'sh-rating',
  templateUrl: './rating.html',
  providers: [RatingLogic, RatingService]
})
export class RatingComponent {
  private ratingService;
  private trends;
  private collectedNews;
  private ratedNews;

  constructor(rs:RatingService) {
    this.ratingService = rs;
    this.trends = rs.getTrends();
    this.collectedNews = rs.getNews();
```

```
      this.ratedNews= rs.rateNews();
   }
 }
```

Notice that we have specified two providers in the meta data section of the component: the rating logic and service.

All the heavy lifting has been done inside the previous two classes already. That's why this component looks so light. We only have four private variables that get their values from the service we have created and pass them on to the template.

Technically, we are going to feed our template with three values:

- The current trends
- The news we have saved already
- The rank for each news

Let's see how we can organize these items inside the template.

This is just an example and you are free to choose the items you like to collect from the service and organize them the way suits you best inside your choice of template.

The rating template

Let's say we need three columns to show the trending keywords, recorded news, and the ranked news. The simple HTML structure for that scenario could be as follows:

```
<div class="row">
  <div class="col-md-3">
    <h3>Hot Trends</h3>
    <ul>
      <li *ngFor="let trend of trends">
        {{trend.keyword}} ({{trend.rank}})
      </li>
    </ul>
  </div>
  <div class="col-md-4">
    <h3>Collected News (Collector Component)</h3>
    <div *ngFor="let item of collectedNews|async; let o=odd;">
```

```
    <div [style.backgroundColor]="o ? 'Khaki':'ivory'">
      {{item.description}}
    </div>
  </div>
</div>
<div class="col-md-5">
  <h3>Ranked News (Rating Component)</h3>
  <div *ngFor="let item of ratedNews">
    {{item.title}} - {{item.rank}} - <a href="{{item.link}}">more</a>
  </div>
</div>
</div>
```

This template generates an output like the following:

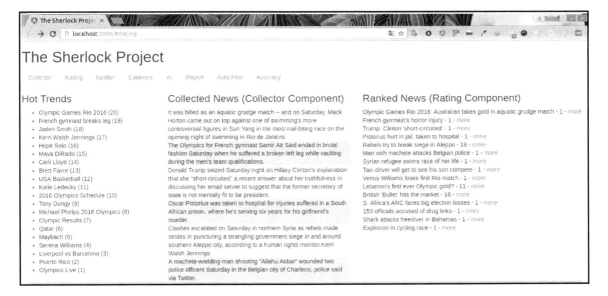

Although it satisfies the major goal for this chapter, it still needs some fine tuning. If you look at the Ranked News column you will see that they are all rated, but they are not sorted properly:

```
Ranked News (Rating Component)

Olympic Games Rio 2016: Australian takes gold in aquatic grudge match - 1 - more
French gymnast's horror injury - 1 - more
Trump: Clinton 'short-circuited' - 1 - more
Pistorius hurt in jail, taken to hospital - 1 - more
Rebels try to break siege in Aleppo - 18 - more
Man with machete attacks Belgian police - 1 - more
Syrian refugee swims race of her life - 1 - more
Taxi driver will get to see his son compete - 1 - more
Venus Williams loses first Rio match - 1 - more
Lebanon's first ever Olympic gold? - 11 - more
British 'Bullet' hits the market - 16 - more
S. Africa's ANC faces big election losses - 1 - more
150 officials accused of drug links - 1 - more
Shark attacks freediver in Bahamas - 1 - more
Explosion in cycling race - 1 - more
```

We can fix this problem via Angular pipes. A Pipe is a fancy name for another TypeScript class that serves a purpose inside a template. There is nothing scary or unusual to it. In the next section, we will see how to create and use one.

Creating a custom pipe

Let's organize all custom pipes in our application in its own folder. So create a 'pipes' folder and add a new class to it as follows:

```
// src/app/pipes/orderby.pipe.ps
import {Pipe, PipeTransform} from '@angular/core';

@Pipe({name: 'orderBy', pure: false})
export class OrderByPipe implements PipeTransform {
  // transform is the only method in PipeTransform interface
  transform(input: Array<any>, property: string, order: boolean):
  // Angular invokes the `transform` method with the value of
  // a binding as the first argument, and any parameters as the
  // second argument in list form.
  Array<string> {
    input.sort((a: any, b: any) => {
      return order
```

```
             ? a[property] - b[property]
             : b[property] - a[property];
        });
        return input;
    }
}
```

The @Pipe function is the metadata that defines this class as a pipe. As you can see, we are implementing the PipeTransform interface, which has a transform() method.

This method is in charge of transforming the input date. In our case, we want to pass an array to it and have it sorted as an array in ascending or descending order.

So we can easily use the sort() function to achieve this goal and based on the value of the'order' parameter, set the ordering type to descending (false) or ascending (true).

Now we need to let our component know about this new pipe. So open the rating component class and add the following pipe to it:

```
// src/app/rating/rating.component.ts
//...
import {OrderByPipe} from '../pipes/orderby.pipe';

@Component({
  //...
  pipes: [OrderByPipe]
})
export class RatingComponent {
  //...
}
```

Having the pipe in place, we just need to use it inside the template as follows:

```
# app/src
<div class="row">
  #...
  <div class="col-md-5">
    <h3>Ranked News (Rating Component)</h3>
    <div *ngFor="let item of ratedNews| orderBy:'rank'">
      {{item.title}} - {{item.rank}} -
      <a href="{{item.link}}">more</a>
    </div>
  </div>
</div>
```

Check out the results and now they are sorted in descending order based on their ranks:

Ranked News (Rating Component)

Rebels try to break siege in Aleppo - 18 - more
British 'Bullet' hits the market - 18 - more
Lebanon's first ever Olympic gold? - 14 - more
Venus Williams loses first Rio match - 1 - more
Olympic Games Rio 2016: Australian takes gold in aquatic grudge match - 1 - more
Man with machete attacks Belgian police - 1 - more
Syrian refugee swims race of her life - 1 - more
Taxi driver will get to see his son compete - 1 - more
French gymnast's horror injury - 1 - more
Trump: Clinton 'short-circuited' - 1 - more
Pistorius hurt in jail, taken to hospital - 1 - more
S. Africa's ANC faces big election losses - 1 - more
150 officials accused of drug links - 1 - more
Shark attacks freediver in Bahamas - 1 - more
Explosion in cycling race - 1 - more
Meet the high-tech cops fighting terror - 0 - more
Who holds the greatest Olympic record? - 0 - more

If you want to sort the output by ascending order, all you need to do is to mention the third parameter of the pipe as follows:

```
<div *ngFor="let item of ratedNews| orderBy:'rank':true">
```

Knowing the power of pipes now you can come up with all sorts of pipe ideas to decorate the templates with a sophisticated look. For example, we can create a pipe to highlight the trends inside the rated news column. That way we can have a better visual concept of top rated items and what made them stand out from the rest of the news.

Summary

In this chapter, we implemented four TypeScript classes for rating logic, rating services, rating components, and a sorting pipe.

We saw how we can achieve a better maintainable code by separating different parts of logic and organizing them in its own classes. We created a new pipe to sort the result array based on their ranks and then we used it inside our template.

In the next chapter, we will see how to delegate the ranking process to the service we have created here and use it in another service called notifier to inform us if something interesting – a high ranked news based on our business logic – is happening in the world.

5
The Notifier Service - Creating Cron Jobs in Angular

This chapter is about utilizing previous services in an automated fashion. The goal that we are going to achieve is implementing a notifier service, which collects and rates news entries and notifies us if their ranks passed a predefined threshold. We can choose to be notified in two ways:

- We can be notified via the application itself. That means the moment we open the application. There should be a badge component where it reflects the number of news entries that have passed the rank threshold and when we click on the badge, it should open the page showing those news items.
- Or we can be notified by email. This provides more freedom because we don't need to open the application to find out what is happening and the moment a news item is qualified as a member of notification list, an email should be sent to us – by application – containing that list.

This introduction suggests two new features for our application. First, we need to come up with some mechanism that runs periodically and executes some tasks such as collecting and rating news automatically. The first thing that pops into our mind is using functions such as `setInterval()` or `setTimeout()`. But we will see why these functions are not the right choices in our case.

The second feature requires a mechanism for sending emails. We will see how to do that without using any backend development library or package.

Cron job versus Interval/Timeout

As you know, there are native JavaScript functions such as `setInterval()` or `setTimeout()`, which can run certain tasks periodically. But the main reason that they are not practical here is their limited lifespan. In other words, their life depends on the JavaScript host (mostly browsers) that executes them. Kill the browser process and they are long dead. This is not ideal, because we need a reliable process that runs in the background – possibly forever – and gathers news and sends emails without requiring to leave a browser window open 24/7.

For that reason, we need something on the system level and Cron jobs sound like a perfect choice for this matter. System administrators have been using them for decades and all we need is to run a command with a bunch of parameters inside a terminal window. With this solution, we can achieve our goal in three steps:

1. First we need to generate a .js file so we can call it from the command line. We can continue creating TypeScript classes and use a TypeScript compiler in watch mode to create the js file from it:

   ```
   $ tsc -w -p --out file.js file.ts
   ```

2. Since that JavaScript file is going to be executed by the node, we need to be sure about which node is running in our system:

   ```
   $ which node
   ```

3. Now we can call that node in a regular cron job and specify how often and when we need to see that task is executed:

   ```
   $ 30 6 1 * * /usr/local/bin/node /path/to/file.js
   ```

But this solution is not ideal either. It seems that now we need to be concerned about the operating system where that terminal is running (moreover, different Cron commands have their own settings and parameters).

The problem is we don't want to be carried away from JavaScript/TypeScript code base to some Shell Script commands or back-end development libraries. So the perfect solution for our problem is a native JavaScript package that runs inside our Angular code base and delivers Cron functionality even if the browser is closed.

Introducing node-cron

Since we don't want to reinvent the wheel, we can benefit from a very useful node package called `node-cron`, which delivers exactly what we are looking for. Simply install the package by running the following command:

```
$ npm install node-cron --save
```

Normally we want to install the typings that are shipped with every node package. But not every node package is designed to be used inside TypeScript classes. Some of them, including node-cron, are plain JavaScript files. To prove that, try the following command:

```
$ typings install node-cron --save
```

As you can see, in the error message we can discover two facts:

```
typings ERR! message Unable to find "node-cron" ("npm") in the
registry.
typings ERR! message We could use your help adding these typings to the
registry:
    https://github.com/typings/registry
```

The first line indicates that node-cron doesn't provide any typings. The second error message denotes that there is a typings registry for all node packages and if you are interested you are most welcome to contribute in creating new typings for plain packages.

We have two options here: we can create the required typings for the new package in our project – and if we are kind enough, we can send it to the registry people later – and then follow the same importing and using notations, the same as what we have done so far for other libraries in this project. Or we can ignore the "typings" hassle completely and "require" the package when we need it in our classes. We will find out how to do that soon.

Dealing with vendors

We bootstrapped the main Angular libraries inside the `src/main.browser.ts` file. But what is the best way to include third-party libraries? As the name suggests, `src/vendor.browser.ts` is the best place to import them. Open the file and add a simple line at the bottom:

```
// src/vendors.browser.ts
//...
// For vendors import them here
import 'node-cron';
```

To prove that it is imported properly we can check the output. As we know, WebPack reads all .ts files and generates equivalent .js files. To see how it works, at the root of your project, open `Webpack.config.js`, and look at the "entry" key inside the webpackConfig variable:

```
// webpack.config.js
//...
var webpackConfig = {
  entry: {
    'polyfills': './src/polyfills.browser.ts',
    'vendor':    './src/vendor.browser.ts',
    'main':      './src/main.browser.ts'
  },
//...
```

As you can see, there are three entry points for adding required tools and libraries to our project. We are interested in the "vendor" key. This is the place where we import the third-party libraries.

Now checkout the contents of the `index.html` file inside the `src` folder. At the bottom of the page, there is a reference to some JavaScript files, which seems to be relevant to the entry keys we saw earlier:

```
# src/index.html
    <script src="/polyfills.bundle.js"></script>
    <script src="/vendor.bundle.js"></script>
    <script src="/main.bundle.js"></script>
#...
```

However, it seems our entries have different naming conventions compared to TypeScript files: [name].`browser.ts`

The question is, how are they transformed to those JavaScript files and where do they get the 'bundle' part in their names? To find out, scroll further down in the Webpack.config.js file and checkout the contents for the `defaultConfig` variable. The answer lies inside the "output" key under the "filename" property:

```
// webpack.config.js
//...
var defaultConfig = {
  output: {
    filename: '[name].bundle.js',
    sourceMapFilename: '[name].map',
    chunkFilename: '[id].chunk.js'
  },
//...
```

To prove this, open the project in the browser, go to the inspect panel, and select the Network tab. There you can see all JavaScript files loaded into the project. Click on vendor.bundle.js and inside the Preview tab, search 'node-cron' and you will see the body of that library has been already loaded and ready to be used in the project.

 Do you remember that we used a CDN link for bootstrap inside the index.html file? With the previously introduced approach, you can now install the node packages for third-party libraries as follows:

```
$ npm install --save bootstrap@3
```

 You can import it into the vendor entry if you like. I personally prefer CDN resources anywhere I have a choice. It boosts the performance in the production.

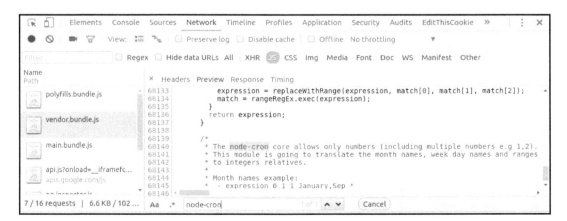

Simply search the term 'node-cron' in this file and you will find that the library has been loaded already.

Getting and rating the news periodically

Let's say we need to fetch fresh news twice a day. That means we need a service that runs every 12 hours, sends a request to the news agencies, and rates and saves them in the Firebase Realtime database. Later we will notify the user about the stored news.

 You might ask why we need to store them in the database. We can email them as soon as we have filtered the right news. That is true for email notifications. But what if we needed to show them inside the application?

The first part of this scenario sounds familiar and we have already implemented it in the Collector service. However, we cannot use it right away and we need to modify the business logic a little.

The current Collector service saves the SELECTED news only. In other words, a news item will be persisted to the database, only if the user CLICKS on the checkbox for that item. The challenge is if we change this service to satisfy the automated tasks then we will lose the user interactivity.

One solution to this challenge is to create a new persistent logic inside our new notifier service. That way we can still benefit from the Collector service (the collecting part) and just add a new mechanism for persisting chosen news items.

Fortunately, the second part of this scenario – rating the news – doesn't have any obstacle and we can use the Rating service that we have created before and apply it on the Collector outlet directly. The following diagram demonstrates the strategy that we are going to use for implementing the Notifier service:

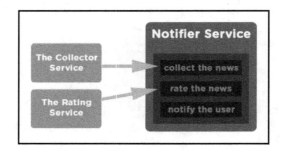

The Notifier template and business logic

Now we can build the UI for the Notifier and decide how it is going to perform. To begin with, let's say we need a switch in this component that declares that some tasks should be done automatically. Having that in mind, open the notifier template and modify it as follows:

```
# src/app/notifier/notifier.html
<h2>Notifier</h2>
#...
      <h3>Current Settings</h3>
      <div class="input-group">
        <span><input type="checkbox" /></span>
        <label >Find, Rate & Save News </label>
      </div><!-- /input-group -->
#...
```

Now we can check the status of the checkbox and pass its value as an optional parameter to the related services.

Next we need to define how the user is going to be notified. The default option should be the built-in application notification system; however, we want to notify them via emails as well:

```
# src/app/notifier/notifier.html
<h2>Notifier</h2>
#...
      <div class="input-group">
        <label class="input-group-addon">notify me via:</label>
        <select class="form-control">
          <!--app/email: to be populated via component class-->
        </select>
      </div>
#...
```

We need to set a threshold for the notifier. In other words, we need to declare a limit for qualifying ranks. In the previous chapter, we had a TypeScript class where all business logic for rating news was defined. Here we need to use it as a bar for all news. Any news with a rank higher than the threshold we define here will be added to the notifying list. The template for this feature can be implemented as follows:

```
# src/app/notifier/notifier.html
<h2>Notifier</h2>
#...
      <div class="input-group">
        <label class="input-group-addon">news threshold:</label>
```

```
        <select class="form-control">
          <!--options to be populated via component class-->
        </select>
      </div>
  #...
```

And finally, we need a section to display qualified news items:

```
# src/app/notifier/notifier.html
<h2>Notifier</h2>
#...
    <div class="col-lg-9">
      <h3>Suggested News</h3>
      <div></div>
    </div><!-- /.col-lg-9 -->
  #...
```

The initial look for the notifier template should look something like the following:

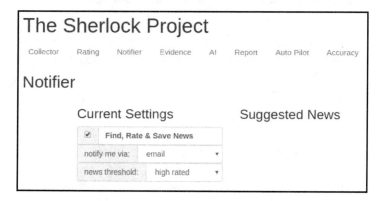

The next step would be implementing the Notifier service and the component to interact with this template and call other services on demand.

The Notifier component

We can set the default values for the form controls inside the Notifier component, but ideally we need a mechanism that loads the configuration settings for the notifier template from a database. That means when we update the settings inside the notifier page to something like `notify me via email about the news with ranks higher than 7`, then we need to save this settings somewhere to make sure the next time we open the application we won't roll back to the default settings.

That sounds like posting a JSON object to the Firebase database. The JSON object can be defined as follows:

```
'notifier-config': {
  'notify'    :'true',
  'notifier' :'email',
  'threshold':'medium rated'
}
```

So let's start by defining the default values. Although we can hard code them inside the Notifier component itself, the best practice is to create an independent class and export it. So create a new TypeScript class named `notifier.config.ts` and construct the properties as follows:

```
// src/app/notifier/notifier.config.ts
export class NotifierConfig {
  constructor(
    public notify: boolean,
    public notifier: string,
    public threshold: string
  ) {}
}
```

Now we can modify the initial Notifier component and make it update the template with available database settings or persist the template changes to the database. That sounds like two way bindings. Let's develop the required code in the component first:

```
// src/app/notifier/notifier.component.ts
import {Component} from '@angular/core';
import {NotifierConfig} from './notifier.config';

@Component({
  selector: 'sh-notifier',
  templateUrl: './notifier.html'
})
export class NotifierComponent {
  private notify   = [true, false];
  private notifier = ['app', 'email'];
  private threshold= ['high rated', 'medium rated', 'low rated'];
  private model    = new NotifierConfig(false,'app','low rated');

  constructor() {}

  // ToDo: Fetch stored settings from db and initialize
  // the component's private variables with them
  updateUI() {}
```

```
    // Todo: Listen to element's change event and persist any
    // change to the Firebase Database
    updateDB() {}
}
```

The model variable is an object that carries the values for each property to the template. With that object in place, let's update the template and provide entries where data can flow back and forth.

Two-way data binding

In previous chapters, we used the [] notation for property binding, which represents the data flow from the component to the template. We also used the () notation for event binding, which represents the data flow from the template to the component.

In both of them, data flows in one direction. In this chapter, we will benefit from two-way data binding in our component. Logically, the [()] notation is the right choice for two way data binding.

 In a two way binding notation, in case you forget which one comes first (brackets or parentheses), just remember what [()]resembles. That notation is also called "banana in the box".

The [(ngModel)] directive both reads and writes values to input elements. In other words, changes to a value in the component class and the value of the related input element in the template – which is bound through [(ngModel)] – will be updated instantly. On the other side, changing the value of input fields inside the template and the member variables inside the component class will be updated as well. This is how we bind the input elements to member variables:

```
# src/app/notifier/notifier.html
<h2>Notifier</h2>
#...
  <div class="input-group">
    <span class="input-group-addon">
      <input type="checkbox" [(ngModel)]="model.notify"
               (ngModelChange)="updateDB(model.notify)"/>
    </span>
    <label>Find, Rate & Save News </label>
  </div><!-- /input-group -->

  <div class="input-group">
    <label class="input-group-addon">notify me via:</label>
```

```
          <select class="form-control" [(ngModel)]="model.notifier"
                  (ngModelChange)="updateDB(model.notifier)">
           <option *ngFor="let n of notifier" [value]="n">{{n}}</option>
          </select>
        </div>
        <div class="input-group">
          <label class="input-group-addon">news threshold:</label>
          <select class="form-control" [(ngModel)]="model.threshold"
                  (ngModelChange)="updateDB(model.threshold)">
          <option *ngFor="let t of threshold" [value]="t">{{t}}</option>
          </select>
        </div>
     #...
```

There are two things that are worth noticing in the preceding code. First, we are using the array elements for each property to populate the input options inside the template. Using arrays all we need is a *ngFor directive to loop through them and assign their elements to drop down options. Secondly, we are calling the updateDB() function as soon as any UI element fires a change event. So the next obvious step would be implementing these methods inside the component class.

Updating the template

After initializing the model variable, before using those values to populate the UI, we need to make sure we haven't saved the UI configuration before. So import the angularfire2 module to this component and get ready to read the configuration key as follows:

```
// src/app/notifier/notifier.component.ts
import {AngularFire,FirebaseObjectObservable} from 'angularfire2';
//...
export class NotifierComponent {
  //...
  private config: FirebaseObjectObservable<any>;
  constructor(af: AngularFire) {
    this.config = af.database
      .object('/Notifier/config', {preserveSnapshot: true});
    this.updateUI();
  }
//...
}
```

We are calling the `updateUI()` method inside the constructor because the first thing that we need to do is load the configs from the database (if they are available). Also note the `preserveSnapshot` key inside the object() function. With this property set to true, now we have the power to gain access to individual keys and values under the provided path. As you can see, we are saving configurations under '/Notifier/config':

```
// src/app/notifier/notifier.component.ts
//...
export class NotifierComponent {
  //...
  updateUI() {
    this.config.subscribe(snapshot => {
      if(snapshot.exists()) {
        //object exists
        this.model = {
          'notify':    snapshot.val().notify,
          'notifier': snapshot.val().notifier,
          'threshold': snapshot.val().threshold
        };
      } else {
        //object doesn't exist save the initialized model to db
        this.config.set(this.model);
      }
      // ToDo: Schedule a cron job based on the values of UI
    });
  }
  //...
}
```

We are subscribing to the config object in the database. In case this object exists, through the snapshot that we preserved in the previous step, we access its individual properties and save them into our model. Then they are served to the template instantly via two way binding.

However, if that object does not exist then we use the model we initialized at the beginning of this class. To prove that both the template and the component are in sync, visit your Firebase console and double-click on a key and set a new value there. Now checkout the UI and see that change.

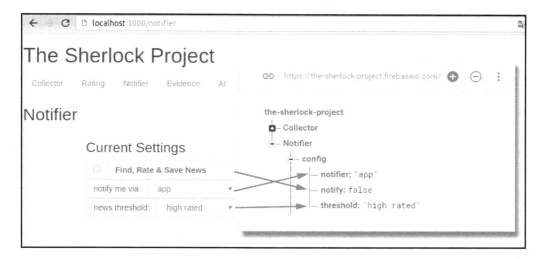

Thanks to the preserved snapshot, you can check out the keys and values on the browser console as well:

```
//object exists
console.log(snapshot.key)
console.log(snapshot.val().email)
```

Updating the database

Now we need to update the database when some changes happen in the UI:

```
// src/app/notifier/notifier.component.ts
//...
export class NotifierComponent {
  updateDB(value) {
    switch(value) {
      case true || false:
        this.model.notify = value;
        break;
      case 'email' || 'app':
        this.model.notifier = value;
        break;
      case 'high rated' || 'medium rated' || 'low rated':
        this.model.threshold = value;
        break;
    }
```

```
        this.config.update(this.model);
    }
}
```

The logic in this function is really straightforward. We set the values of properties inside the model, based on the choices that have been made inside the UI. At the end when using the `update()` function, all changes will be saved to the database.

The Notifier service

Having the UI and the database in place, now it is time to implement the service that delivers the actual tasks for the notifier. Earlier in this chapter, we mentioned three tasks for the notifier: collect the news, rate and store them (in case they pass the threshold), and finally notify the user. The important feature for this service is that it should run periodically at specific times:

```
// src/app/notifier/notifier.service.ts
import {Injectable} from '@angular/core';
import {CollectorService} from '../collector/collector.service';
import {RatingService} from '../rating/rating.service';
import {FirebaseListObservable, AngularFire} from 'angularfire2';

@Injectable()
export class NotifierService {
  private cron = require('node-cron');
  private collectorService;
  private ratingService;
  private angularFire;
  private task;

  constructor(cs: CollectorService, rs: RatingService,
              af: AngularFire) {
    this.collectorService = cs;
    this.ratingService = rs;
    this.angularFire = af;
  }

  scheduler() {
    // stop previous tasks first, otherwise you will have
    // multiple notifiers with different settings running
    if(this.task != null)
      this.task.stop();
    var self = this;
    this.task = this.cron.schedule('* */12 * * *', function () {
      self.collectRateNotify();
```

```
    });
  }

  // ToDo: implement the logic for collect, rate
  // and notify the news
  collectRateNotify(notifier, threshold) { }
}
```

We installed the node-cron library earlier in this chapter, but notice that we didn't import it like other modules. Instead we "required" it inside the cron variable. Now that variable has access to all functions available in the node-cron library.

Let's say we want to execute the collect/rate/notify cycle twice a day (every 12 hours). All we need to do is to feed the schedule function with the desired cycle plus the actual function that is in charge of delivering collect/rate/notify duties:

```
      scheduler() {
    this.task = this.cron.schedule('* */12 * * *', function () {
      self.collectRateNotify();
    });
  }
```

A quick tip about the stars: you can mention six starts in the schedule function, where the first one is optional and represents seconds. Use it if you need to run a task on seconds intervals. However, if you mention only five stars in this function it will start the calculation straight from minutes. The following pattern describes the meaning for each star:

```
 ┌──────────────────────── second (optional): 0-59
 │ ┌────────────────────── minute: 0-59
 │ │ ┌──────────────────── hour: 0-23
 │ │ │ ┌────────────────── day of month: 1-31
 │ │ │ │ ┌──────────────── month: 1-12 (or names)
 │ │ │ │ │ ┌────────────── day of week: 0-7 (or names)
 * * * * * *
```

Instead of hard-coding the period here, we could add another option to our config model and read it from the database. But it will require us to inject that value to the constructor and deal with its own limitations. So to keep things simple, let's just roll with the current code.

Checking the rates for collected news

In this section, we implement the `CollectRateNotify()` function. But first we need to define a value for thresholds. Again we can do it by modifying the configuration model (notify.config.ts) and pass the threshold to the service constructor, but let's keep things simple and define them directly inside the service class:

```
// src/app/notifier/notifier.service.ts
//...

@Injectable()
export class NotifierService {
  //...
  private threshold = [1, 5, 10];
  private items: FirebaseListObservable<any>;
  //...

  collectRateNotify(notifier, threshold) {
    var self = this;
    var thresholdRank = this.thresholdToRank(threshold);
    this.items = this.angularFire.database
      .list('/Notifier/rated-news');
    this.collectorService.getHeadlines().subscribe(
      data => { data.forEach((item: any) => {
        var trendRank =  self.ratingService.rl
            .rateTrends( item.title + item.description);
        var dateRank=self.ratingService.rl.rateDate(item.PubDate);
        var newsRank = trendRank + dateRank;
        if (newsRank >= thresholdRank) {
          var ratedItem = {
            'title': item.title,
            'description': item.description?item.description:'',
            'rank': newsRank,
            'date': item.pubDate?item.pubDate:'',
            'link': item.link
          };
          self.items.push(ratedItem);
          if (notifier == 'email'){
            this.emailNotification(ratedItem);
          }
        }
    })
  }
}
```

This function takes two string parameters and does all the expected tasks from the service.

Since thresholds are expressed as strings (for example, "high rated") we need to define a correspondent array for those values and create a function to calculate a numeric value for each threshold. We call this function `thresholdToRank()` and will implement it in the next section:

```
var thresholdRank = this.thresholdToRank(threshold);
```

To access rated news later we need to store them in another address inside the FireBase database. Since they are related to the notifier service, let's store them under the same key and give them the 'rated-news' name:

```
this.items=this.angularFire.database.list('/Notifier/rated-news');
```

As you have noticed in the constructor, we initiated objects from `CollectorService` and `RatingService`. That's because now we are going to delegate the collecting and rating tasks to these object. As you can see, we are using `getHeadlines()` to fetch the latest news first, then we loop through each news item, calculate their ranks, and if their rank is higher than the threshold we defined earlier, that news item will be pushed as a new item to the new object we created in the Firebase database:

```
if (newsRank > thresholdRank)
  self.items.push({
    'title': item.title,
    'description': item.description,
    'rank': newsRank,
    'date': item.pubDate,
    'link': item.link
  });
```

Now we have the rated news stored somewhere safe and they are ready to be used in the notification list. Notification via app is easy, and as before we can do it by passing the news list to the template. But for notification via email, we need to take an extra step and delegate the sending email task to another function.

The helper functions

From the previous topic, we need to implement two functions. These types of functions don't have a direct communication point to the outside world, but they help to calculate or perform something for the service itself. That is why they are called helpers.

We can define them inside their own class (for example, `notifier.helper.ts`) and inject them to the service class when they are needed, or we can define them directly in the service class and get away from the hassle of importing and injecting steps.

The first function is `thresholdToRank` and we use it to calculate the rank number for a given threshold string:

```
// src/app/notifier/notifier.service.ts
//...
@Injectable()
export class NotifierService {
  //...
  thresholdToRank(threshold) {
    var rank = this.threshold[0];
    if (threshold == 'high rated')
      rank = this.threshold[2];
    else if (threshold == 'medium rated')
      rank = this.threshold[1];
    return rank;
  }
}
```

Since we have already defined the threshold rank array, all we need to do is check the input string and return the equivalent rank for it. As you can see, we set the default value to the lowest rank and in case something else has been decided, we set the return value to that threshold.

Next we need a function for sending emails in case the notification type is set to "email":

```
emailNotification(ratedItem) {
  console.log('email notification mechanism to be decided');
}
```

For now, just leave a console.log() command there and let's see what other options we have.

Automating tasks with Zappier

As we know, Angular is a frontend framework and we need a server side mechanism to send emails. My original solution – which was functioning very well up until a few weeks ago – was a mechanism to connect all backend players together and trigger them to take the necessary action at the right time. Go to zapier.com and have a look at the amazing job those people have done in connecting different web applications and cloud services.

With their service all I needed to do was create a new zap and connect Firebase to Sendgrid (the service for sending emails). That way Firebase will act as a trigger and every time there is a new child added to the 'rated-news' table, it will signal zappier about it. On receiving this signal, Zapppier will make the Sendgrid send an email – containing all the useful info about the new child – to the user.

It might sound like a lot of configurations (Zappier account, Firebase console, and Sendgrid keys) but believe me when I say it turns the whole procedure to a very neat and professional process. Even better, we don't need to add a single line in our Angular services to send emails. In other words, the whole backend activities happen in a block outside of our project. All we care about is pushing a new entry to the Firebase and after that, sending emails is not our problem anymore. The following diagram describes the process better:

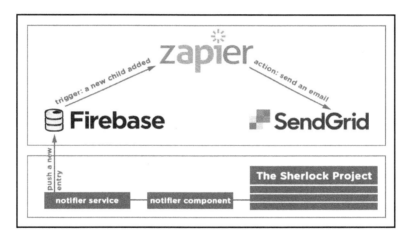

But again, life is not always that easy. As I have mentioned earlier, this solution was working beautifully until recently. Unfortunately, the people at Firebase decided to block all third-party webhooks, promising that they will introduce their own libraries soon. You can read the official announcements from both Firebase and Zappier here:

```
https://github.com/sendgrid/docs/issues/1491
```

In my humble opinion, this is neither acceptable nor professional, but it is what it is and we need to come up with plan b until they settle their problems. So in the next topic, I'm going to sort out the email sending challenge in the simplest way possible. However, the reason that I mentioned Zappier here was for you to keep an eye on it and replace any back-end requirements in your Angular projects with the services provided by Zappier. It has a lot to offer and you can benefit immensely from the potentials available in their triggers and actions.

Sending Notification e-mails

The way that we are going to handle email requirement is by sending a POST request to a service, which can send emails for us. Please remember that sending emails through Angular is possible, but it is NOT advised, because the account credentials will be exposed to the world. Perhaps the simplest solution for most Linux and Mac machines is to use the default mail application available in the system.

 It really doesn't matter what mail program you are using (sendgrid, postfix, ssmtp, and so on). But if by any chance you don't have any mail program simply install it with commands such as: $ sudo apt-get install ssmtp You can then follow the installation process. After it is done, PHP will call it internally for sending emails. Configuring the SMTP settings for various mail libraries and mail servers is beyond the scope of this book. But all mail programs mentioned previously have a robust documentation for configuration.

What we are going to do is write a few lines in PHP and call the default mail application to send emails for us. So create a new file and add the following contents to it:

```php
<?php
    header('Access-Control-Allow-Origin: http://localhost:3000');
    $message = $_POST['message'];
    $to_email = '<your email address>';
    $email_subject = "Notification from Sherlock app";
    mail($to_email,$email_subject,$message)
?>
```

This file could be saved anywhere in your system. Just make sure it is served via any virtual hosts available in your machine. I personally save it in /var/www/html/mail,php so later I can access it through http://localhost/mail.php.

The important thing to notice here is the header() function. To prevent the CORS (Cross Origin Resource Sharing) challenge that we experienced earlier in Chapters 2 and 3 we need to declare that it is perfectly fine that our Angular project (served on http://localhost:3000) sends requests to this PHP script (available on localhost).

 Please note, although both codes (the Angular project and the PHP script) might live in the same computer, technically your machine perceives them as they are on different servers. This fact will be helpful when you deploy your application on a live server.

And that is it for the PHP part. Now head back to the Notifier service and modify the emailNotification() function as follows:

```
// src/app/notifier/notifier.service.ts
//...
  emailNotification(ratedItem) {
    var headers = new Headers({'Content-Type': 'application/x-www-form-
urlencoded'});
    var options = new RequestOptions({headers: headers});
    var body = 'message=Hi,\n there is a new rated item in firebase
database with following details:\n'+
      'title: '+ ratedItem.title +'\n'+
      'description: '+ ratedItem.description+'\n'+
      'rank: '+ ratedItem.rank+'\n'+
      'date: '+ ratedItem.date+'\n'+
      'link: '+ ratedItem.link+'\n'+
      'Please click on the link if you are interested to know more about
this news item.';

    this.http.post('http://localhost/mail.php', body, options)
      .subscribe(res => {
        console.log('post result %o', res);
      })
  }
```

All we do here is assemble the message body with the contents of a qualified (rated) news and send a post request to the email script we created earlier. To test this, set the news threshold to "low rated" and check your email. If there is any news that is passing the rating threshold, you should get an email with contents similar to the following:

```
Hi,
    there is a new rated item in firebase database with following details:
title: Giant leaps in space exploration description: From Sputnik to the
International Space Station, take a look back at a few of the greatest
moments in space exploration. rank: 4 date: Thu, 06 Oct 2016 19:44:18 GMT
link:
http://www.cnn.com/videos/health/2016/10/05/giant-leaps-in-space-exploratio
n-orig.cnn
    Please click on the link if you are interested to know more about this
news item.
```

In App notifications

As we know so far, the qualified news for notifications are saved under the `Notifier/rated-news` object. So listing and showing them inside the notifier template will satisfy the in app notification goal. So start by creating a new list observable object inside the component and point it to the Notifier/rated-news node:

```
// src/app/notifier/notifier.component.ts
import {
  AngularFire, FirebaseObjectObservable, FirebaseListObservable
} from 'angularfire2';
//...

export class NotifierComponent {
  //...
  private ratedNews: FirebaseListObservable<any>;
  constructor(af: AngularFire, ns: NotifierService) {
    //...
    this.ratedNews = af.database.list('Notifier/rated-news');
  }
//...
}
```

Now inside the template, loop through the news item and format them the way you like. One option could be as follows:

```
<h2>Notifier</h2>
<div class="container">
  <div class="row">
    #...
    <div class="col-lg-9">
      <h3>Suggested News</h3>
      <div *ngFor="let item of ratedNews|async">
        {{item.title}} - <a href="{{item.link}}">more</a>
      </div>
    </div><!-- /.col-lg-9 -->
  </div><!-- /.row -->
</div>
```

News maintenance

With the current setup everything works as expected, except that we have the maintenance problem. The cron job here is adding the qualified news on each running cycle. But what happens to the old news? The rated-news object is the home for notification items and we need to implement a mechanism to loop through previous news items and throw them out if a specific condition is met.

To create this logic, inside the Notifier service add a new function to the scheduler as follows:

```
// src/app/Notifier/notifier.service.ts
//...
@Injectable()
export class NotifierService {
//...

  scheduler(notifier: string, threshold: string) {
    //...
    this.task = this.cron
      .schedule('*/15 * * * *', function () {
      self.removeOldNews();
      self.collectRateNotify(notifier, threshold);
    });
  }
//...
}
```

It is important to call the `removeOldNews()` function before collecting any new items. Since the final list is assembled based on the current items under /rated-news object, if we don't tidy up first, the old news will slip into the notification list.

Now we need to create that function. To do so, first we need a fresh AngularFire object, so we can use it as an access point to the list of news.

Keep the list assembly object (`this.items`) and house keeping object (this.maintenance) separate otherwise you will face a major headache when you are trying to figure out what weird games the Observable objects are playing. Please keep in mind that the Observable objects offered by AngularFire are a superset of objects that originally existed in React.

After accessing the list of news items, what we need to do is go through them and check their dates, and if they are older than a specific time span, erase them. That means we need to define that time span in this class. Here is the code to implement these steps:

```
// src/app/Notifier/notifier.service.ts
//...
export class NotifierService {
  private eraseFactor = 72; // 3 days (72 hours)
  //...
  removeOldNews() {
    var self = this;
    this.maintenance = this.angularFire.database
      .list('/Notifier/rated-news', {preserveSnapshot: true});
    this.maintenance.subscribe(snapshots => {
      snapshots.forEach(
        function (snapshot) {
          var date = snapshot.val().date;
          if (self.isOldNews(date) == true)
            self.maintenance.remove(snapshot.key);
        })
    });
  }
}
```

As you can see, checking the news date and finding out if they have to be erased is happening inside the isOldNews() function:

```
// src/app/Notifier/notifier.service.ts
//...
export class NotifierService {
  //...
  isOldNews(newsDate) {
    var eraseFactor = this.eraseFactor *60 * 60 * 1000;
    var now = new Date().getTime();
    var then= new Date(newsDate).getTime();
    if((now - then) > eraseFactor) {
      console.log(now - then);
      return true;
    }
    return false;
  }
}
```

What is happening here is very similar to what we did in the previous chapter. We find the difference between now and the news date in milliseconds and compare it to the erase factor – which is three days at the moment. If the difference is older than the erase factor, that means the news has to go.

As we saw, the actual elimination happens inside the `removeOldNews()` function and here we just send the signal (true or false) for elimination.

Summary

In this chapter, we implemented the logic for automated tasks. We saw how to import and use node packages that don't contain Typings and where we can find the registry for adding new type definitions.

We used a cron job to call services created in the previous chapters for collecting, rating, and storing qualified news in a list ready to be fetched and notified by the application or later via email. We also saw how to implement the helper functions for calculating dates, finding out dated items, and keeping the database clean on each cron job cycle.

In the next chapter, we will see how to use clustering algorithms to find related resources (articles, images, videos, and so on) to the news of our interest.

6
The Evidence Tree Builder Service - Implementing the Business Logic

In the previous chapter, we managed to save the top-ranked news items, so now we can choose the item of our interest and build an evidence tree around it. An evidence tree is basically a collection of concepts which directly or indirectly relate to the subject we want to find more facts about. We can visualize it as a network of nodes which are connected to each other via edges and each node contains valuable information regarding the subject of our interest.

Sometimes we might have a question in our mind and want to find the answer related to that news. It shouldn't always be a question. Sometimes we just want to gather more information about the news itself. That question or intention forms the subject of our interest and whatever our intention might be, we need to create an evidence tree which supports the subject of our interest.

 The evidence board is not a new concept and detectives use a physical board to stick up photos, phone numbers, pieces of newspaper, and so on. They usually put the subject of their interest in the middle of the board and connect other pieces of evidence to it via threads. Having an evidence board visually helps to find a faster and more accurate answer to a problem. The best part: it triggers creative thinking during the process.

The overall process would be something like this:

- First, we choose the news item that we would like to investigate more.
- Then, we measure the value of that news item by looking into its words and their frequency.
- Next, we search the Web and try to find links similar to our subject.
- Finally, we scrape the contents of collected links and try to measure the distance between the original news and each of them. The items with closer distance can be added to a cluster of similar nodes.

The result will be a network of observations (nodes) which gives us valuable insights about our investigation. It is valuable because sometimes they provide hints and clues that we cannot find with the traditional search and click approach. To do so, let's start by processing an article and finding a measure for similarity.

Clustering and similarity – retrieving documents of interest

The main questions are how do we measure similarity and how do we query over articles? If you think about it, we need to have some kind of scale (or a model if you like) to decide whether a specific document is close enough (similar) to our selected article.

Perhaps the simplest way to measure similarity between articles is count the similar words. We can simply create an object in which each word in the document will be the key, and the number of occurrences of that word in the document will be the value:

```
similarity-factor: { word1: 5 times, word2: 3 times,  ...}
```

Then we can have an array of those objects for each document and use it as a factor for measuring similarity between two documents. For example, we take the following paragraph (from CNN news):

> *"Billy Bush ashamed of Donald Trump tape. Angry comments piled up on Billy Bush's Facebook page …"*

> *– CNN*

Then we organize it into a data structure like the following figure:

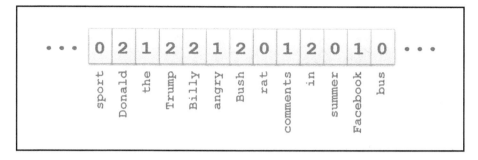

Looking at the screenshot, there are some fields with 0 value (for example, sport). Those fields represent words which are available in English vocabulary, but they are not necessarily available in our article. We will see those 0 values will nullify the uninteresting words and narrow down our search for similar articles.

There are also words with other values. For example, `Trump` has been repeated twice, so it has a value of 2, and `Facebook` was repeated once so it has the value of 1. In JavaScript, we can use JSON objects to represent the preceding screenshot as follows:

```
{[
  {"Billy":2},{"Bush":2},{"Donald":2},{"Trump":2},{"tape":2},
  {"in":2},{"ashamed":1},{"Angry":1},{"comments":1},{"piled":1},
  {"up":1},{"on ":1},{"Facebook":1},{"page":1},{"from":1},
  {"men":1},{"and":1},{"women":2},{"who":1},{"were":1},
  {"disgusted":1},{"by":1},{"the":2},{"contents":1},{"of":1},
  {"2005":1},{"which":1},{"brags":1},{"graphic":1},{"terms":1},
  {"about":1},{"being":1},{"able":1},{"to":1},{"grope":}
]}
```

So our first job is simple. We need to implement a service which finds unique word instances and counts their occasions in a given document.

The evidence service

Let's start by creating an empty service and creating a very basic structure for its functions. Create a new TypeScript file inside the `evidence/` folder and add the following contents to it:

```
// src/app/evidence/evidenc.service.ts
import {Injectable} from "@angular/core";
```

```
@Injectable()
export class EvidenceService {
  private words = [ {key:"w1",value:1}, {key:"w2",value:2} ];
  wordCounts(url) {
    // ToDo: get a url subscribe to its response and call other
    // functions to count the words and their occurrence in it.
    // Ideally it will return an array of objects.
    return words;
  }
}
```

So the draft version of our service is very simple. It gets a URL which contains the article of our interest and then finds and returns all unique words and number of their instances.

Before implementing these functions, we need to get the URL and find a way to extract *useful* content out of it. The important question here is how we distinguish between HTML tags and useful content. To answer this question, let's implement the component and the template and see the output as it evolves.

The evidence component

As we know, the news link itself comes from items saved under the /Notifier/rated-news path. So let's pull out the news item with the highest rank from rated-news and pass it to the service for counting its words. To do so, open the component file and edit the contents as follows:

```
// src/app/evidence/evidence.component.ts
import {Component} from '@angular/core';
import {EvidenceService} from "./evidence.service";
import {AngularFire} from "angularfire2";

@Component({
  selector: 'sh-evidence',
  templateUrl: 'evidence.html'
})
export class EvidenceComponent implements OnInit{
  private angularFire;
  private evidenceService;

  constructor (es:EvidenceService, af: AngularFire) {
    this.evidenceService = es;
    this.angularFire = af;
  }

  ngOnInit() {
```

```
this.angularFire.database.list('/Notifier/rated-news', {
  query: {
    orderByChild: 'rank',
    limitToFirst: 1 // lets fetch 1 item for now
  }}).subscribe(data => {
    this.newsItems = data;
  });
}
}
```

We have something new in this component. It is implementing the OnInit interface, which means we are going to hook into one of the most popular component's life cycles. Each component, from the moment that Angular creates it till the moment it is destroyed, has various life cycles. We can hook into those life cycles and make the component do a specific task at a specific moment. For example, here, we are putting part of business logic into the ngOnInit() function and saying the moment this component initializes, we want it to do some query tasks.

Let's expand this concept by exploring the AngularFire query inside the ngOnInint() function. We didn't see that before, but it is possible to narrow down the Firebase query results to specific items and here we want to get those results as soon as the component is initialized.

 We could make that query directly inside the constructor. But one of the Angular best practices is to keep the constructor as light as possible and move initialization tasks into the ngOnInit() function.

This query object holds all the necessary keys which define the search criteria. Since we are looking for the rated news with the highest rank, we should focus on the rank property. Moreover, we need only one result – for now – so we can set the number of results in the limitToLast property:

```
query: {
  orderByChild: 'rank',
  limitToLast: 1
}
```

The other alternative to setting the number of results is using `limitToFirst: 1`. But since the search results are sorted in ascending order by default, we used `limitToLast` here. For a complete list of available properties and their usage, check the query documentation in the AngularFire repository:
https://github.com/angular/angularfire2/blob/master/docs/4-query ing-lists.md

Now we need to find the link value in the given result and pass it to the evidence service for the word count:

```
.subscribe(item => {
  this.evidenceService.wordAnalyzer(item[0].link);
});
```

We will implement `wordAnalyzer()` soon. It will be the host for all required calculations, including counting words and finding their true values.

Notice how we got direct access to the link property via the object index. To see where is that index come from, log the query result and check out the console:
`console.log("Result: ", item);`

Now it is time to discuss the critical function in this component. As you can see, extracting the link from a news object is not good enough. We need to find a way to extract valuable words in a given HTML page. What we want to avoid is parsing the HTML tags (for example, head, body, div, and so on) and consider them as a word instance. Let's see how we can achieve this via **Yahoo Query Language** (**YQL**).

Parsing HTML pages into JSON content

We used YQL before to pick selected keys from a JSON response (CNN RSS feed). It was easy because that JSON page was generated by the CNN website already. But how can we convert a HTML page to JSON?

You might ask why we can't use the contents of the title and description keys in a given RSS news object. It is because they only contain a small portion of the whole story. We need to extract the words from the complete article. That is why we need to follow the link and find a way to make a JSON structure out of it.

There are various motives behind the way news agencies shorten the contents in their RSS feeds. Among them are putting more contents in a limited space and encouraging people to click on links so they can gain more traffic to their websites.

Luckily, we can delegate the task of parsing HTML pages to the Yahoo API. Using the following query, we say we want all DOM elements in a given URL to be converted into a bunch of keys:

```
q=select * from html
```

Using the format parameter, we can define the response type as JSON:

```
&format=json
```

Let's try a sample link using these query parameters and see what the response looks like:

```
https://query.yahooapis.com/v1/public/yql?q=select * from html where
url="http://edition.cnn.com/2016/10/14/politics/yemen-us-role-in-war/index.
html"&format=json
```

As you can see, in the response, we can find almost every single DOM element, property, and so on:

```
- results: {
    - body: {
        class: "pg pg-vertical pg-politics pg-leaf pg-article international t-light",
        data-eq-pts: "xsmall: 0, medium: 460, large: 780, full16x9: 1100",
        - div: [
            - {
                class: "user-msg",
                - div: {
                    class: "user-msg--container",
                    - div: [
                        - {

                            • • •
```

Now, the challenge here is we don't want to parse every single DOM element or property. In other words, we are not interested in the contents of data-eq-pts or class properties. So we need to find a way to limit the output to something more meaningful.

For that purpose, we can use xpath. As we know, in most websites, news content is held inside the <p> elements; however, there are exceptions such as the CNN website which use <div> tags to represent news content but use CSS classes to distinguish between normal divs and the ones which are used for paragraphs, so we can add those elements to the xpath condition as follows:

```
https://query.yahooapis.com/v1/public/yql?q=select * from html where
url="
http://edition.cnn.com/2016/10/14/politics/yemen-us-role-in-war/index.html
" and xpath="//*[contains(@class,'paragraph')]|//p"&format=json
```

Now try the query link in your browser again and it should show the valuable content separated from DOM noises.

As we go through different websites with unique DOM and styling rules, we will always need to update the xpath conditions and add more rules to it. Because we need to extract as much as valuable content as possible. All you need to do is use the OR operand as follows:
… and xpath="rule1|rule2|etc"…

Looking at the query link, we see there is only a news link which changes depending on the selected news. So we can use a function to embed the unique news links into the query URL and then call it before passing on the JSON response to the evidence service:

```
// src/app/evidence/evidence.component.ts
//...
export class EvidenceComponent {
  constructor (es:EvidenceService, af: AngularFire) {
    //...
    .subscribe(item => {
        this.evidenceService
          .wordAnalyzer(this.getYahooQueryUrl(item[0].link));
      });
  }

  getYahooQueryUrl (link) {
    return "https://query.yahooapis.com/v1/public/yql?" +
        "q=select * from html where url=""+ link +"" and "+
        "xpath="//*[contains(@class,'paragraph')]|//p"" +
        "&format=json&diagnostics=true&callback=";
  }
}
```

Now we can do some basic tests and see how this component works in the template.

The evidence template

We know that we are going to start with word instances and their counts and later on we are going to add more calculations to it. So let's create a table structure and add columns to it as we proceed.

Open the `evidence.html` file and modify its contents as follows:

```
# src/app/evidence/evidence.html
<div class="col-md-6">
  <div class="panel panel-default ">
    <!-- Default panel contents -->
    <div class="panel-heading">Processing words</div>
    <!-- Table -->
    <table class="table">
      <thead>
      <tr>
        <th>#</th><th>Words</th><th>Raw Value</th>
      </tr>
      </thead>
      <tbody *ngFor="#w of evidenceService.words; #i=index">
      <tr>
        <th>{{i+1}}</th>
        <td>{{w.word}}</td>
        <td>{{w.count}}</td>
      </tr>
      </tbody>
    </table>
  </div>
</div>
```

Let's check out the result so far and see what it looks like in the browser:

Please keep in mind this template will change as we continue.

Saving all valuable words

So far, we managed to get a news link, parse its HTML contents, and narrow it down into a selective JSON response and pass it on to the Evidence service. Now it is time to process that response and get the unique word instances and their counts.

The first thing to notice in the JSON response is the words that we are looking for are saved under the result key. So we need a function to map to the JSON response and return that portion of the JSON body which is held inside the results key. That way, we can filter out – even more – unnecessary keys and values:

```
// src/app/evidence/evidence.service.ts
// ...
export class EvidenceService {
  // ...
  wordAnalyzer(url) {
    this.getArticle(this.getYahooQueryUrl(url))
      .subscribe(
        data => {
          // ToDo: Do something with the mapped data
        });
  }
  getArticle(url) {
    return this.http.get(url)
      .map((res:Response) => res.json())
      .map(data => data.query.results)
  }
}
```

Next, we see that the real news is mostly saved under the content key. Check out this paragraph code snippet, for example:

```
...
p: {
    class: "zn-body__paragraph",
    cite: {
        class: "el-editorial-source",
        content: " (CNN)"
    },
    content: "Just when you thought the complicated, tangled web of who's
fighting who in the Middle East couldn't get more complicated, the rules
have changed. Again."
}
...
```

So we need to find a way to extract the contents in the content key. Let's create a function which finds and returns texts inside a given key.

That might sound easy, but since we are dealing with complex JSON structures from different news agency websites, we need to find a solution which parses each branch recursively and drill down for more content if there are still more depths to explore.

So let's create that function as follows and feed it with the subscribed data coming from the previous function:

```
// src/app/evidence/evidence.service.ts
// ...
export class EvidenceService {
  private article='';
  // ...
  wordAnalyzer(url) {
    this.getArticle(url)
      .subscribe(
        data => {
          this.findKey(data, 'content');
        });
  }

  // ...
  findKey(object, string) {
    for (var key in object) {
      if (object[key] && typeof(object[key]) == "object") {
        this.findKey(object[key], string);
      } else if (
        key == string ||
        typeof (key) == "string" &&
        key != 'class' &&
        key != 'id' &&
        key != 'href'
      ) {
        this.article += object[key];
      }
    }
  }
}
```

The findKey() is a recursive function which receives two input parameters: the object which it is going to parse and the name of the key (a string) which it is looking for in the object. While we are parsing the JSON tree, if the current node is an object, then we pass it to the findKey() function again for further processing.

But if the current node is a content key, then we simply append its value at the end of the article variable (it is a private variable). Check out the contents of the article variable:

```
console.log(this.article);
```

We will find all texts stored in content keys are saved there.

Counting the unique words

Now that we have most of the valuable words saved in a variable, we can move on to counting them. This is a two-step task: first we need to sanitize the words and remove all symbols, white spaces and so on. Then we need to implement a mechanism which increments a word count if it finds a duplicate for any words. So add the following functions to the evidence service and call them inside the subscriber (don't forget to remove the hardcoded values from the words variable; we don't need them anymore):

```
// src/app/evidence/evidence.service.ts
// ...
export class EvidenceService {
  private words;
  // ...
  wordAnalyzer(url) {
    this.getArticle(this.getYahooQueryUrl(url))
      .subscribe(
        data => {
          this.findKey(data, 'content');
          this.words =
            this.countInstances(this.extractWords(this.article));
      });
  }

  extractWords(article) {
    // remove all symbols from the article
    var pure=article.replace(/[\.,-\/#!$%\^&\*;:{}=\-_`~()]/g,"");
    // extract all words available between white spaces
    return pure.split(/\s+/);
  }

  countInstances (allWords) {
    // create an object for word instances and their counts
    var instances = {};
    allWords.forEach(function (word) {
      if (instances.hasOwnProperty(word)) {
        instances[word]++;
      } else {
```

```
        instances[word] = 1;
      }
    });
    return this.sortWords(instances);
  }
```

In the `countInstances()` function, we simply loop through the array of cleansed words and if they are new, we just give the value of 1 to them, otherwise we increase their previous count by one.

You may have noticed there is another function which sorts the results before returning them. That is not necessary but if you want to have the word instances sorted, we can implement and apply the `sortWords()` function as follows:

```
// src/app/evidence/evidence.service.ts
// ...
export class EvidenceService {
  private words;
  // ...
  sortWords(instances) {
    var words = [];
    var sortedWords = Object.keys(instances).sort(function(a, b){
      return instances[b] - instances[a]
    });
    sortedWords.forEach(function (word) {
      words.push({word: word, count: instances[word]});
    });
    return words;
  }
}
```

Here, we used the `sort()` function, which is the default JavaScript function for sorting arrays and explicitly here, we created a logic to sort the array elements descending based on their occurrences. The result is saved as an array of objects.

Lets do another road test and see what all these methods look like in the template. But before checking the browser, please make sure that you do have some items saved under the Notifier/rated-news object. We don't have hard-coded values anymore so we need real data to work with:

Those words were extracted from the following link (which at the time of writing this chapter was one of the highest-ranked news items – automatically saved in my Firebase account):

```
http://cnn.com/politics/
```

I can show all the words in that image but our service extracted 376 unique words out of this article and, as you can see, words such as "the", "of", and "to" have the highest occurrence in this article – which makes sense – whereas words such as "Trump" were repeated less than them. We will see how to find the true value in the extracted words.

Understanding the bag of words model

In this book, we are going to choose a popular machine learning model called the bag of words to represent a document. To give you a better idea about this concept, imagine that we take all the words in a document, throw them in a bag, shake them well, and take them out in no particular order. This new random document might not have a meaningful value to a human being, but to machines it has the same value as the original document. That's why we implemented all of those functions in our service so far.

Basically, when we demolish the grammar structure, it gives us freedom to focus more on the word instances, their weights, and how often they are repeated in the document. We will find out why and how we can benefit from this model in our application.

Imagine that we have applied this model on our original document, and there are two other documents out there. Now we want to find out which one of the other two samples has the highest similarity to our original article. As we saw, the original article is about Donald Trump. Lets say the second article is about agricultural machines and the third document is about the US presidential election. Lets assume, after counting the individual words in each document, we came up with the following results for each of them:

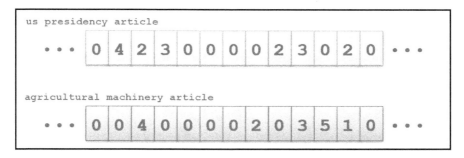

Now, to find out the similarity rank between our selected news and these articles, we need to multiply the weight of each word in both articles and sum them up as follow:

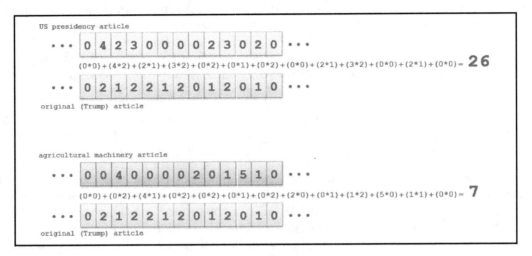

The result shows that the similarity factor between the presidential election article and our original article is 26, while for agricultural machines, this value is down to 7.

Please keep in mind we are showing only fraction of the two articles for demonstration purposes only. In the real world, those streams of words are way longer and the weight of each word much higher than what we see here. For example, in our coding example, we saw there were over 300 words and some words, such as "the" were repeated over 20 times.

From a human perspective, that makes sense. We don't need to count words to find out which articles are related. We just glance at the titles and the decision will be made in our brains instantly. But that decision could be a little tricky when there are thousands of articles in the corpus and most of the given articles are about the presidential election. So the bag of words model could be a big help here.

The flaws in the bag of words model

The "bag of words" has some flaws and we need to optimize this model a little bit before using it in a real-world problem. For example, this model can be fooled easily. If we duplicate the original contents of the presidential election article and measure the similarity factor again, it will jump from 26 to 52 (and that number could potentially be much higher in real examples).

So, again from a human perspective, we can recognize the duplication and we won't give any credit to that, but our computer model doesn't see that as a problem and can be led to inaccurate results.

To address this issue, we can normalize the word count factor. First we need to calculate the normalize factor via the following formula:

```
Norm factor = Square Root of (Sum of(each word value power 2));
```

Then we can divide each individual element by this factor. In our original example, the word values will change as follow:

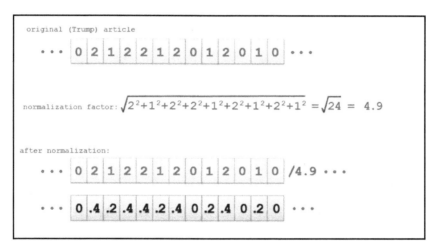

As you see, the value 2 from the original document becomes `0.4` and that helps us to level out (normalize if you like) all word counts to a more realistic value, regardless of article length. Now lets modify our Evidence service and add normalization to it:

```
// src/app/evidence/evidence.service.ts
// ...
export class EvidenceService {
  //...
  wordAnalyzer(url) {
    this.getArticle(this.getYahooQueryUrl(url))
      .subscribe(
        data => {
          this.findInKey(data, 'content');
          this.words= this.evaluateWords(
            this.countInstances(this.extractWords(this.article))
          );
        });
```

```
    }

    evaluateWords(instances) {
      var words = [];
      var normFactor = this.calculateNorm(instances);
      instances.forEach(function (w) {
        var normalized = w.count/normFactor;
        words.push({
            word:w.word,
            count:w.count,
            normalized:normalized
          })
      });
      return words;
    }

    calculateNorm (rawWords) {
      var total = 0;
      rawWords.forEach(function (w) {
        total += w.count * w.count;
      });
      return Math.sqrt(total);
    }
    // ...
  }
```

Here, we added another function called `evaluateWords()` and passed the output of `countInstances()` to it. The `evaluateWords()` function would be in charge of all required calculations, including the normalization. After normalizing the words, the result will be returned as an array of objects.

The normalization process happens inside `calculateNorm()`. The `calculateNorm()` function does exactly what we earlier mentioned in plain English. It returns the square root of all squared words summed.

Now we add another column to the template and show the normalized value for each word as follow:

```
# src/app/evidence.evidence.html
#...
  <table class="table">
    <thead>
      <tr>
        <th>#</th>
        <th>Words</th>
        <th>Raw Value</th>
        <th>Normalized Value</th>
```

```
      </tr>
    </thead>
    <tbody *ngFor="let w of evidenceService.words; let i=index">
      <tr>
        <th>{{i+1}}</th>
        <td>{{w.word}}</td>
        <td>{{w.count}}</td>
        <td>{{w.normalized}}</td>
      </tr>
    </tbody>
  </table>
#...
```

Check the browser now and you will see after normalization, the word occurrence value has been brought down tremendously and it feels like words are way closer to each other now:

Please note that we didn't round up/down the float numbers. We will see how to do that soon. But remember, in real-world situations, as the corpus grows and we are dealing with a larger number of articles and more words in each article, we will see every single digit after the floating point plays a critical role in accuracy. In other words, if we modify values here by epsilon, later on we will miss the targets by miles.

The next problem that we have here is the real value of words. Even after normalization, it is not fair to give the same value for all words just because they were repeated equally. If you think about it, the words "Trump" and "the" shouldn't have the same value. (In my opinion, the word "the" should have a higher value! *Kidding... :)*). What we need here is a mechanism which prioritizea important words.

Introducing the TF-IDF factor

To extract and prioritize important words from an article, we are going to use the **Term Frequency – Inverse Document Frequency (TF-IDF)** factor. It is a tool which we are going to use for hunting important words.

Before we continue, you might think, in the rating (Chapter 4, *The Rating Service – Data Management*) and notifier (Chapter 5, *The Notifier Service – Creating Cron Jobs in Angular*) services, we used trending keywords to rate and recognize the articles of our interest, so why we can't continue the same line of logic for finding similar articles? The answer lies in the difference between linear logic and multidimensional thinking. Yes, we could search for the same keywords and make our collector service hit the servers with some predefined orders. But if you think about it, there is not much of AI is happening here and the search result would be painfully predictable and boring. In fact, why did we need to create these services in the first place when the Google search engine does an amazing job at finding things? What makes our application different is the ability to dive into the unknown, looking for hints and clues which might not be visible at first glance. That is why this project called The Sherlock Project.

The question is, how do we define important words? Obviously, if we declare important words based on repetition in the original document (TF), it doesn't get us anywhere, because popular words such as "the" or "to" will drown the real value of important words.

But if we add the corpus – other documents in the sample pool – to the equation (IDF), we can create a mechanism which intensifies the value of important words and almost nullifies the effect of unimportant words. So the TF-IDF formula goes like this:

```
# of occurance for a specific word * log((# of docs in the corpus)/(1+#
of docs contain a specific word))
```

Lets put this in perspective and see how it works. Imagine we have 1,000 documents in our corpus and we want to find the value of the word "the". Because almost all documents have this word, most likely we will end up with the following result:

```
IDF = log (1000/1+1000) = log 1 = 0
```

So the value of a popular word such as "the" is literally lowered to 0. This means it doesn't matter how many times this word is repeated in the current document, because when it times by 0, the result will be 0.

Now lets see how it works for a word such as "election" in the same corpus. Lets assume there are only 86 documents in our corpus which contain the word "election". So the IDF factor produces the following result:

```
IDF = log (1000/1+87) = log (11.36) = 3.5
```

That is impressive. It means if this word is repeated a few times in the current document (for example, five times), we get a noticeable value for it (TF*IDF = 5 x 3.5 = 17.5). Now we have a tool that at the same time intensifies important words while nullifies unimportant words in a given article. Don't worry about the corpus and how we can gather all articles in there at the moment. We will get to that later. For now, lets equip our service with the TF-IDF formula.

Implementing the TF-IDF factor

To calculate the TF-IDF factor, first we need to find out the IDF value for each word. Open the evidence service and add a new function to it as follow:

```
// src/app/evidence/evidence.service.ts
//...
export class EvidenceService {
  //...
  saveIDFs (word) {
    var corpusSize   = 1000;
    var docsWithWord = 55;
    return Math.log2(corpusSize/(1+docsWithWord));
  }
```

```
}
```

The hard-coded values here are just for testing the output and, as usual, we will replace them with real functions soon. To see how it looks in the browser, add new columns to the template as follow:

```
# src/app/evidence/evidence.html
# ...
    <!-- Table -->
    <table class="table">
      <thead>
      <tr>
        <th>#</th>
        <th>Words</th>
        <th>Counts</th>
        <th>Normalized</th>
        <th>IDF factor</th>
        <th>TFIDF(C)</th>
        <th>TFIDF(N)</th>
      </tr>
      </thead>
      <tbody *ngFor="#w of evidenceService.words; #i=index">
        <tr>
          <th>{{i+1}}</th>
          <td>{{w.word}}</td>
          <td>{{w.count}}</td>
          <td>{{w.normalized}}</td>
          <td>{{w.idf}}</td>
          <td>{{w.tfidf_C}}</td>
          <td>{{w.tfidf_N}}</td>
        </tr>
      </tbody>
    </table>
  #...
```

The new columns will look for the TF-IDF factor as a property for each word. This property does not exist at the moment so lets find out where we can assemble the word objects and add the TF-IDF property to it. As you can see, it happens inside the evaluateWords() function so edit this function as follow:

```
// src/app/evidence/evidence.service.ts
//...
export class EvidenceService {
  //...
  evaluateWords(instances) {
    var self = this;
    var words = [];
    var normFactor = this.calculateNorm(instances);
```

```
instances.forEach(function (w) {
  var normalized = w.count/normFactor;
  var idf = self.saveIDF(w);
  words.push({
      word:w.word,
      count:w.count,
      idf:parseFloat(idf).toFixed(5),
      normalized:normalized.toFixed(5),
      tfidf_N:(normalized*idf).toFixed(5),
      tfidf_C:(w.count*idf).toFixed(5)
  })
});
return words;
}
}
```

Here, we calculated two versions of TF-IDF. tfidf_N uses the normalized value for each word and tfidf_C uses the raw counts. We keep them both so we can compare the values side by side and see how normalization works in action.

Now check the output and the TF-IDF factor is calculated for each column – based on the hard-coded values:

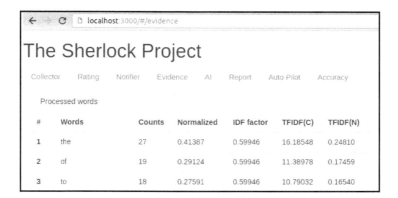

This new function suggests a lot of subtasks. We need to do the following:

- Assemble a corpus (an array of documents)
- Find how many documents there are in the corpus
- Count the number of documents that contain a specific word
- Calculate and return the TF-IDF factor based on the given formula

Let's begin by creating a corpus.

Corpus – how to build the body

"Corpus" is a Latin word which means "body". If it sounds like "corpse" (dead body), well, that is because it literally got its meaning from the concept of dead body and later on it branched out into many fields, including linguistics, music, literature, religion, and so on. What they all have in common is the meaning: "corpus" means "body".

Our evidence service needs a body to perform its magic. As we saw in the previous section, the TF-IDF factor cannot be calculated if we don't have body made out of hundreds of articles. So lets begin by creating a corpus.

Lets go back to the selected news item from the previous section.

Lets say we want to see if our application can find and organize enough evidence related to that news title and provide us some insight. One way to build the corpus around this article is to find articles related to important keywords in the original news item. Checking the contents of that news, we can find the following names and keywords:

- Summer Zervos
- Kristin Anderson
- Jessica Leeds
- Mar-a-Lago
- *People* magazine

We can dig in for even more keywords but, for now, lets keep it simple. We are going to find articles for each keyword in specific time-period patterns. In order to cover as much investigation ground as possible, lets set the periods as follow:

last 24 hours, last week, last month, last 6 months, last year, last decade.

We want to find 10 articles per each period for the given keywords (that will lead to a maximum of 60 articles per keyword). We can see, in the given news item, there are direct connections between each keyword and "Trump" so we need repeat the process with "Trump" + keyword and that will leave us with 600 items in the corpus for the given example. Compared to what real data scientists use, it is not very big, but it is enough for our experiment.

It is important to mention that the corpus won't contain exactly 600 items. There are requests which will end up with 400 or 404 response codes and will be ignored.

Before we start coding for corpus functions, we need to update our template a little and add missing pieces to it.

Making the template Corpus aware

What we need in the template is a section where we can select the document of our interest and a click event which shows the contents of document when it is selected. It will be even more democratic if we don't limit the user to the high-ranked news saved under `Notifier/rated-news` object. So lets put another input box where they can enter a URL for any article of their choice, regardless of what has been suggested by the media.

In fact, sometimes we had better stay away from the way the mainstream media or hot trends decide what we need to read, hear, and watch. Since I started writing this book, I have been watching closely how news agencies prioritize subjects and categorize them into important or trivial groups. There have been times which I failed to see the value in a news item which was considered to be an important one. We will discuss this soon. For now, lets give the user the choice to select between high-ranked news or the URL of their choice and focus on the technical side.

Finally, we need input boxes to catch the main keyword and supporting keywords for the nominated article. These inputs will be passed to our – yet to be implemented – corpus functions for further processing.

Open the template and add the following section to it:

```
# /src/app/evidence/evidence.html
<div class="container">
  <div class="col-md-5">
    <div class="panel panel-default ">
      <div class="panel-heading">Available News Items</div>
      <ul class="list-unstyled">
        <li *ngFor="let item of newsItems">
          <div class="media-right">
            <input type="radio" (click)="onSelect(item, true)">
            {{item.title}} <a href="{{item.link}}">(read more)</a>
          </div>
        </li>
```

```
        </ul>
        <div class="input-group">
          <input type="text" class="form-control" placeholder="other
news/article url..." #url>
          <span class="input-group-btn">
          <button class="btn btn-default" type="button"
(click)="onSelect(url.value, false)>Go!</button>
          </span>
        </div><!-- /input-group -->
      </div>
      <div class="panel panel-default ">
        <div class="panel-heading">
          Nominated keywords for corpus
        </div>
        <input type="text" [(ngModel)]="supportKeywords" class="form-control"
placeholder="Comma separated keywords">
        <input type="text" [(ngModel)]="mainKeyword"
class="form-control" placeholder="Keyword of interest">
        <button type="submit" (click)="buildCorpus()" class="btn btn-default
btn-block">Fetch Articles For Corpus</button>
      </div>
      <div class="panel panel-default ">
      # HTML tags for article content
    </div>
    <div class="col-md-7">
      # HTML tags for words
    </div>
</div>
```

Here, we divided the page into two columns. On the left-hand side, we have all the
required inputs for calculations and evaluations, and on the right-hand side, we have the
processed words and evaluated number. Here is what the page looks like without selecting
or entering anything:

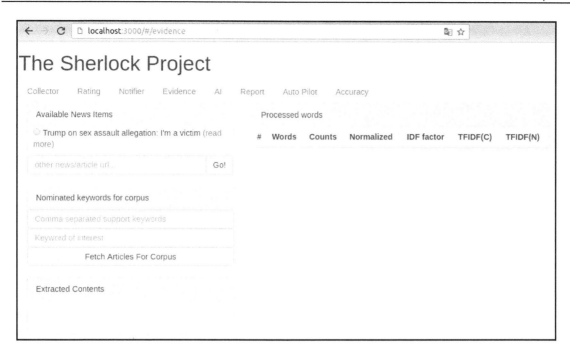

Notice that the (click) event for both radio buttons and the URL input box trigger the same `onSelect()` function inside the component. We have just added an extra input parameter of type boolean to distinguish between the sources of the click. We see how to modify the `onSelect()` function to serve both type of inputs.

Making the component Corpus aware

Changing the template requires updating the business logic in the component as well. In other words, we need more than one result from the Notifier/rated-news object; moreover, we need to consider any other URL that the user might provide as well. On top of that, calling the evidence service should be bound to user selection and we can't let that happen by default. With these requirements, update the business logic as follow:

```
// src/app/evidence/evidence.component.ts
// ...
import {EvidenceService} from "./evidence.service";

export class EvidenceComponent {
  private newsItems;
  private supportKeywords;
  private mainKeyword;
```

```
//...

constructor (es:EvidenceService, af: AngularFire) {
  this.evidenceService = es;
  this.angularFire = af;
}

ngOnInit() {
  this.angularFire.database.list('/Notifier/rated-news', {
    query: {
      orderByChild: 'rank',
      limitToFirst: 5 // lets fetch 5 items
    }}).subscribe(data => {
      this.newsItems = data;
    }
  );
}

onSelect(item, isRadio){
  this.resetCounters();
  var url = isRadio?item.link:item;
  this.evidenceService.wordAnalyzer(url);
}

buildCorpus() {
  // ToDo: get input keywords and fetch related articles/news
}
}
```

The first thing to notice in the modifications is increasing the query limit to five items and subscribing the component variable to them. Now the users have the power to choose the news item they want to investigate.

When they select an item or enter a URL of their choice, the `onSelect()` function triggers and, based on the source of click event (radio button or input text), sets a proper value for URL before sending it to the Evidence service for further processing:

```
url = isRadio?item.link:item;
```

Also notice that at the beginning of `onSelect()` function, we call a method to reset the previous values. This method simply nullifies all previous content of words and articles:

```
// src/app/evidence/evidence.service.ts
//...
export class EvidenceService {
  //...
  resetCounters() {
```

```
      this.article = null;
      this.words = null;
    }
  }
```

If we don't do that, every time the user clicks on a news item, or pushes the Go button, the related article will be appended to the previous one and the word instances of the new selection will be added to the previous numbers, making our calculations inaccurate. This function will be moved to the corpus builder soon.

The Corpus functions

Now it is time to replace recent hardcoded values for the corpus with real functions, so open the evidence service and add the following modifications to it:

```
// src/app/evidence/evidence.service.ts
//...
@Injectable()
export class EvidenceService {
  private corpusSize;
  private corpus: FirebaseListObservable <any>;
  private IDFs: FirebaseListObservable <any>;
  //...
  constructor(http: Http, af: AngularFire) {
    this.http = http;
    this.angularFire = af;
    this.corpus = af.database.list('Evidence/Corpus/Articles');
    this.IDFs = af.database.list('Evidence/Corpus/IDFs');
  }

  corpusBuilder(keywords) {
    // ToDo:
    // 1. Fetch links for each keyword
    // 2. Pass the link to EvidenceService for extracting contents
    // 3. Save them under corpus key for further caluculation
  }
}
```

Please notice that we have created two children under the Evidence/Corpus key. Apart from articles, we need to keep all IDF calculations somewhere, because as we proceed to build clusters, we need to read IDFs.

Now, here is the critical question. The first ToDo step in the `corpusBuilder()` involves fetching links. Which search engine shall we use to fetch the related links for each keyword?

Introducing the Google Custom Search Engine

As we saw in `Chapter 3`, *The Collector Service – Using Controllers to Collect Data*, not every website is open to HTTP requests coming from unknown sources. We experienced **cross-origin resource sharing** (**CORS**) issues before and we saw how to use Yahoo APIs to work around it. So what we need here is a list of links related to searched keywords. Assembling a URL which uses Google to search for keywords is easy. What is not easy is passing that search result to the Yahoo API for extracting the contents. If you do that, you will get an "access denied" response from Google.

That makes sense because if Google people don't set any control over the source and number of queries that hit their servers, they will be vulnerable and a few lines of code can put a lot of pressure on, or even crash, their servers. Basically, what they say is: you are welcome to use our search engine in browser/mobile applications but if you are going to make requests via code or command line, we need to know who you are and we need to set a quota for your usage.

The **Google Custom Search Engine** (**CSE**) provides such a facility to webmasters so they can customize the Google search engine and use it in their websites / Web applications. It comes with an API which we are going to use to fetch links for our corpus.

Enabling the Custom Search API And creating a new CSE

Adding a search feature to our application is a two-step process. First, we need to enable the Custom Search API for our project and then we need to create a new search engine and use its id in our application.

In order to enable the Custom Search API – assuming that you have already logged in to your Google Developers console – head to the following link:

`https://console.developers.google.com/apis/api/customsearch/overview`

Then, hit the **Enable** link at the top of the page:

If this is the first time you are doing this, you will be led to the following page:

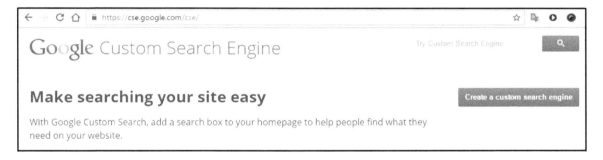

Hit the blue button to create a new custom search engine. On the next page, all you need to do is set the name for your new search engine and push the Create button at the bottom of the page:

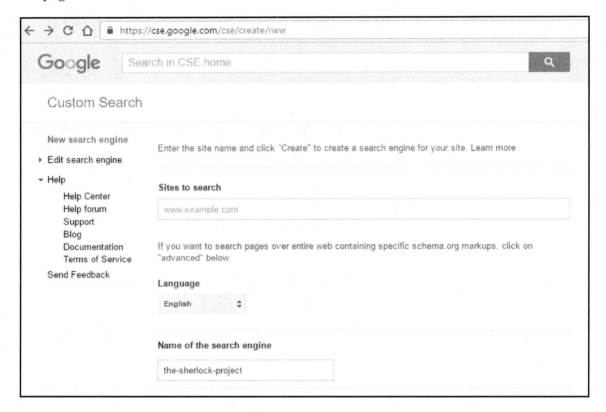

The default search settings will force the search engine to look for everything (image, video, text, and so on). But you can limit the search options by going to the advanced section of this window. You can visit schema.org to find out what other options you have and what each option does.

After the search engine is created successfully, the following page will be shown:

What we are interested in on this page is the cx code. The combination of this code and the API key for our project is required every time we need to use the custom search engine. So lets export them globally and make sure they are available application-wide.

Open the app.module.ts file and export the following constant in it:

```
// src/app/app.module.ts
//...
export const googleSearchConfig = {
  apiKey: 'your-google-api-key',
  cx     : 'your-custom-search-engine-code'
};
```

In case you need these keys in the future, you can find apiKey by looking under the credentials tab inside the Google Developers console:
https://console.developers.google.com/apis/credentials
You can find the cx value by checking the settings for the search engine that you have just created:
https://cse.google.com/cse/all

Having all players in place, lets see what we can do with our new search engine. We don't need to create a new http.get() request inside our app to check the new search engine. Simply open your browser and try something like this:

```
https://www.googleapis.com/customsearch/v1?key=your-google-api-key&cx=your-cust
om-search-engine-code&q=keyword
```

The response will be a robust JSON object with loads of details. It extracts every valuable detail out of searched pages and summarizes them into objects like this:

```
"queries": {
  "request": [
    {
     "title": "Google Custom Search - keyword",
     "totalResults": "85800000",
     "searchTerms": "keyword",
     "count": 10,
     "startIndex": 1,
     "inputEncoding": "utf8",
     "outputEncoding": "utf8",
     "safe": "off",
     "cx": "001410267427255255168:nfviboevhri"
    }
  ],
  ...
},
"context": {
 "title": "the-sherlock-project"
},
...
"items": [
  {
   "kind": "customsearch#result",
   "title":"How To Do Keyword Research-The Beginners Guide ",
   "htmlTitle": "How To Do \u003cb\u003eKeyword",
   "link":"https://moz.com/beginners-guide-to-seo/keyword",
   "displayLink": "moz.com",
   "snippet": "It all begins with words typed into ...
   ...
  },
 ]
}
```

We are interested in the "items" part and, to be more specific, we want the value stored in the "link" key. This is the URL that we get from our search engine response and pass it to Yahoo APIs to get the HTML contents of the page associated with that URL.

In this book, we are going to use only a few options in our search and we will discuss them during the implementation, but be aware that there are many parameters that we can use in our search queries, which you can find out about here:

```
https://developers.google.com/custom-search/json-api/v1/reference/cse/list#para
meters
```

Now we have a clear idea about implementing the functions for fetching links and processing their contents, but before getting on with coding, lets talk about the quota for the Custom Search API. Please keep in mind we are using a free account and we are limited to 100 queries per day. Since each query can generate a response with up to 10 links, that gives us a total of 1,000 links per day. It is more than enough for our experiment.

If, at any stage, you need to check your usage, you can go to the Custom Search API dashboard and click on the Quotas link at the top of the page:

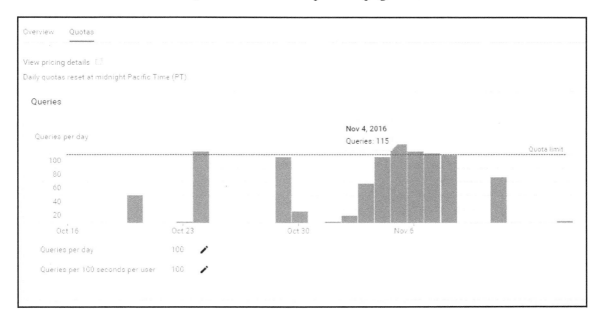

Before moving on, there are a few things to notice on this page:

- First of all, the 100 queries per day is not a strict quota. As you can see, in my account, there have been days when I used 95 queries, and then I requested a burst of an extra 20 queries (November 4). As you can see, I went over the quota but my request was accepted and processed gracefully.
- Second, please keep in mind that no matter where you are located in the world, the quota will be reset at midnight Pacific Time. This is just a heads-up in case you want to plan your usage during the day or night.
- Third, if you have decided to take your code to the next level and a free account with a limited quota is not good enough anymore, you can always upgrade your services. Click on **View pricing details** and keep in mind that prices are always subject to change (they are always going down).

Implementing the corpusBuilder() function

We have a working search engine in place. Now it is time to use it in our application. Start by reviewing the corpusBuilder() function and modify it as follow:

```
// src/app/evidence/evidence.service.ts
//...
export class EvidenceService {
  //...
  corpusBuilder(mainKeyword, supportKeywords) {
    this.resetCounters();
    var keywords = this.setKeywordArray(
      mainKeyword, supportKeywords
    );
    keywords.forEach((keyword: any) => {
      this.fetchLinks(keyword);
    })
  }
}
```

Since calling this function will generate a new set of articles and word counts, we need to make sure any previous records of content and words are erased from the template. Calling the resetCounters() function will serve this purpose.

Now we need to create an array of keywords from the provided main and supported keywords in the template. Please remember the corpus will be built around those keywords we will implement and use setKeywordArray() for building the keyword array.

Next, we will loop through the keyword array and fetch the related group of links for each of them. Lets implement the keyword array here and fetch the links in the next section:

```
// src/app/evidence/evidence.service.ts
//...
export class EvidenceService {
  //...
  setKeywordArray(mainKeyword, supportKeywords) {
    var keywords = [];
    if (supportKeywords)
      keywords = supportKeywords.split(",");
    keywords.forEach(k => {
      keywords.push(mainKeyword+' '+k);
    });
    keywords.unshift(mainKeyword);
    return keywords;
  }
}
```

It is a simple logic which saves a string of comma-separated elements into an array (if support keywords are provided in the template), then adds the combination of each support keyword and main keyword as a new element and finally adds the main keyword to the beginning of the array using the `unshift()` function. It is not a big deal and you can add the main keyword to the end of the array (using the `push()` function), but adding it at the beginning gives that array a sense of priority.

Couldn't we push the main keyword first then deal with the support keywords afterward? Yes, that is possible too but then you have to create two variables and deal with merging two arrays later. The current implementation is shorter, it does the job in one shot, and it satisfies the purpose with one variable only.

Fetching the links

To fetch the links, we need to define a couple of time spans. As we mentioned before, we need to find links, for a given keyword, over a predefined time span (last 24 hours, last week, last month, and so on). That means we have to create nested loops, where the outer one loops through the keyword list and the inner one calls the search engine for various time spans.

So the `fetchLinks()` function can be implemented as follow:

```
// src/app/evidence/evidence.service.ts
//...
import {googleSearchConfig, timeSpans} from "../app.module";
export class EvidenceService {
  //...
  fetchLinks(keyword) {
    var self = this;
    timeSpans.forEach(function (period) {
      self.getSearchResults(
        self.getGoogleQueryUrl(keyword, period)
      ).subscribe(data => data.forEach(function (item) {
        self.wordAnalyzer(item.link);
      }))
    });
  }
}
```

You may have noticed that we imported googleSearchConfig and timeSpans from the application module. That means we need to define timeSpans in app.module.ts as well:

```
// src/app/app.module.ts
//...
export const timeSpans = [
```

```
    {"span":"d1",  "sort":"date:d"},
    {"span":"w1",  "sort":"date:a"},
    {"span":"m1",  "sort":"date:a"},
    {"span":"m6",  "sort":"date:a"},
    {"span":"y1",  "sort":"date:a"},
    {"span":"y10", "sort":"date:a"}
];
```

timeSpan here is a simple JSON object with two properties. The span property defines the time range that we are going to use to perform the search. The values for this property are provided as "d1" (last day), "w1" (last week), and so on, which are the predefined values that Google can recognize and respond to.

The sort property defines the order (d for descending and a for ascending) in which the search results should be shown. We cannot let sort orders for all time spans be descending, because most likely we get the same result sets for all six of them. Please note that since the search results are sorted based on the latest showing first, it doesn't matter whether your time span is within a day or a month. Chances are, the first 10 results would be similar.

But if we sort the results from the last 24 hours in descending order (newest first) and sort the rest of the ranges in ascending order (oldest first), we can cover a lot of searching ground. The following figure shows the differences between the approaches:

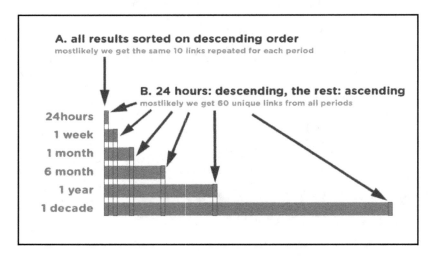

Now remember, the objective is to find links for given keywords and time spans and pass them on to the word analyzer for further processing. That means now we are ready to hit our custom search engine with some parametric queries using the getGoogleQueryUrl() function.

Creating queries and processing search results

Implementing the `getGoogleQueryUrl()` function is very straightforward. We have all the required parameters already. All we need to do is put it all together and return a URL string:

```
// src/app/evidence/evidence.service.ts
//...
export class EvidenceService {
  //...
  getGoogleQueryUrl(keyword, range) {
    return "https://www.googleapis.com/customsearch/v1?" +
      "key=" + googleSearchConfig.apiKey +
      "&cx=" + googleSearchConfig.cx + "&q=" + keyword +
      "&sort=" + range.sort + "&dateRestrict=" + range.span;
  }
}
```

Next, we need to pass this URL string to the `getSearchResults()` function and make an actual `get()` request there:

```
// src/app/evidence/evidence.service.ts
//...
export class EvidenceService {
  //...
  getSearchResults(url) {
    return this.http.get(url)
      .map((res: Response) => res.json())
      .map(data => data.items);
  }
}
```

If you remember from our manual tests a few pages ago, in the JSON response, the search results are saved under the "items" property. But we don't need all properties for each search result item. All we need is the "link" child for each item.

That's why in the `getSearchResults()` function, we return the `items` property as an observable object:

```
.map(data => data.items);
```

Then later, in the `fetchLinks()` function, we subscribe to this observable object and pass only the contents of the `link` child to the `wordAnalyzer()` function for further processing:

```
.subscribe(data => data.forEach(function (item) {
  self.wordAnalyzer(item.link);
}))
```

Now we can create and instantiate two observable objects as follows:

```
this.corpus = af.database.list('Evidence/Corpus/Articles');
this.IDFs = af.database.list('Evidence/Corpus/IDFs');
```

We can then save the articles under the Evidence/Corpus/Articles key. Also, we should find unique words and calculate their IDFs and save them under the `Evidence/Corpus/IDFs` key.

Probably, we would do that after wordAnalyzer() was called. If we did that and tested the result in the browser, we would see the application blow up with a bunch of errors popping up in the console. But none of those errors are as critical as the warning that might get from the Firebase.

Testing the application at that stage by selecting a link (any link from a rated news object) and – to keep it light and simple – providing only ONE keyword for building the corpus would cause a stack overflow issue:

```
469 FIREBASE WARNING: Exception was thrown by       firebase.js:276
    user callback. RangeError: Maximum call stack size exceeded
        at va (http://localhost:3000/main.bundle.js:7999:41)
        at wa (http://localhost:3000/main.bundle.js:7999:90)
        at Yg (http://localhost:3000/main.bundle.js:8163:94)
```

Firebase simply complains that it cannot keep up with the demands coming from our application.

We can give some breathing space to Firebase by setting the traditional JavaScript timeouts. Or we can use the modern observable timers and initialize them inside `ngOnInit()` as follow:

```
ngOnInit() {
  // wait 1 sec, then call wordAnalyzer on 2 sec intervals
  Observable.timer(1000,2000).subscribe(this.wordAnalyzer);
}
```

But do not follow this approach. This is a hacky solution which doesn't fix the root cause of the problem. Lets see how to deal with this issue properly.

Refactoring the service logic (removing IDF calculations)

The problem that we have here is caused by IDF calculations. Lets do a sanity check and study the data flow inside the evidence ecosystem (template, component, and service).

- In component: five top-rated news items are selected and displayed inside the template
- In template: we select a link and fire a click event
- In component: we catch that event and call a service function
- In service: several functions work together to find words and calculate counts, normalization value, IDF, and TFIDF for each word and they return the result as an array back to the component
- In template: the specific part of the screen which is bound to article and its words will be updated

That logic was good enough before to demonstrate concepts such as normalization or the IDF factor for one article. But now we are dealing with hundreds of articles which demand to burst into our corpus in a few seconds and generate a vocabulary of over 50,000 words.

The last thing that we want to do is to update the IDFs object (Evidence/Corpus/IDFs) on every cycle that a new item is added to the Articles object (Evidence/Corpus/Articles). Instead, we need to wait for the corpus to be fully populated, then we can issue a command to calculate all IDFs in one cycle.

So lets begin with the wordAnalyzer function and modify it as follow:

```
// src/app/evidence/evidence.service.ts
// ...
export class EvidenceService {
  //...
  wordAnalyzer(url) {
    this.getArticle(this.getYahooQueryUrl(url))
      .subscribe( data => {
        this.resetCounters();
        this.findKey(data, 'content');
        if (this.article) {
          this.evaluateWords(
            this.countInstances(
              this.extractWords(this.article)
            )
          ).then(data => {
            this.corpus.push(
```

```
                {article: this.article, link: url, bag_of_words: data});
                })
            }
        });
    }
```

wordAnalyzer() is mostly like it was before except now we expect evaluateWords() to return a promise. That promise will contain a bag of words for the evaluated article and will be saved as part of a child inside the Evidence/Corpus/Articles object.

This means that now we need to refactor the evaluateWords() function. First, we need to make sure it will return a promise. Second, we need to take any sign of IDF calculations out of this function. They will have their own place soon:

```
// src/app/evidence/evidence.service.ts
// ...
export class EvidenceService {
  //...
  evaluateWords(instances) {
    var self = this;
    var normFactor = this.calculateNorm(instances);
    return Promise.all(instances.map(function (w) {
      if (w.word.length < 20) {
        var normalized = w.count / normFactor;
        w['normalized'] = normalized.toFixed(4);
        self.words.push(w);
      }
      return w;
    }));
  }
}
```

When we call for Promise.all(), we make sure that the return value from this function will be a promise and at the same time we make sure any other promises inside this code block will be resolved before returning any value to the callback function. This is a good practice, because since we are going to deal with a lot of words in each article, and dealing with each word might take some time, using all() we guarantee that all promises are resolved before moving on to the next task.

Did you notice the word length check (`if (w.word.length<20 )`) in the code? It wasn't there before and the reason that we need it is to make sure all concatenated nonsense words are filtered out and they are prevented from being saved to the database. It reduces some overhead and optimizes the overall performance a little. To see what kind of words might be generated if we don't have that check – later – comment out the condition and you will see wrong word instances such as: pleasevisitourfacebookpage. The bottom line is we might lose words which legitimately are longer than 20 characters, for example, some medical terms such as `pneumonoultramicroscopicsilicovolcanokoniosis`. Personally, I don't know how to read such words and don't see how I'd possibly be interested to get insight into these terms. But if, for any reason, you needed to consider long words in your investigation, by all means feel free to change the length condition inside the code. (I bet some of you tried to read that medical term ;))

Now we have an independent logic for processing words in each article and our resources won't be wasted on calculating IDFs in each cycle. The next step is refactoring the template and adding a new table which will be populated with IDF calculations on demand.

Refactoring the template

In order to have word-related calculations in one place, lets divide the current table into two separate ones where the left-hand side is used for analyzed words and the right-hand side is used for IDF calculations. Moreover, lets put a button for IDF calculations on top of the right-hand table. So edit the previous template as follow:

```
<div class="container">
  <div class="col-md-5">
    # ...
  </div>
  <div class="col-md-7">
    <div class="panel panel-default ">
      <!-- Default panel contents -->
      <div class="panel-heading">Processed words
        ( corpus: {{evidenceService.corpusSize}} items
        - vocabulary: {{evidenceService.vocabularySize}} words )
        <button class="btn btn-default btn-xs pull-right"
          type="button" (click)="onIDFs()">Calculate IDFs</button>
      </div>
      <!-- Table -->
      <div class="col-md-7">
```

```
<table class="table">
<thead>
<tr><th>#</th><th>Words</th><th>Counts</th><th>Normed</th>
</tr>
</thead>
<tbody *ngFor="#w of evidenceService.words;#i=index">
<tr>
  <td>{{i+1}}</td>
  <td>{{w.word}}</td>
  <td>{{w.count}}</td>
  <td>{{w.normalized}}</td>
</tr>
</tbody>
</table>
</div>
<div class="col-md-5">
  <table class="table">
  <thead>
  <tr><th>IDF</th><th>TF-IDF(C)</th><th>TF-IDF(N)</th></tr>
  </thead>
  <tbody *ngFor="#w of evidenceService.words; #i=index">
  <tr>
    <td>{{w.idf}}</td>
    <td>{{w.tfidf_C}}</td>
    <td>{{w.tfidf_N}}</td>
  </tr>
  </tbody>
  </table>
  </div>
  </div>
 </div>
</div>
```

Since the word calculations need more space, we assigned seven columns to the left-hand table (`class='col-md-7'`) and five columns to the IDF table on the right (`class='col-md-5'`).

Also, notice the statistic information that we put in the header of the IDF table:

```
<div class="panel-heading">Processed words
  ( corpus: {{evidenceService.corpusSize}} items
  - vocabulary: {{evidenceService.vocabularySize}} words )
  <button class="btn btn-default btn-xs pull-right"
    type="button" (click)="onIDFs()">Calculate IDFs</button>
</div>
```

Being informed about the number of articles in the corpus and the number of words in the vocabulary provides a better understanding about the size of the current investigation.

After these modifications, the template will look like this:

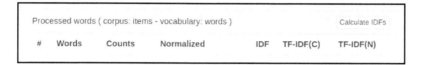

Now it is time to go back to the component and the service and add the missing pieces.

Updating the component and the service

In order to respond to the Calculate IDF button inside the template, all we need to do in the component is catch the click event and call the related function from the service. So just add the onIDFs() function as follow:

```
// src/app/evidence/evidence.component.ts
// ...
export class EvidenceComponent implements OnInit{
  // ...
  onIDFs() {
    this.evidenceService.saveIDFs();
  }
}
```

However, on the service side, we have a lot of work to do. We can summarize the required steps for IDF calculations as follow:

1. Remove previous IDF calculations: every time a new article is added to the corpus, it makes all previous IDF calculations invalid, so we need to erase them before starting the new calculations.
2. Loop through articles and gather all unique words by looking into bag of words for each article. This will be a corpus-level bag of words or a bag of words made out of all available bags of words if you like.
3. Loop through unique words and find the number of articles that each unique word exists in.
4. Calculate the IDF.
5. Save IDFs as an array of {word:", number_of_docs:", idf:"} objects.

Also, we need to add two private variables which we are going to use as informative bits in the heading of the IDF table. With that requirement in mind, add a new function called saveIDFs() to the Evidence service as follow (to make the implementation easier to understand, I have added comments which indicate where each step begins in the code):

```
// src/app/evidence/evidence.service.ts
// ...
export class EvidenceService {
  private vocabularySize;
  private corpusSize;
  //...
  saveIDFs() {
    var uniqueBagOfWords = {};
    // step 1 ...........................................
    this.IDFs.remove();
    this.corpus._ref.once("value")
      .then(snapshot => {
        this.corpusSize = snapshot.numChildren();
        // steps 2 & 3 ..................................
        snapshot.forEach(item => {
          item.child('bag_of_words').val().forEach(w => {
            uniqueBagOfWords.hasOwnProperty(w.word) ?
              uniqueBagOfWords[w.word]++ :
              uniqueBagOfWords[w.word] = 1;
          });
        });
        var words = Object.keys(uniqueBagOfWords);
        this.vocabularySize = words.length;
        // step 4 .......................................
        words.forEach(word => {
          var idf = Math.abs(Math.log2(
            this.corpusSize / (uniqueBagOfWords[word] + 1)
          ));
          // step 5 .....................................
          this.IDFs.push({'word': word, 'doc_with_word':
            uniqueBagOfWords[word], 'IDF': idf});
          this.words.some(function (item) {
            if (item.word === word) {
              item['idf']    = idf.toFixed(4);
              item['tfidf_C'] = (idf*item.count).toFixed(4);
              item['tfidf_N'] = (idf*item.normalized).toFixed(4);
              return true;
            }
          })
        });
      });
  }
}
```

There are two things that we need to discuss a little. First of all, notice the moment we get a value for corpus size or vocabulary, we save them in the private variables so later we can show them in the template:

```
this.corpusSize = snapshot.numChildren();
//...
this.vocabularySize = words.length;
```

Second, look at the some() function at the end of this code block. Since we need to display IDF calculations for the current article, if somehow we manage to utilize the current loop and add more properties to the 'this.words' variable, it saves our processing time noticeably.

In other words, we don't need to create another loop *after* all the IDFs are calculated and look for words which are currently showing on the screen. We calculate and assign them to the this.words variable as we proceed.

The even more clever move is to break the loop the very moment that we find a match for an IDF word. Both the forEach() and some() functions are designed to loop through array elements. But forEach() forces you to follow the loop till the last element in the array, while the some() loop can be broken the moment a condition is met.

Knowing that our vocabulary can grow to over 50,000 words, having a choice to stop the loop can give a tremendous boost to our application's performance.

How to choose a subject for a road test

Based on the current design, we can choose one of the high-ranked news items or enter a URL of our own choice to build a corpus around it. The logic in our code works the same for both of them. But the reason that I'm going to choose an independent link as the subject of our investigation is because I can not trust the hot trends or mainstream media any more. As I mentioned earlier in this chapter, as part of the R&D for the Sherlock Project, I had to watch closely the news agency outlets and follow all the pulses when an important news story breaks out. At the same time, I watched how trends respond to news on an hourly basis. And finally, I watched how our application works with the given data.

I encourage everyone to do some experiments with a couple of hot trends and see it for yourselves. When I followed what was suggested by news agencies and supported by hot trends, I expected some insights which would give me a better understanding about the subject and perhaps a clear direction to formulate my next question. But, most of the time, what I got was a bunch of bland and not very interesting links which didn't provide the value that I was expecting. The problem was input. At the end of the day, what we are dealing with here is an algorithm and we can't expect good results out of poor data: garbage in, garbage out.

To give you an example, for the past 6 months, the news agencies bombarded their audiences all around the world with the US presidential elections, Democrats and Republicans, the private life of their nominees, how they will affect the financial markets, how they will impact the current conflicts and wars in the world, and so on. Quora, which used to be my favorite social network where you could meet and talk to intelligent people, turned into a battleground.Affected by hot trends, most of the polite and mature communication was replaced by rants where people called each other names and used very graphic literature to prove their points.

So the question is, do we really want to be part of this? News agencies surf the current waves to make money as much as possible. They are not with or against anyone. Simply put, they are just following the money. The question is, should we fall for it? I mean, think about it, does it really matter how many ladies are groped by Donald Trump? If something is unethical, it is unethical. And if we use an algorithm to get some insight about it, what value do we get out of it?

I can talk about this forever but the moral of story is this: make sure you are facing the right direction before focusing on technical stuff.

For that reason, I'm going to ignore what is supposed to be high-ranked news and focus on subjects such as 3D printing, biofuel, or living on Mars.

How can we live On Mars?

To kick-start the test, lets use the following link and have a look at the contents:

`http://www.universetoday.com/111462/how-can-we-live-on-mars`

Just by looking at its bag of words (864 unique words) and skimming through the contents, it sounds like an interesting article.

It discusses – objectively – reasons to go and reasons not to go to Mars. It provides some facts about the red planet, discusses the scientific obstacles, and offers possible solutions for that challengApart from the article itself, there are comments from other people sharing their point of view on this. For example, PHILW1776 suggests the following:

Short Term...

Bring hydrogen. React with CO2 to produce methane CH4 to power rockets and land vehicles and O2. All this should be done before colonists land...

PHILW1776

It seems this article has some good potential to gather some facts, get some insight, and learn something about our other neighbors in the solar system. So lets pick a few key words and build a corpus for this article.

For this test, I chose the following keywords:

```
Support keywords: Climate Change,regolith,Elon Musk,SpaceX,Solar
System,oxygen,radiation,toxic soil,NASA,Martian,hydroponic
Main keyword: Mars
```

As you can see, that is a lot of queries. That means the final keyword array will have 25 elements and since each element will be queried over 6 different periods, that will leave us with 150 queries. This is beyond our quota (100 queries per day). I did it here to test Google's patience plus show you the missing items. You guys at home, DON'T DO THAT or your account might be suspended:

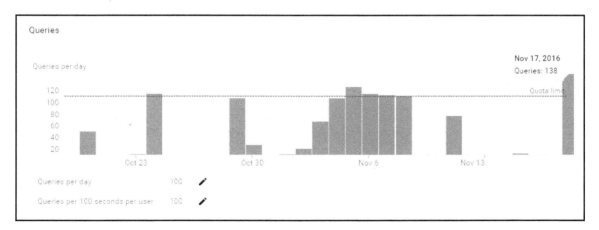

If you need more queries, you can always come back the next day when the quota is reset. Keep in mind that the corpus is saved in the Firebase database and you can always add more items to it.

Now, here is the question: we expected 150 queries, so why does the control panel show only 138? What happened to the 12 missing queries? Remember we talked about some requests which come back with 400 or 404 responses? These 12 queries are among them. Open your browser console and spot them there if you like.

Testing the IDF calculations

Queries went down well and it seems we have a healthy number of articles in our newly created corpus. So simply push the Calculate IDFs button in the browser and watch them be calculated. After about 30 seconds or so, you should be able to see the output:

Processed words (corpus: 342 items - vocabulary: 37247 words)						Calculate IDFs
#	Words	Counts	Normalized	IDF	TF-IDF(C)	TF-IDF(N)
1	the	59	0.5811	0.2580	15.2209	0.1499
2	of	40	0.3940	0.2630	10.5214	0.1036
3	and	28	0.2758	0.2630	7.3650	0.0725
4	a	23	0.2265	0.3146	7.2350	0.0712
5	in	20	0.1970	0.3198	6.3964	0.0630
6	water	17	0.1674	2.3093	39.2586	0.3866
7	to	17	0.1674	0.2783	4.7311	0.0466
8	on	17	0.1674	0.4521	7.6852	0.0757
9	Mars	15	0.1477	1.2681	19.0216	0.1873
10	is	13	0.1280	0.3572	4.6430	0.0457

Let's study the output for a moment. Among the top 10 popular words in this article, we can spot the words "water" and "Mars". Comparing them with the neighbors, we can see the IDF calculations serve the purpose we are looking for brilliantly. For example, the words "water" and "to" are both repeated 17 times in the current article but the normalized TF-IDF value for "water" is 0.3866 while for "to", this value is 0.0466. That means we managed to evaluate and separate valuable words from common ones no matter how many times they are repeated in the article.

The other thing to notice is the information inside the table heading. It says in our vocabulary we have 37,247 words and we saved 342 articles in our corpus. This is suspicious. We managed to slip in 138 queries and since each query should contain 10 results, the corpus should contain around 1,380 articles. Even considering empty pages and bad requests (from Yahoo APIs), ending with only 342 articles in the corpus is way below the expected number. What is going on here?

The thing is I'm responsible for that loss. I just added another parameter to our custom search engine and forced it to return, instead of 10 items, only 3 items per query. That means the corpus size should be around 414 articles (342 is still 72 items short from 414 but it is bearable).

So the question is, how did I set the number of items per query and why did I do it? To set the number, simply add the 'num' parameter at the end of the query string inside the `getGoogleQueryUrl()` function as follows:

```
// src/app/evidence/evidence.service
//...
  getGoogleQueryUrl(keyword, range) {
      return "https://www.googleapis.com/customsearch/v1?" +
        "key=" + googleSearchConfig.apiKey +
        "&cx=" + googleSearchConfig.cx +
        "&q=" + keyword + "&sort=" + range.sort +
        "&dateRestrict=" + range.span +"&num=3";
  }
```

 You can chose any number between 1 and 10 and if you don't set any value, the default is `10`.

Now, the reason I was aiming for a smaller corpus size was to save some processing time. As you continue playing with different subjects, ranges, and keywords, you will notice no matter how much you demand from your application, it always calculates the IDFs in less than a minute; in other words, whether you are dealing with 1,000 articles with a vocabulary made up of over 50,000 words or 300 articles with a vocabulary of 25,000.

Thanks to Angular's two-way binding and clever logic in our service (using the `some()` function instead of `forEach()`, for example), the moment IDF calculations for current words are ready, they are populated in the IDF tables instantly. But that does not mean the fight is over.

Go to your Firebase account and drill down to the Evidence/Corpus/IDFs object. Now open your application in another browser and put them side by side. Now hit the Calculate IDFs button again and watch what happens. Even after the application screen is updated, the Firebase window contents (under the IDFs key) turn yellow, green, and gray for about 10 minutes:

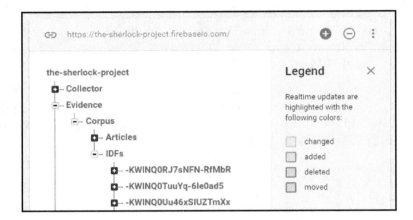

That means regardless of what is happening in the application screen, it takes a while to calculate and organize all IDFs in Firebase. So be very careful if you decide to go party size. Keep in mind the complete English vocabulary contains slightly over 1 million words. The number we are dealing here is around 50,000 (just a fraction) and yet they take about 10 minutes to be fully processed.

So if, one day, you decide to take your application to the next level, you should have some serious planning about strategies and timing.

Getting insights via clustering

So far, we got articles, analyzed their words, and measured the value of them, but how can staring at a bunch of words and numbers possibly provide some insight?

We need to create clusters around the keywords that we are interested in. Since we know the value of the words, we can easily navigate through the bags and see which one of them is a close match to our insight. In other words, what we need to do is group similar articles together.

To be more specific, a keyword will be used as a cluster center, and a group of articles which have the highest similarity (value of words) will be considered to be in closer distance with the cluster center and so eligible to be clustered in one group. This group of articles (called a cluster) provides the insight we are looking for.

For example, if we want to get some insight into the practicality of growing food, building houses, transportation, and so on on Mars, we need to look for related keywords in the corpus and find articles with the highest value that contain those keywords and cluster them together.

Having said that, what we need to do is modify the template, component, and service to create a data flow for creating and displaying clusters.

Making the template and the component cluster aware

Since the clusters are built around keywords, all we need to do in the template is provide input boxes for collecting insight keywords and a button to fire click events:

```
# src/app/evidence/evidence.html
<div class="container">
  <div class="col-md-5">
   #...
    <div class="panel panel-default ">
      <div class="panel-heading">
        Nominated keywords for cluster centers
       </div>
      <input type="text" [(ngModel)]="mainKeyword"
        class="form-control"
        placeholder="Keyword of interest (same as corpus)">
      <input type="text" [(ngModel)]="clusterKeywords"
        class="form-control"
        placeholder="Comma separated cluster keywords">
      <button type="submit" (click)="buildClusters()"
        class="btn btn-default">Build Clusters</button>
    </div>
  </div>
  #...
</div>
```

Please note that we are using the same private variable (`mainKeyword`) that we used for building the corpus. We will see in the service code why we need that. But to clarify its role in the template, imagine the main keyword as the root node for the graph with the cluster centers connected to it directly. The following diagram describes their relationship better:

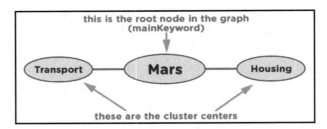

The click event will trigger the `buildClusters()` function, so the next step is updating the component.

First, we need to define the private variable which holds the cluster keywords. Then we need to call and implement the service function which builds clusters:

```
// src/app/evidence/evidence.component.ts
export class EvidenceComponent implements OnInit{
  private clusterKeywords;
  //...
  buildClusters() {
    const self = this;
    this.evidenceService
      .clusterBuilder(this.mainKeyword, this.clusterKeywords);
  }
}
```

This new function simply passes a couple of keywords to the service and delegates the cluster building task to it.

Making the service cluster aware

The logic for building clusters is going to be a little bit complex, because we are going to use all previous bits that we have created so far in one code block. We can break down the cluster builder logic into three parts:

- First, we need to convert the comma-separated string of keywords – coming from the template – into an array.

- Then, we need to implement a nested loop: the outer ring loops through the keywords (keywords for cluster centers) and the inner ring goes through the corpus and looks into each article's bag to find out whether the word "Mars" (mainKeyword) and the current cluster center are available in the bag. If the answer is yes, the frequency of the keyword will be compared to the previous records (it is 0 at the first cycle) and in the event that it is higher, the article is considered as the cluster center. At the end, we save all eligible articles in an array of objects. Later, we will use them as a measure to find similar articles.

These two first steps can be implemented as follow:

```
// src/app/evidence/evidence.service.ts
//...
export class EvidenceService implements OnInit {
  private clusters;
  //...
  clusterBuilder(main, centers) {
    var self = this;
    var count;
    var max;
    var clusterCenters = {};
    var flag;
    var keywords = centers.split(",");
    var records = this.corpus._ref.once("value");
    return Promise.all(keywords.map(function (word) {
        records
          .then(snapshot => {
            max = 0;
            snapshot.forEach(article => {
              count = 0;
              flag = false;
              article.child('bag_of_words').val().forEach(w => {
                if (w.word == word) count += w.count;
                if (w.word == main) flag = true;
              });
              if (flag && count > max) {
                max = count;
                clusterCenters[word] = {
                  id: article.key,
                  bag_of_words:article.child('bag_of_words').val()
                }
              }
            })
            return clusterCenters;
          })
          .then(/* ToDo: Logic for finding similar articles */)
    }));
```

```
      }
   }
```

The important note here is that we used the frequency of a keyword to be considered as a measure for cluster centers. Although it is a good indicator to begin with, it is definitely not accurate. In other words, if we add other parameters to our measure, there might be other articles in the same cluster which could be a better fit to serve as cluster centers.

If that is true, it can cause a lot of trouble, because when we move the center to other articles, that means the similarity measure will change and the previous calculations are not valid anymore. As a result, all distance calculation for finding the closest neighbors should be repeated.

Don't worry, we won't change the measures in this chapter because for the time being we need them as they are. But in Chapter 9, The Accuracy Component, we will come back to this issue and show how to refine the clustering solution and shift the center to the right location and make the cluster converge to the most accurate neighborhood. For now, lets get on with the last bit of clusterBuilder( ) logic.

Now we have the cluster centers which are returned as an array of objects from previous step. So we need to loop through the corpus one more time and calculate the distance between the cluster center and each article. Then we can save these calculated objects in an array and sort them based on the distance property. The cluster that we are looking for will consist of the closest articles to the cluster center. Lets choose only the top seven articles for now:

```
// src/app/evidence/evidence.service.ts
//...
export class EvidenceService implements OnInit {
  //...
  clusterBuilder(centers) {
    var observations = {};
    //...
    return Promise.all(keywords.map(function (word) {
        //...
        .then(centers => {
          var i = 1;
          return records
            .then(snapshot => {
              snapshot.forEach(article => {
                var sum = 0;
                var d = 0; // this is the distance variable
                centers[word].bag_of_words.forEach(k => {
                article.child('bag_of_words').val().forEach(w=>{
                    if (k.word == w.word)
                      sum += k.normalized * w.normalized;
```

```
        })
      })
      d = 1 - sum;
      observations[word].push({
        id: article.key, distance: d.toFixed(4)
      });
    })
    // sort the result based on distance
    observations[word].sort(function (a, b) {
      return a['distance'] - b['distance'];
    });
    // take only top 7 closest articles
    observations[word]=observations[word].slice(0,6);
    return observations;
  }) // end of second then()
  }) // end of first then()
  })); // end of map() function
  }
}
```

You can see the result of this calculation by logging them in the console:

```
console.log(observations);
```

We can make some more modifications to the template and show the clusters in the form of text and number back to the user. But this is not ideal. What would suit us best is a graph which shows the clusters and useful information about them.

Data visualization

There are several definitions for data visualization and many articles talk about how beneficial it is when it is about communicating with data. I think that old idiom "a picture is worth a 1,000 words" summarizes it better. Since we are dealing with – literally – thousands of words, lets see how we can benefit from data visualization libraries in our project in order to get the insight we have been talking about since the beginning of this chapter.

In this section, we are going to use a graph to represent clusters (centers and their articles). We can use the current template to show the graph, but instead we are going to introduce another Angular concept called child components and see how we can use other views as the children of the current view. So, as usual, let's create the blueprints first and develop them progressively as we proceed.

The modal component

When we click the Build clusters button, it does the job, but doesn't show anything back to the user. Lets keep the current template as it is and open a new modal window when a user clicks that button. Later, we will use that modal window to host the graph we mentioned earlier. For now, create a new folder in app/ and add the following files to it:

```
app
  |_ modal
        |- modal.component.ts
        |- modal.html
        |_ modal.css
```

Starting from the component class, add the following contents to it:

```
// src/app/modal/modal.component.ts
import {Component} from '@angular/core';

@Component({
  selector: 'sh-modal',
  templateUrl: 'modal.html',
  styleUrls  : ['./app/modal/modal.css']
})

export class ModalComponent {
  public ModalIsVisible: boolean;
  constructor() {}
  showModal() { this.ModalIsVisible = true; }
  hideModal() { this.ModalIsVisible = false; }
}
```

Perhaps this is by far the simplest component that we have seen in this chapter. It has a template with some styling and a private variable which defines whether the modal is visible or not. Now lets see what the template looks like:

```
# src/app/modal/modal.html
<div *ngIf="ModalIsVisible" class="modal fade" role="dialog">
  <div class="modal-dialog">
    <div class="modal-body modal-content">
      <button type="button" class="close" data-dismiss="modal"
        (click)="hideModal()">&times;</button>
      <div class="mynetwork"></div>
    </div>
  </div>
</div>
```

This is a simple Bootstrap modal with the required bells and whistles, including the Close button. The only custom classes we have here are defined as follow:

```
# src/app/modal/modal.css
.mynetwork {
  width: 968px;
  height: 550px;
  border: 1px solid lightgray;
}
.modal-dialog {
  width:1000px;
  margin: 5px auto;
}
```

Now let's see how we can call this component when the cluster button is pushed in the main component.

Adding child view to the main component

Adding our new Modal component as the child of Evidence component, is as simple as importing it and creating a new variable of type ModalComponent inside EvidenceComponent, except we do it with decorators. That is how we say we are dealing with a child component. So modify EvidenceComponent as follow:

```
// src/app/evidence/evidence.component.ts
import {Component, OnInit, ViewChild} from '@angular/core';
import {ModalComponent} from "../modal/modal.component";
//...
@Component({
  selector: 'sh-evidence',
  templateUrl: 'evidence.html',
  styleUrls  : ['./app/evidence/evidence.css']
})
//...
export class EvidenceComponent implements OnInit{
  @ViewChild(ModalComponent) modal: ModalComponent;
  //...
  buildClusters() {
    this.evidenceService.clusterBuilder(this.clusterKeywords);
    this.modal.showModal();
  }
}
```

Notice that we imported the ViewChild decorator from angular/core before defining a new variable of type ModalComponent. Now we display the modal window as soon as the Build Clusters button is pushed. Before trying that, we need to add the modal selector to the Evidence template. So at the bottom of the evidence.html template, add the following line:

```
# src/app/evidence/evidence.html
#...
<sh-modal></sh-modal>
```

And the last step – of course – is informing the app module about the new component. So open app.module.ts and import and add the new component definition over there:

```
# src/app/app.module.ts
import {ModalComponent} from './modal/modal.component';
//...
@NgModule({
  declarations: [ //...
    , ModalComponent
  ],
/...
})
```

Now we are good to go. If we press the Build Clusters button in the browser, an empty modal window will pop up, which can be closed by hitting the little x in the top-right corner.

Creating a network graph for clusters

There are wonderful JavaScript libraries for data visualization. Feel free to go for your own choice but in this chapter, we are going to use VisJs. They have great documentation in which you can learn all about it here: http://visjs.org.

Lucky for us, we don't need to go through a complicated setup process to use this library. Thanks to Severine (https://github.com/seveves/ng2-vis), we have a ready-to-use Angular wrapper for the VisJs library and we can integrate it into our project in three easy steps:

1. Install the module via the following command:

```
$ npm install ng2-vis
```

2. Import it to the vendors library:

```
# src/vendor.browser.ts
import 'vis';
```

3. Add it to the application module:

```
# src/app/app.module.ts
import {VisModule} from 'ng2-vis';
#...
@NgModule({
  //...
  imports     : [ //...
    ,VisModule ],
})
```

Now we have a fully functional data visualization library which can be used on the data we feed to it. Since we are interested in network graphs, lets have look at the required data types and see how we can create them. Here is a sample network graph:

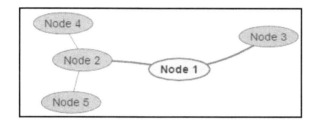

In the simplest form, a network graph consists of two elements:

- Nodes: These represent individual observations from the dataset
- Edges: These show the relationship (connections) between nodes

So we can imagine a network object has two properties as follow:

```
network: { nodes:[], edges:[]}
```

The nodes and edges are considered as arrays here. That means we need to come up with an object definition for each element inside node and edge arrays. Moreover, those definitions should be meaningful so they can represent the network graph as a whole.

Consider the graph shown in the previous figure, for example. We can save nodes as a array of labels and ids like this:

```
nodes: [
    { id: '1', label: 'Node 1' },
    { id: '2', label: 'Node 2' },
    { id: '3', label: 'Node 3' },
    { id: '4', label: 'Node 4' },
    { id: '5', label: 'Node 5' }
```

```
        ]
```

We can define the relationship between each node as follow:

```
edges: [
        { from: '1', to: '3' },
        { from: '1', to: '2' },
        { from: '2', to: '4' },
        { from: '2', to: '5' }
    ]
```

This means the network graph shown earlier can be created from node and edge arrays. We are going to use the same principle for the clusters generated by our application, except the nodes will be more complex here. In other words, we need more than id and label to get insight. Perhaps a link to the original article, the size of the article, the distance between each article and cluster center, and so on would be more insightful. So lets begin by modifying `clusterBuilder()` in the evidence service and make it generate the output that can serve as network data set.

Adding the network data to the cluster builder

The network graph data can be generated in various sections of `clusterBuilder()` functions. There are several variables that need to be initialized and a couple of bits of logic that need to be added in different parts of the current function.

Starting with the network building blocks, we need to create two arrays for nodes and edges and since they are going to form a network, lets create an empty network object as well. Since the root node is created once, we are going to create the first node of this graph, before entering the calculation logic. So we can modify the beginning of corpusBuilder() as follow:

```
// src/app/evidence/evidence.service.ts
//...
export class EvidenceService implements OnInit {
  //...
  clusterBuilder(centers, main) {
    //...
    var network = {};
    var nodes = []; //{id, label}
    var edges = []; //{from, to}
    var currentCenterId;
    var id = 10;
    nodes.push({ id: 1, label: main });
    //...
  }
```

```
}
```

We simply used the main keyword (Mars) and set it as the root node for the graph by assigning its id to 1. Now lets create some nodes for cluster centers and connect them (via edges) to the root node. To do so, go to the code block where cluster centers are calculated and add the following code to the end of it:

```
// src/app/evidence/evidence.service.ts
//...
export class EvidenceService implements OnInit {
  //...
  clusterBuilder(centers, main) {
    //...
    return Promise.all(keywords.map(function (word) {
        observations[word] = [];
        records
          .then(snapshot => {
            //...
            currentCenterId = id++; //clusterCenters[word].id;
            nodes.push({ id: currentCenterId, label: word });
            edges.push({from: 1, to: currentCenterId});
            return clusterCenters;
          })
          //...
    }));
  }
}
```

The logic here is very simple: we use the keyword for each cluster center as the node label and then connect that node to the root node (id:1) via an new entry in the edges array.

You may have also noticed that we created some variables (`id` and `currentCenterId`) to hold id values for each node. The question is, why do we need that? Couldn't we use the same article ids generated and saved in Firebase for node ids? Yes, we could and, as a matter of fact, I highlighted the part of the code that shows this alternative (look at the commented area in front of id assignments):

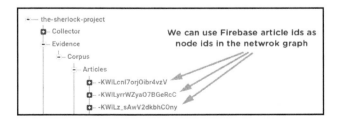

But there are two factors which prevent us from using Firebase ids. First of all, no matter what id we use for nodes, at the end, VisJs completely ignores them and it uses some 10-digit unique ids which are created internally. We can see that by logging and checking the network object in the console.

Secondly, during the development and test, using simple numbers such as 10,11, and 12 (compared to articles ids such as -KWlLcnI7orjOibr4vzV, -KwlLyrrWZyaO7BGeRcC, and -KwlLz_sAwV2dkbhCOny) is way more convenient and productive.

So far, we added root node and the cluster center to the network graph and connected them via an edge array. Now lets do the same for selected articles in each cluster center. To do so, proceed to the second `then()` function and add the following code after finding, sorting, and slicing the top seven closest articles:

```
// src/app/evidence/evidence.service.ts
//...
export class EvidenceService implements OnInit {
  //...
  clusterBuilder(centers, main) {
    //...
    return Promise.all(keywords.map(function (word) {
        observations[word] = [];
        records
          //... first then()
          .then(centers => {
            //...
            return records
              .then(snapshot => {
                var node = nodes.find(node => node.label=== word);
                observations[word].forEach(item => {
                  nodes.push({ id: id, label: item.distance });
                  edges.push({ from: node.id, to: id });
                  id++;
                });
                colorIndex ++;
              })
          })
        network = {nodes: nodes, edges: edges};
        return network;
    }));
  }
}
```

After deciding the nearest articles, we add them to the 'nodes' array using the current id value for id and the distance as the label. At the same time, we connect them to the cluster center via the 'edges' array.

To make sure that we are connecting the articles to the right center, first we find the id of current cluster by looking for its label. The following line does the trick:

```
var node = nodes.find(node => node.label=== word);
```

At the end, the 'nodes' and the 'edges' array are added to the network object and returned to the Evidence component.

Processing the network graph data

So far, we have created and returned the network graph data from the service back to the component. Since this graph is going to be shown inside the modal component, we cannot process the graph data here. Instead, we have to pass it on to the modal component.

That means inside EvidenceComponent, we need to modify the buildClusters() function again and use it as bridge between EvidenceService and ModalComponent as follow:

```
// src/app/evidence/evidence.component.ts
//...
export class EvidenceComponent implements OnInit {
  //...
  buildClusters() {
    const self = this;
    this.evidenceService.clusterBuilder(this.mainKeyword,
      this.clusterKeywords).then(data => {
        self.modal.showModal(data[0]); });
  }
}
```

Please notice that since clusterBuilder() returns a promise, we need to get the output data via then() and pass it as a parameter in the showModal() function.

Having said that, the next step would be making the Modal component process the network data and display the network graph inside the modal.

Showing the graph inside the Modal component

We passed the network data to the `showModal()` function. That means now we need to make it parametric and after receiving the data, we need to pass it to VisJs so it can do its job and display a graph upon receiving it.

So the first obvious step here is importing the VisJs library, setting up a couple of private and public variables, and modifying the constructor to reflect these changes. Open `ModalComponent` and make the following changes:

```
// src/app/modal/modal.component.ts
import * as Vis from 'vis';
import { VisNetworkService } from 'ng2-vis/components/network';

//...
export class ModalComponent{
  public ModalIsVisible: boolean;
  public visNetwork: string = 'networkId1';
  public visNetworkData: Vis.IData;
  public visNetworkOptions: Vis.IOptions;
  public visNetworkService: VisNetworkService;

  constructor (vns: VisNetworkService) {
    this.visNetworkService = vns;
    this.visNetworkOptions = {};
  }
  showModal(data)
  {
    this.visNetworkData = data;
    this.ModalIsVisible = true;
  }
  //...
}
```

So we imprted and initialized required variables for VisJs. We also assigned the network data (calculated in EvidenceService) to the vis.NetworkData variable. Now what is next? Technically, that is it! The rest rests on the shoulders of VisJs and (technically) we should be able to see the graph as soon as we hit the Build Clusters button in the evidence template.

But before rushing to the browser and trying the output (and most likely facing an empty modal), lets talk about these new variables a little. To keep it short, each variable has a duty as follow:

- `visNetwork`: The network id for the current graph
- `visNetworkData`: The home for the {nodes:[], edges:[]} object

- `visNetworkOptions`: Where we can decorate the graph
- `visNetworkService`: Where we can interact with the graph and process events such as click, drag, hover, and so on

But here is the problem: when we click on the Build Clusters button, the modal window pops up (instantly!) but it is empty. Checking the console area doesn't show any errors. So what went wrong?

Resolving the timing issue

The challenge that we have here is the timing. Since calculating clusters – depending on the size of our corpus – takes a while, calling the showModal function in EvidenceComponent will result in an empty graph. Technically, we should use an observer (or a promise) and subscribe to it for fetching the network data and there is a function for it:

```
clusterBuilder(this.mainKeyword, this.clusterKeywords).then(data => {
this.visNetworkService.setData("idOfYourNetwork", data); })
```

But at the time of writing this chapter, there are a few bugs in the `setData()` function, which brings us to the other alternative.

For the time being, use timeout so the cluster builder has a chance to recover from all of those heavy calculations and returns the network data on time:

```
// src/app/evidence/evidence.component.ts
//...
export class EvidenceComponent implements OnInit {
  //...
  buildClusters() {
    const self = this;
    this.evidenceService.clusterBuilder(this.mainKeyword,
      this.clusterKeywords).then(data => {
      setTimeout(function() {
        self.modal.showModal(data[0]); }, 10000);
      // this.visNetworkService.setData("idOfYourNetwork", data);
    });
  }
}
```

Later, you can get rid of timeout and uncomment the `setData()` line and it will work the same.

With these modifications in place, go to the evidence page in your browser. In the cluster builder area, set the main keyword to Mars and choose a few keywords for cluster centers (lets say water, transport, and safety) and push the Build Clusters button.

After a few minutes – depending on your hardware setup plus your Internet speed – you should be able to see the following graph:

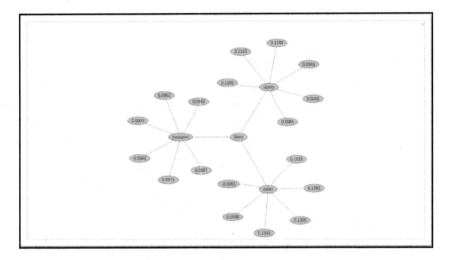

As you can see, the clusters are generated and connected through the cluster centers to the root node.

This graph is generated with default settings and we can test the interactivity features by:

- Clicking outside of nodes and edges and dragging; that will pan the view area around
- Clicking and dragging nodes; that stretches the whole graph around and shows the elasticity between nodes and edges
- Using the mouse wheel to zoom in/out

It feels good to see the result of our efforts. But lets improve this experience a little bit more and make the graph more insightful.

Decorating a network graph

What would be visually appealing is if we could convert this monotonic graph into something more informative. For example, if we put the distance numbers on the edges and, depending on the distance, change the length of the edge, that would be really helpful.

Or how about assigning different color codes to each cluster? That way, we can easily spot different regions without following the edges.

We need to do something with the labels too. If we move the distance numbers from node labels and place them on the edges, then we need to show something else on the nodes.

There are so many options that we can use to make the graph more insightful; lets see how to implement the few items mentioned above.

Decorating the edges

We can define two sets of edges for this graph. The edges that connect the root node (Mars) to the cluster centers (water, transport, and safety) should be a little thicker to express the main branches. We can use the width property and set it to 2 (the default value is 1) to achieve this goal. The edges which connect article nodes to the cluster centers should have various sizes and lighter colors, and should be dashed instead of solid lines. Having these requirements in mind, we can modify the edges as follow:

```
// src/app/evidence/evidence.service.ts
//...
  clusterBuilder(centers, main) {
    //...
    return Promise.all(keywords.map(function (word) {
      //...
      records.then(snapshot => {
        //...
        edges.push({from: 1, to: currentCenterId, width: 2});
      }).then(centers => {
        //...
        return records
          .then(snapshot => {
            //...
            observations[word].forEach(item => {
              //...
              edges.push({from:node.id, to: id, dashes: true,
            label:item.distance,length: 100+item.distance*400,
                font: {color: '#777777',background:'white',
                  align:'middle'},
```

```
        });
  //...
```

Please have a look at the formula which we used to measure the length of each edge from cluster centers to its articles:

```
length: 100+item.distance*1000
```

Since each distance property is a very small number, we need to multiply it by a big number (1,000) to effectively show their differences. Moreover, the first article normally has a distance of 0, so adding 100 to the calculations guarantees that nodes which belong to the first articles won't cover the cluster centers. Before testing the result, lets decorate the nodes as well.

Decorating the nodes

Decorating the nodes is a little bit tricky. Lets say our requirements can be summarized as follow:

- The root node (Mars) should have bigger size font and different color.
- The cluster centers should be a bit smaller and uniform color.
- The articles in each cluster can have the default font size, but they should have uniform colors (for each cluster); instead of ellipses, they should be in boxes with shadows; and, finally, their labels should be multilined text. The first line should represent the website they are coming from and the second line should show how many words are there in that article.

Let's start by decorating the root node:

```
// src/app/evidence/evidence.service.ts
//...
  clusterBuilder(centers, main) {
    //...
    nodes.push({
      id: 1, label: main, font: {size:40}, color: this.colors[0],
      borderWidth: 3, borderWidthSelected: 4
    });
    //...
  }
```

Here, we used the font property to change the size; also, we used two border properties to set the border size in normal and selected states. The important note here is the color property. This property is basically an object which can have a complex structure to define various colors for different states. Since we are going to use this complex structure, in various nodes, lets create an array of color objects and refer to their indices for different node types. We will come back to this definition at the end of this section.

Now lets move on to the cluster center nodes. Almost the same principles apply here as well, except that we have a different font size, a slightly thinner border, and a different color object:

```
// src/app/evidence/evidence.service.ts
//...
  clusterBuilder(centers, main) {
    //...
    return Promise.all(keywords.map(function (word) {
        //...
        records.then(snapshot => {
            //...
            nodes.push({ id: currentCenterId, label: word,
              color: self.colors[1], borderWidth: 2,
              borderWidthSelected: 3, font: {size: 28} });
          })
        //...
```

Finally, lets decorate the nodes for articles in each cluster:

```
// src/app/evidence/evidence.service.ts
//...
  clusterBuilder(centers, main) {
    //...
                observations[word].push({
                  id: article.key,
                  distance: d.toFixed(4),
                  link: article.child('link').val(),
                  size: contents.split(' ').length
                });
                //...
                nodes.push({
                  id: id,
                  label: (item.link)?item.link
                    .replace('http://','')
                    .replace('https://','')
                    .replace('www.','').split("/")[0]
                    +'\n'+item.size+' words'
                  :'4xx', // for 404 or 400 responses
                  shadow:{ enabled: true, size:11, x:3, y:3,
```

```
                    color: 'rgba(0,0,0,0.5)' },
                  color: self.colors[colorIndex],
                  shape: 'box'
               });
         colorIndex ++;
    //...
  }
```

The same rules apply here and we have extra properties to set the shadows and the shape of the node. Perhaps the label property here deserves extra attention. Since we have limited space, we want to make most of it and truncate the URLs by removing any `http://` or `https://` and `www.` from beginning and also by removing any path comes after the host name. We also need to show the word counts at the second line. That is why we added two properties (link and size) to each observation object so that later we can use them in the label property of the node objects.

The color object

The color property that we used in the previous section is actually an object which holds all details about node colors. Each node can be in one of these three states:

- Normal
- Selected
- Hover

The following objects address the background color and border color for each state:

```
// src/app/evidence/evidence.service.ts
//...
export class EvidenceService implements OnInit {
  private colors = [{  // root node
    border: '#555555', background: '#BBBBBB',
    highlight: { border: '#444444', background: '#EEEEEE' },
    hover: { border: '#444444', background: '#EEEEEE' }
  },{ // cluster centers
    border: '#777777', background: '#DADADA',
    highlight: { border: '#555555', background: '#EFEFEF' },
    hover: { border: '#555555', background: '#EFEFEF' }
  },{ // article nodes
    border: '#CC9900', background: '#FFCC00',
    highlight: { border: '#FF9900', background: '#FFEE55' },
    hover: { border: '#FF9900', background: '#FFEE55' }
  }, /* rest of colors */ ];
  //...
}
```

To see the hover color in action, in the modal component's constructor we have to activate the hover options:

`this.visNetworkOptions={interaction:{`**`hover:true`**`}};`

Feel free to see the complete list of colors that I have created for this project in the repository:

`https://github.com/soolan/the-sherlock-project`

With this private variable in place, when we need a specific color theme, all we need to do is reference the required colors using the array index (for example, `color: this.colors[0]` is used for the root node).

Now, with all of these decorations in place, build the same clusters (Mars as the root node and water, transport, and safety as cluster centers) again and watch the output:

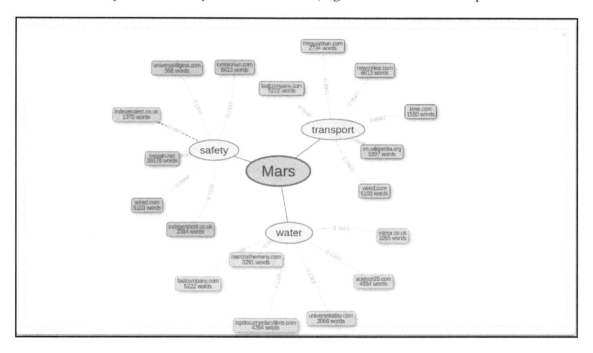

Now this is the graph we deserve. The root node and cluster centers are distinguishable; each cluster has its own color code and article nodes are distributed in various distances based on their similarity (the more similar to the cluster center, the closer they are to it). In the next section, we see how to deal with events in the graph.

Processing custom events

Let experiment with a few things in the current graph. Grab the root node and move it around very fast. As you can see, it will stretch out then, a few milliseconds later, all cluster center nodes and their children follow its lead. It proves that, behind the scenes, a complete physics engine takes care of all elasticity before finally the graph stabilizes again. From the user perspective, it shows that we have click and drag events already in place:

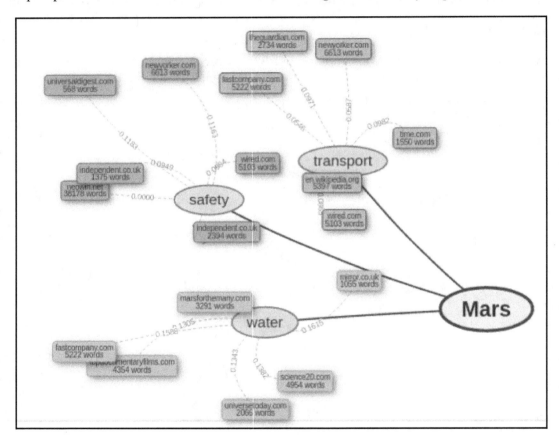

Let's try something else. Rotate the mouse wheel toward yourself while the pointer is in the modal and it will zoom in the graph. Now click on a empty area and drag the graph up. It will pan down to the lower part of the graph. Finally, click on a node and see how it highlights the node and the edge(s) connected to that node:

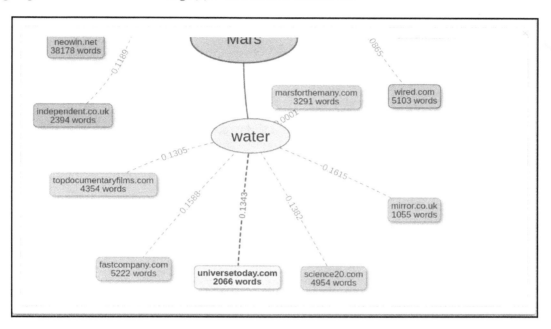

So these are all default configurations that come out of the box whenever we create a network graph. Lets see how we can catch an event and perform a custom action.

For example, when we click on an article node, lets open the page which contains its URL in a new tab.

In VisJs, there should be a function where events can be caught and processed. As we saw in the Modal component, we injected an object of type `VisNetworkService`. This object is the home or processing event. To see how it works, we are going to use it inside the `networkInitialized()` function as follow:

```
// src/app/modal/modal.component.ts
//...
export class ModalComponent {
  //...
  public networkInitialized(): void {
    // now we can use the service to register on events
    this.visNetworkService.on(this.visNetwork, 'click');
```

```
        // open your console/dev tools to see the click params
        this.visNetworkService.click
          .subscribe((eventData:any[]) => {
             console.log(eventData); //{networkId:'',{node:[{id:''}]}
          }
        });
    }
```

As its name suggests, this function is called the very moment the network graph is initialized. So we won't miss any event since the beginning. For our click event example, we simply subscribed to the event data and logged it inside the console. Create a new set of clusters and click on any node and check the result in the console.

 For a complete list of events and their return objects, visit http://visjs.o rg/docs/network/#Events.

eventData is an object with two properties. The second property contains the id of the node that we just clicked on it. So what we need to do is to find URL by the node id and then open it in a new tab. But not all the nodes are the same. In other words, what if we click on the root node, or the cluster centers? The following modifications on the click event listener can resolve that issue:

```
// src/app/modal/modal.component.ts
//...
export class ModalComponent {
  //...
  public networkInitialized(): void {
    this.visNetworkService.on(this.visNetwork, 'click');
    this.visNetworkService.click
      .subscribe((eventData: any[]) => {
        if (eventData[0] === this.visNetwork) {
          let url = this.findUrlById(eventData[1].nodes[0]);
          (url.indexOf('http') !== -1)?
            window.open(url,'_blank'):
            console.log('This is root or a cluster center');
        }
      });
  }
```

We are calling a new – yet to be implemented – function called `findUrlById()` and passing the node id to it. This function supposed to return a string. If that string is a legitimate URL then we open it in a new tab. Otherwise, nothing will happen on the screen and we just log a message in the console. Here is the implementation of `findUrlById()`:

```
findInfoById(id) {
    let nodes = this.visNetworkData.nodes;
    let i = (nodes as Array<any>)
        .map(function (n) {return n.id; }).indexOf(id);
    return nodes[i].title;
}
```

Here, we simply go through the array of nodes and find the array index associated with the given node id. With that array index, now we can acquire other properties in the node object. As we can see, here, we are returning the title property of the found node. But what is this title property? We didn't have it before. That is correct and it means we need to modify our node objects one more time and add a new title property every time we add a new node object to the nodes array.

Final modification on the nodes array

For the last time, open the evidence service and spot all three places where we push node objects to the `nodes` array and add the `title` property at the end:

```
// src/app/evidence/evidence.service.ts
//...
  clusterBuilder(main, centers) {
    //...
    nodes.push({ /* previous properties */, title:main });
    //...
    nodes.push({ /* previous properties */, title:word });
    //...
    nodes.push({ /* previous properties */, title: item.link });
  }
```

Notice that for the root node and the cluster centers, we are using the keywords as the value for the title property. But for article nodes, we are using a real link. That is how the logic block inside the Modal's click event distinguishes between these different nodes and takes the proper action.

Please note that although we used the title property to slip in some extra data to the network graph, its real purpose is showing tool tips. In other words, when we hover over a node, the contents of the title property will be shown over the node in a pop-up tool tip.

Now, with these updates in place, generate the network graph one more time and click on any link. While clicking on the root node and cluster centers logs a message in the console, clicking on an article node will open its link in a new tab.

Final thoughts on data visualization

So the question is, can we pass more data to the network graph via the title property? Yes, it is possible. Instead of assigning a simple string to the title property, you can use objects, an array of objects, or any sophisticated data structure that you have in mind. Just make sure you process the data on the other side (in the Modal component) accordingly. However, depending on your needs, there are better solutions in the VisJs library. For example, we can cluster our clusters. In other words, depending on the zoom level, we can show a certain number of nodes on screen.

Lets expand this idea a little. Currently, the article nodes are the outermost nodes in the graph. But if you decided to add more children nodes to each article (for example, phrases which contain the keyword appearing in the cluster center, the top 10 words with the highest TF-IDF, and so on), that makes the final graph very crowded and hard to read.

By clustering the clusters, we can keep the graph tidy and show only what is needed. Here is a good example which shows how it works (zoom in/out and watch nodes snap out/in to their parents):

```
http://visjs.org/examples/network/other/clusteringByZoom.html
```

Just keep in mind adding more nodes to the graph means modifying the code, everywhere the nodes and edges are referenced. Feel free to use your imagination and create the most complex network graph on the planet.

Gathering other types of evidence

So far, we have just discussed words and textual evidence. But what about visual evidence? Finding photos that relate to the subject of interest could be helpful too. The same applies to audio evidence and video clips.

The fact is, the same principles studied in this chapter apply for images as well. Except we are dealing with pixels here. The relationship between an image and a bunch of pixels which form a pattern in that image is like an article and the unique words that construct that article. So it is just a different type of building block. That means we can use the same algorithms we used here for other types of media, including images, audio, videos, and so on.

We are not going through the implementation process for each of them here (it needs around extra 100 pages for each media type) but just keep in mind the bag of words/patterns model applies to any problem where we need to find highest similarity and closest distance between items in a cluster.

It is worth mentioning that there are other tools and APIs that become handy especially when you want to commercialize your ideas and need to process data on a huge scale. For example, the Google Prediction API and Vision API are packed with all you need to implement or use any machine-learning-related problem.

Gathering evidence from social networks

The original plan was to include major social networks (Facebook, Twitter, and so on) in the investigation field but shortly I hit two major obstacles.

First, according to recent updates in the terms and conditions and privacy policy, it is illegal to scrape the contents of any social network. Please note it is not impossible, but it is illegal. You do that and they can sue you. However, there are solutions if you want to read something legally from social networks. For example, Facebook provides the Graph API which you can use to read from (and write to) Facebook social graphs. The problem is, you need to know what are you looking for and know exactly where to look for it; then you might have a chance – *if* the part of the social graph that you are investigating grants you permission to read its contents. So it is not like diving into the unknown to discover something new. It is more like spending some time on familiar content and at the end getting the predefined results.

The second problem is **return on investment** (**ROI**). Even if you invest your resources on searching familiar places in the social graph and get something from there, chances are the contents are so shallow that you won't consider it insightful to your investigation. For those reasons, social networks are off the list.

Summary

In this chapter, we started with the idea of gathering evidence which supports investigation into an article of our interest. We looked at how we can have a general evaluation for an article and how to measure, weigh down, and lift up the value of certain words in any article.

We learned how to see an article as a bag of words and how to use this concept to calculate similarity. We set up and used Custom Search Engine and Yahoo APIs to query and fetch the contents of Web pages in periodic time spans.

Finally, we learned how to get some insight by clustering the gathered articles – corpus – around specific subjects and we saw how to visualize the cluster using a third-party data visualization library (VisJs) and an Angular wrapper module (ng2-vis).

In the next chapter, we take one step back and try to organize what we have created so far into an informative report.

7
The Report Generator Service - Creating Controllers to Set Report Template

In this chapter, we are going to create a service to read the network graph data (generated from the previous chapter), mix it with summary details created from the corpus, and generate various reports. The report will solely rely on the data that we feed it. So the first two requirements are:

- Corpus summary (corpus size, vocabulary size, average article size, and so on)
- Network graph data

When these information sources are in place, we can feed them (as raw data) to the Report Generator and make it generate different types of reports (with different levels of details).

That means the report generator should have controllers to set the template for the report (child views) and those templates should get their setup from a configuration mechanism saved permanently somewhere. It is nice to have a mechanism that creates and saves various configurations for different themes as well. At the end we need to have another service to print reports. Let's start by saving the network graph into Firebase.

Saving network graph data to the database

In the `clusterBuilder()` function inside the evidence service, when we pushed a new element to the observations array, we used the article key – generated by Firebase – as the value for the "id" property in each observation element:

```
// src/app/evidence/evidence.service.ts    line number: 344
observations[word].push({
  id: article.key, //...
});
```

But we never used that value. Technically, we could use that id as the node id, but for the sake of simplicity and easier debugging we didn't.

 If you want to use article ids, keep in mind that graph node ids should be unique, otherwise you will get an error message from VisJs. In our case, that means the same article cannot appear on two or more clusters. So if you want to use the article id as the node id, make sure that you have a code that checks for duplicates and deals with them before adding a new node to the network.

Now it is time to put the article id (that we never used before) in better use. We need the article contents for generating reports. So we need to access them via the network data. One option could be slip the article contents into the "title" property of each graph node. This is a very bad idea because we will create redundant data in our database (the article contents appear in the corpus and the network data simultaneously).

The better solution would be saving the id of article in the network data and when we need that article later, query it via its id. So modify the `clusterBuilder()` function as follows:

```
// src/app/evidence/evidence.service.ts
  //...
  clusterBuilder(main, centers) {
    //...
      nodes.push({ /* previouse properties */,
        title: [item.link, item.id] });
    //...
  }
```

Now before showing the graph we need to persist the network data to the database. So open the evidence component, create a new private variable to hold the network data, and save them before calling the `showModal()` function:

```
// src/app/evidence/evidence.service.ts
//...
private network: FirebaseObjectObservable <any>;
constructor (es:EvidenceService, af: AngularFire) {
  //...
  this.network =
    af.database.object('Evidence/Corpus/network-graph');
}

buildClusters() {
  const self = this;
  this.evidenceService
    .clusterBuilder(this.mainKeyword, this.clusterKeywords)
    .then(data => { setTimeout(function() {
      self.network.set(data[0]);
      self.modal.showModal(data[0]);
    }, 25000);
  });
}
```

Now try the evidence page again, build new clusters, and check out the Firebase console:

As we can see, every time we generate a new graph, the same network data structure is created in Firebase. So from now on, we can use that as a reference to generate the reports we are looking for. This also means that in the future we can skip all of those heavy calculations inside the evidence service and in case we need to regenerate the same graph, we can read the graph data directly from Firebase.

The report generator component

We are going create the basic structure of the main component and add the required features as we proceed. So create the main component first:

```
// src/app/report/report.component.ts
import {Component, OnInit} from '@angular/core';
@Component({
  selector: 'sh-report',
  templateUrl: './report.html'
})
export class ReportComponent implements OnInit {
  constructor() {}
  ngOnInit() {}
}
```

Next, check out the application routes and make sure the new component is visible to the routing system:

```
// src/app/app.routes.ts
//...
import {ReportComponent} from "./report/report.component";
export const rootRouterConfig: Routes = [
  //...
  {path: 'report', component: ReportComponent},
];
```

Then import and declare the new component to the application module:

```
// src/app/ap.module.ts
//...
import {ReportService} from "./report/report.service";
//...
@NgModule({
  declarations: [
    AppComponent, NavigationComponent, CollectorComponent,
    RatingComponent, NotifierComponent, EvidenceComponent,
    OrderByPipe, ModalComponent, ReportComponent
  ]
```

```
    //...
})
export class AppModule {}
```

Finally we can create a very basic view for this component with the following items:

```
# src/app/report/report.html
<div class="container">
  <ul class="nav nav-tabs">
    <li class="active">
      <a data-toggle="tab" href="#config">
        <span class="glyphicon glyphicon-cog"></span>
      </a>
    </li>
    <li *ngFor="let report of items">
      <a data-toggle="tab" href="#">template name</a>
    </li>
  </ul>
  <div class="tab-content"
    <div id="config" class="tab-pane fade in active">
      <div> PLACE HOLDER FOR CONFIGURATION TAB CONTENTS</div>
    </div>
    <div  class="tab-pane fade">
      <div> PLACE HOLDER FOR REPORTS CONTENTS</div>
    </div>
  </div>
</div>
```

We are using two bootstrap structures here:

- On top of the page we will have a tab system, which the first tab belongs to, the report configurations, and the rest is used for each new report template that we will create
- Inside the configuration tab, we will use an accordion system where each item belongs to one of the tabs on top of the page

Ideally, after we have filled all the place holders with real elements, the end result should look like this:

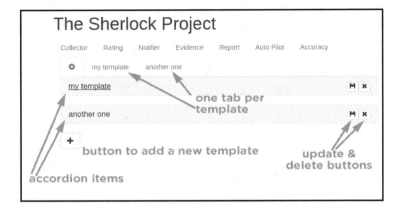

We will implement the contents of the configurations tab soon. But before that, let's study the way parent/child components talk to each other.

The mechanics of component interaction

We need to define report templates and then generate the reports based on those configurations. It means if we put each functionality in its own component, our application would be easier to maintain. So we need to implement a mechanism to share information between different components.

In the previous chapter, we saw how to connect two components and build a parent/child interaction via the @ViewChild decoration. But it was not that much of a communication because the parent (EvidenceComponent) delivered some data (Network Graph) to the child (ModalComponent) and expected it to do something (render the graph). But what if we needed more? For example, what if we needed:

- The parent and child to communicate in both directions
- When the input data changes, the child to sense them and update its view
- When the child fires an event, the parent to catch that event and respond to it

In this section, we are going to explore the component interaction in Angular.

The report generator template

We are going to put all required elements to render the configuration accordion in its own component, and then use property binding and even binding techniques to deliver the messages and requests back and forth. To see how the view of this component will look like, check out the following screenshot (this is when the 'my template' pane inside the accordion is open):

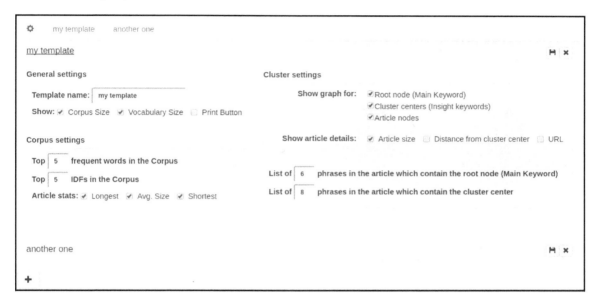

Start by creating a basic component and add the following contents to it:

```
// src/app/report/report-template.component.ts
import {Component} from '@angular/core';
@Component({
  selector: 'sh-report-template',
  templateUrl: './report-template.html'
})
export class ReportTemplateComponent {}
```

Right after creating this new component, call its selector inside the `report.html` so we know it is available immediately. In other words, replace the place holder line:

```
# src/app/report/report.html
#...
<div id="config" class="tab-pane fade in active">
    <div> PLACE HOLDER FOR CONFIGURATION TAB CONTENTS</div>
```

```
#...
```

With the following code:

```
# src/app/report/report.html
#...
<div id="config" class="tab-pane fade in active">
      <sh-report-template></sh-report-template>
#...
```

Looking at the image for this component, the view is certainly one big complex structure. We are going to start by studying the heading:

```
// src/app/report/report-template.html
<div class="panel-group" id="accordion" role="tablist" aria-
multiselectable="true">
   <div class="panel panel-default">
     <div class="panel-heading" role="tab" id="heading+unique id">
       <h4 class="panel-title">
         <a role="button" data-toggle="collapse"
           data-parent="#accordion"
           href="#collapse+unique id" aria-expanded="true"
           [attr.aria-controls]="'collapse'">
           name place holder</a>
         <button class="btn btn-default btn-xs pull-right"
           type="button" (click)="">
           <span class="glyphicon glyphicon-remove"
             aria-hidden="true"></span></button>
         <button class="btn btn-default btn-xs pull-right"
           type="submit" (click)="">
           <span class="glyphicon glyphicon-floppy-disk"
             aria-hidden="true"></span></button>
       </h4>
     </div>
   #...
```

The first thing to notice is the id name set for the panel heading. This is how we distinguish between various accordion items. The same logic applies to the `href` property of each anchor element. Using the id specified here, we know which accordion element should be collapsed/expanded when we click on it.

Next to the template name, there are two buttons that collect click events and trigger a related – yet to be implemented – function immediately. As their names suggest, one button is for deleting the template and the other one for updating any changes.

The next part of this template, as shown in the following snippet, is in charge of handling general settings for the report:

```
// src/app/report/report-template.html
#...
    <div id="collapse+unique id" class="panel-collapse collapse"
        role="tabpanel" [attr.aria-labelledby]="heading+unique id">
        <div class="panel-body">
          <form>
            <div class="row">
              <div class="col-md-5">
                <label>General settings</label>
                <div class="well well-sm">
                  <label> Template name: <input type="text"
                    class="input-sm" name="template-name"></label>
                  <label>Show:</label>
                  <label class="checkbox-inline">
                    <input type="checkbox" name="corpus-size"/>
                    Corpus Size</label>
                  <label class="checkbox-inline">
                    <input type="checkbox" name="vocabulary-size"/>
                    Vocabulary Size </label>
                  <label class="checkbox-inline">
                    <input type="checkbox" name="print-button"/>
                    Print Button</label>
                </div>
                #...
```

Technically, this is part of the UI, which expands/collapses when we click on the header. That is why they have the same naming conventions as in the previous section.

As we will see very soon, all code snippets such as: `[attr.aria-labelledby]="heading+unique id"` will be replaced by true unique IDs, which come from a model: `[attr.aria-labelledby]="'heading'+model.$key"`.

This general settings section has three checkboxes that decide if any checked item should be shown in the report or not.

At the bottom of the general settings, corpus settings exists, which has a more complex structure:

```
// src/app/report/report-template.html
#...
                <label>Corpus settings</label>
                <div class="well well-sm">
                  <label>Top <input type="text" size="1"
```

```
                     class="input-sm" name="max-freq-words"/>
                     frequent words in the Corpus</label>
                   <br>
                   <label>
                     Top <input type="text" size="1" class="input-sm"
                     name="max-idfs" /> IDFs in the Corpus</label>
                   <br>
                   <label>Article stats:</label>
                   <label class="checkbox-inline">
                     <input type="checkbox" name="longest-article"/>
                     Longest</label>
                   <label class="checkbox-inline">
                     <input type="checkbox" name="avg-article"/>
                     Avg. Size</label>
                   <label class="checkbox-inline">
                     <input type="checkbox" name="shortest-article"/>
                     Shortest</label>
                 </div>
               </div>
     #...
```

Apart from checked/unchecked items, this section has input fields that get a number. As we will see soon, these numbers will be used in a query to limit the result set.

Perhaps the most complex part of the view is the cluster settings:

```
     // src/app/report/report-template.html
     #...
                 <div class="col-md-7">
                   <label>Cluster settings</label>
                   <div class="well well-sm">
                     <dl class="dl-horizontal">
                       <dt>Show graph for:</dt>
                       <dd><input type="checkbox" name="root-node"/>
                         Root node (Main)</dd>
                       <dd>
                         <input type="checkbox" name="cluster-node"/>
                         Cluster centers (Insight keywords)</dd>
                       <dd>
                        <input type="checkbox" name="article-node-show"
                         nodes</dd>
                     </dl>
                     <div>
                       <dl class="dl-horizontal">
                         <dt>Show article details:</dt>
                         <dd><label class="checkbox-inline">
                           <input name="article-node-size"
                             type="checkbox" />Article size</label>
```

```
      <label class="checkbox-inline">
        <input name="article-node-distance"/>
          Distance from cluster center</label>
      <label class="checkbox-inline">
        <input name="article-node-url"
           type="checkbox"/>URL</label></dd>
  </dl>
  <label>List of
    <input type="text" size="1" class="input-sm"
      name="max-root-phrase"/>phrases in the
      article which contain the root node
      (Main Keyword)</label>
  <label>List of
    <input type="text" size="1" class="input-sm"
      name="max-center-phrase"/>phrases in the
      article which contain the cluster center
  </label>
</div>
#...
```

This is the simplest structure for this section. Later we will see how to show/hide only part of the elements in this section based on the checkbox status of a higher element. For example, the cluster center's checkbox should be shown only if the root node is checked. The same way, the article nodes and their details should be shown only if the root node and the cluster centers are selected. That involves a bit of logic implementation inside the component class. We will get to that soon.

The configuration parameters

Now we have a separate component for report configuration. No big deal, so far we were just calling components inside each other. It is time move on to the interaction part and make the components talk to each other. To do so, we need a model to act as a vessel for carrying data.

Add a new TypeScript class and define the following structure in it:

```
// src/app/report/report.config.ts
export class ReportConfig {
  constructor(
    public templateName: string,
    public corpusSize: boolean,
    public vocabularySize: boolean,
    public printButton: boolean,
    public maxFreqWords: number,
    public maxIDFs: number,
```

```
    public longestArticle: boolean,
    public shortestArticle: boolean,
    public avgArticleSize: boolean,
    public rootNode: boolean,
    public clusterNode: boolean,
    public articleNode: {
       show: boolean, size: boolean, distance: boolean, url:boolean
    },
    public maxRootPhrases: number,
    public maxCenterPhrases: number
   ) {}
}
```

All public properties defined here are a one-to-one match to the DOM elements in the configuration component.

In the parent, add a new `private` variable to handle that model and initialize that model with the following values. Remember this is just for testing and later we will replace that with real data coming from Firebase:

```
// src/app/report/report.component.ts
//...
export class ReportComponent implements OnInit {
  private templates;
  ngOnInit() {
    this.templates  = new ReportConfig(
      'test',true,true,false,5,6,true,true,false,true,true,
      {show:true,size:true,distance:true,url:true},11,22);
  }
}
```

Feed that model to the child template. We can do that via property binding. So use the `templates` property of the `ReportComponent` in the `<sh-report-template>` selector and then loop through its elements and bind them to the `template` property of `ReportTemplateComponent`:

```
#  src/app/report/report.html
<sh-report-template *ngFor="let template of templates"
  [template]="template">
</sh-report-template>
```

Although there is only one item at the moment, we need to create a loop for templates here. Because soon enough we will remove the hard-coded values and we will read a bunch of template objects from Firebase. So having a loop in place is a good practice.

Now that we are passing some data from parent to the child, we need to make the child aware of this new input. So open the child component and decorate it with the @Input function. The @Input decorator is simply in charge of any incoming data to the component. On the other hand–as we will find out soon–@Output is the decorator that handles any outgoing data from the current component:

```
// src/app/report/report.component.ts
import {Component, Input} from '@angular/core';
import {ReportConfig} from "./report.config";
//...
export class ReportTemplateComponent {
  @Input('template') model: ReportConfig;
}
```

Notice that we made the child to be receptive of the 'template' input and at the same time defined an alias called model for this input. Since the input type is ReportConfig (which is the model for our template configuration), defining the 'model' name as an alias makes sense.

Now we can modify the child view and replace all of those hard-coded values with the properties coming from the parent. Here is an example:

```
# src/app/report/report-template.html
#...
    <div class="col-md-5">
      <label>General settings</label>
      <div class="well well-sm">
        <label>
          Template name:
          <input type="text" class="input-sm" name="template-name"
            [(ngModel)]="model.templateName"></label>
        <label>Show:</label>
        <label class="checkbox-inline">
          <input type="checkbox" name="corpus-size"
            [(ngModel)]="model.corpusSize"/>Corpus Size</label>
        <label class="checkbox-inline">
          <input type="checkbox" name="vocabulary-size"
            [(ngModel)]="model.vocabularySize"/>Vocabulary Size
        </label>
        <label class="checkbox-inline">
          <input type="checkbox" name="print-button"
            [(ngModel)]="model.printButton"/>Print Button</label>
      </div>
#...
```

The child view is very big and there is no point in diving into plain HTML codes. Kindly refer to the repository and see the complete template at the following link:
`https://github.com/Soolan/the-sherlock-project/tree/master/src/app/report/report-template.html`

A closer look at the accordion and tab navigations

Since we are using the bootstrap tabs and accordion features, we need to come up with the unique IDs for particular `div` tags. For example, look at the following code snippet for accordions (let's use id values such as `headingTwo` and `collapseTwo` to see the point):

```
# src/app/report/report-template.html
#...
<div class="panel-group" id="accordion" role="tablist"
  aria-multiselectable="true">
  <div class="panel panel-default">
    <div class="panel-heading" role="tab" id="headingTwo">
      <h4 class="panel-title">
        <a role="button" data-toggle="collapse" data-parent="#accordion"
          href="#collapseTwo" aria-expanded="true"
          aria-controls="collapseTwo">
          {{model.templateName}}</a>
        #...
      </h4>
    </div>
    <div id="collapseTwo" class="panel-collapse collapse in"
role="tabpanel"
        aria-labelledby="headingTwo">
      #...
    </div>
  </div>
</div>
```

Since we will repeat the same code in a loop, we can't use the same ID for each report template, because IDs are supposed to be unique. To solve this problem we can use Firebase object keys as ids for each template. We will see how to get and use Firebase objects in the following section:

```
# src/app/report/report-template.html
#...
<div class="panel-group" id="accordion" role="tablist"
  aria-multiselectable="true">
```

```
<div class="panel panel-default">
  <div class="panel-heading" role="tab"
    id="heading{{model.$key}}">
    <h4 class="panel-title">
      <a role="button" data-toggle="collapse"
        data-parent="#accordion"
         href="#collapse{{model.$key}}" aria-expanded="true"
         [attr.aria-controls]="'collapse'+model.$key">
         {{model.templateName}}</a>
       #...
    </h4>
  </div>
  <div id="collapse{{model.$key}}" class="panel-collapse
    collapse" role="tabpanel"
       [attr.aria-labelledby]="'heading'+model.$key">
    #...
```

The right place for holding Firebase objects

Before reading the data and passing it to the template, the important question to ask is: where is the best place for keeping data? In other words, if we could get the same results, what is the difference between:

- Putting the model inside the child component, and
- Putting the Firebase Object in the parent and feeding the child with it

If we put the Firebase object in the template child, when we need those data in the render child, we have to pass them first from template child to the parent and then pass them again from parent to the render child. But if we keep the Firebase object in the parent, we cut the journey one step shorter. For that reason we are going with the second solution. The Firebase object stays in the parent and will be fed to the render child on demand.

Creating new report templates

We are ready to create our first–empty–report template and save it to Firebase as an object. Clearly we need to do some modifications on the parent's component. So add the Firebase object and modify the previous `templates` property as follows:

```
//src/app/report/report.component.ts
import {FirebaseListObservable, AngularFire} from "angularfire2";
import {ReportConfig} from "./report.config";
//...
export class ReportComponent implements OnInit {
```

```
private templates: FirebaseListObservable<any>;
private items = [];
constructor(af: AngularFire) {
  this.templates = af.database.list('/Report/templates');
}

ngOnInit() {
  this.templates.subscribe(data => {this.items = data;});
}

newReportTemplate() {
  this.templates.push(new ReportConfig('untitled333', false,
    false, false, 0, 0, false, false, false, false, false,
    {show: false, size: false, distance: false, url: false},0,0)
  );
}
```

These changes suggest that when a new report template object is created, it will be saved under the `/Report/templates` key in Firebase. Moreover, the moment this component is initialized, it will fetch the available templates from the database and save them in the `items` property. We will need that property later to loop into it and build the accordion items in the configuration tab.

The last, but not least thing to notice is the `newReportTemplate()` function, which basically generates a new `ReportConfig` object with some initial values. The DOM element, which catches the click event and triggers this function, lives inside the parent view:

```
# src/app/report/report.html
#...
  <div class="tab-content">
    <div id="config" class="tab-pane fade in active">
      <sh-report-template *ngFor="let template of items"
        [template]="template"
        (onSaveReportTemplate)="onSaveReportTemplate($event)"
        (onDeleteReportTemplate)="onDeleteReportTemplate($event)">
      </sh-report-template>
      <button type="button" class="btn btn-default"
        (click)="newReportTemplate()">
        <span class="glyphicon glyphicon-plus" aria-hidden="true">
        </span>
      </button>
    </div>
```

So the moment we hit the plus sign at the bottom of the configuration tab, a new `ReportConfig` model is initialized and pushed to the templates array. Since this array is subscribed to the Firebase object our job is done. Thanks to Firebase's three-way binding, any changes to the templates array will be seen and required modifications on the database side will be done automatically.

As we can see, there are new players added to the `<sh-report-template>` selector. The `(onSaveReportTemplate)` and `(onDeleteReportTemplate)` event binders will be used to save any changes to the current report template and delete the current report template, respectively. Let's find out how they work.

Updating the report template

The updating process should be considered as a child to parent interaction. In other words, when we update a value inside one of those accordion elements and hit the save button, we need to trigger a function inside the child component. That's why we need to bind a click event to the save button (the disk icon in the header):

```
# src/app/report/report-template.html
#...
<button class="btn btn-default btn-xs pull-right" type="submit"
  (click)="saveReportTemplate(model)">
 <span class="glyphicon glyphicon-floppy-disk" aria-hidden="true">
 </span>
</button>
#...
```

In the component class we need to catch that event–and since all Firebase-related operations are handles in the parent–we need to emit a new event to the parent:

```
// src/app/report/report-template.component.ts
import {Component,Input,EventEmitter,Output} from '@angular/core';
//...
export class ReportTemplateComponent {
  @Input('template') model: ReportConfig;
  @Output() onSaveReportTemplate = new EventEmitter<any>();

  saveReportTemplate(model) {
    this.onSaveReportTemplate.emit(this.setOptions(model));
  }

  setOptions(model) {
    if (!model.rootNode) {
      model.clusterNode = false;
```

```
            this.deactivateNodes(model);
            return model;
        } else if (!model.clusterNode) {
            this.deactivateNodes(model);
            return model
        } else if (!model.articleNode.show) {
            this.deactivateNodes(model);
        }
        return model;
    }

    deactivateNodes(model) {
      model.articleNode =
        {show: false, size: false, distance: false, url: false};
      model.maxRootPhrases = 0;
      model.maxCenterPhrases = 0;
    }
  }
```

There is a lot happening here. From the angular/core module we have imported `Ouput` and `EventEmitter`:

- The `@Output` decoration is how we tell the parent that the child has something to say. We need to indicate which function name in the parent should be triggered (`onSaveReportTemplate()`) when a new event is emitted by the child.
- The `EventEmitter` is the property that carries (emits) events from the child to the parent.

Looking at the code it is clear that we are emitting a Firebase object for the current report template from child to parent.

Before we pass the model to the parent we need to set the options based on the hierarchy defined under the cluster section. We saw before how to show/hide the elements in this section via their higher elements. But inside the report-template component we use a bunch of nested conditional blocks in the `setOptions()` function to save those UI values to Firebase. That way we will make sure the updated version of settings will be rendered the next time we open the reports.

How parent component deals with the output data from child component

Now on the parent side we need to get this new event and do something about it. The first signals for this interaction should be sensed via the parent's template. This is where the event binding mechanism that we have added to the parent component earlier (inside the `<sh-report-template>` selector) comes to play:

```
# src/app/report/report.html
# ...
  <sh-report-template *ngFor="let template of items"
        [template]="template"
        (onSaveReportTemplate)="onSaveReportTemplate($event)"
        (onDeleteReportTemplate)="onDeleteReportTemplate($event)">
  </sh-report-template>
# ...
```

Here we bound that event emitted from the child component to a function called `onSaveReportTemplate` inside the parent component. So the next obvious step would be implementing that function as follows:

```
// src/app/report/report.component.ts
//...
export class ReportComponent implements OnInit {
  // ...
  onSaveReportTemplate(report) {
    this.templates.update(report.$key, report);
  }
}
```

That is a simple Firebase `update()` function, which basically updates an object (with the given ID) with the properties provided as data. But we have a serious problem here. If we test the app we will get the following error:

```
EXCEPTION: Error in ./ReportComponent class ReportComponent - inline
template:13:26 caused by: Firebase.update failed: First argument contains a
function in property 'Report.templates.-KXtWqfDkwPJScSB-1DQ.$exists' with
contents: function () {}
```

What this function complains about is the wrong properties inside the data object. If we log the `report` parameter, we will get the following data:

```
                                    report.component.ts:44
  Object {articleNode: Object, avgArticle: true,
▼ avgArticleSize: false, clusterNode: true, corpusSize:
  true…}
  ▶ $exists: function ()
    $key: "-KXtWqfDkwPJSc0B-lDQ"
  ▶ articleNode: Object
    avgArticle: true
    avgArticleSize: false
    clusterNode: true
    corpusSize: true
    longestArticle: true
    maxCenterPhrases: "2"         The disturbing properties
    maxFreqWords: "8"
    maxIDFs: "7"
    maxRootPhrases: "9"
    printButton: true
    rootNode: true
    shortestArticle: true
    templateName: "lavender"
    vocabularySize: true
```

It was very convenient that we had all we need in one object. But now we need to come up with a solution to separate the 'key' property from the data before passing it to the `update()` function.

The question here is couldn't we update the Firebase objects instantly while we change the input fields in the child template? The answer is yes we could and we did it before (in `Chapter 4`, *The Rating Service – Data Management*, when we had a few elements for the notifier form). But here we have a reasonably bigger form with complex field structure. So it is better to submit all changes in one shot and not to disturb Firebase for every single click or key strike.

Although we can do that in the child side of the interaction, the simpler way is to handle it from the parent side as follows:

```
// src/app/report/report.component.ts
//...
export class ReportComponent implements OnInit {
  // ...
  onSaveReportTemplate(report) {
    var key = report.$key;
    delete report.$key;
    delete report.$exists;
    this.templates.update(key, report);
```

```
      }
   }
```

Here we saved the object id in a separate local variable and then we got rid of redundant properties via the delete command. Now change the report template data and check out the Firebase console and we should be able to see the template update properly on both sides.

Deleting The Report Template

The delete event can be processed the same way as the update event. We need to assign a click event to the delete button in the child template:

```
# src/app/report/report-template.html
#...
   <button class="btn btn-default btn-xs pull-right" type="button"
              (click)="deleteReportTemplate(model)">
      <span class="glyphicon glyphicon-remove" aria-hidden="true">
      </span>
   </button>
#...
```

Then add the function and the event emitter to process that click in the child:

```
// src/app/report/report-template.component.ts
//...
export class ReportTemplateComponent {
  //...
  @Output() onDeleteReportTemplate = new EventEmitter<any>();

  deleteReportTemplate(model) {
    this.onDeleteReportTemplate.emit(model);
  }
}
```

In the parent template bind a function to the event coming from the child:

```
# src/app/report/report.html
#  ...
   <sh-report-template *ngFor="let template of items"
        [template]="template"
        (onSaveReportTemplate)="onSaveReportTemplate($event)"
        (onDeleteReportTemplate)="onDeleteReportTemplate($event)">
   </sh-report-template>
#  ...
```

And finally in the parent component implement the function to process the event:

```
// src/app/report/report.component.ts
//...
export class ReportComponent implements OnInit {
  // ...
  onDeleteReportTemplate(report) {
    this.templates.remove(key);
  }
}
```

Luckily, we only need the object key to remove it from Firebase and don't need to go through separating the key from the data here.

Rendering The Reports

Looking at the report.html template, we are using accordion structure for report template configuration and tab structure for each individual report. The configuration tab has the active class by default. So when we open the report page, we see that the tab has been opened already.

Now what we need is a mechanism to generate tabs for each report template dynamically. That means we need to sense any update to Firebase and the moment an object is created/updated/deleted reflect that change on screen instantly. Since we already have an 'items' property associated with our Firebase object, implementing the first part is easy. Simply remove all hard-coded values from report.html and modify it as follows:

```
# src/app/report/report.html
  #...
  <ul class="nav nav-tabs">
    #...
    <li *ngFor="let report of items">
      <a data-toggle="tab" href="#{{report.$key}}">
        {{report.templateName}}</a>
    </li>
  </ul>
  #...
    <div *ngFor="let report of items" id="{{report.$key}}"
      class="tab-pane fade">
      <p>place holder for {{report.templateName}}</p>
    </div>
  #...
```

Here we simply loop through the `items` property, set unique ids using the template keys saved in Firebase, and assign the tab names using the template names. Go ahead and play with this structure. You can easily create a new template in the config tab (hit the plus (+) button) and see a new tab is generated instantly. You can remove a report template and see it is gone from the current tabs and you can update the name of each report template and watch it change live on the tab name.

Now we need to implement the tricky part. Basically, what we need to do is replace the place holder snippet with the real report contents. To do so we are going to implement a service that reads each report template configuration and renders the report contents. The question is where we should keep the view for report contents. It is absolutely fine to modify the current `report.html` and add all the missing HTML rendering elements over there.

But the better solution–since we know how to use the `@Input` decoration and interact with child components–is to create three more child components–one for each report section–and pass the service data to them. These new children will receive the service data and show them in their own views. Later we will use the selectors assigned to each new child and show their views inside the parent view (`report.html`). So let's start by creating these new children.

Creating new children to render the reports

The process for all these new children is almost the same. We create a new component, set the input parameter for it, feed the input from parent, and finally put the new child's selector inside the parent's view.

Let's start by creating a new component for showing the configuration in general settings. Create a new component and add the following contents to it:

```
// src/app/report/report-general.component.ts
import {Component, Input} from '@angular/core';
@Component({
  selector: 'sh-report-general',
  templateUrl: './report-general.html',
  styleUrls: ['./report-general.css']
})
export class ReportGeneralComponent {
  @Input() general: {};
  constructor() {}
}
```

The input parameter here is called `general`, so we need to set and initialize this parameter in the parent as follows:

```
// src/app/report/report.component.ts
// ...
export class ReportComponent implements OnInit {
  private general = {
    mainKeyword:'MARS', corpusSize:'540', vocabularySize:'15000'
  };
  // ...
}
```

As usual this is a hard-coded value to begin with. Later we will create yet another injectable service and delegate the task of calculating and assigning report values to it. Now we need to pass that parameter from parent to the child. So modify the parent's view as follows:

```
# src/app/report/report.component.ts
  #...
    <div *ngFor="let report of items" id="{{report.$key}}"
      class="tab-pane fade">
      <sh-report-general [general]="general"></sh-report-general>
    </div>
  #...
```

Now the last thing that we need to do is catch what is coming to the child's way and lay it down over the child's view:

```
# src/app/report/report-general.component.ts
<div class="row general">
  <div class="col-md-4 wing move-left">
    <h3>The report is generated based on a corpus with
      <strong>{{general.corpusSize}}</strong> entries</h3>
  </div>
  <div class="col-md-4 circle">
    <div class="circle-inner">
      <h1>{{general.mainKeyword}}</h1>
      <p>This report is generated for evidences found around
        keyword: {{general.mainKeyword}}.</p>
    </div>
  </div>
  <div class="col-md-4 wing move-right">
    <h3>and there are <strong>{{general.vocabularySize}}</strong>
      words in the vocabulary</h3>
  </div>
</div>
```

You may have noticed that there are a bunch of new CSS classes and styles, which are all defined inside the `report-general.css` file. To save some space we won't show them here, but you can find the complete CSS file in the code repository:

```
https://github.com/Soolan/the-sherlock-project/tree/master/src/app/report/report-general.css
```

That file is responsible for turning a bland view to an infographic page, like the following screenshot:

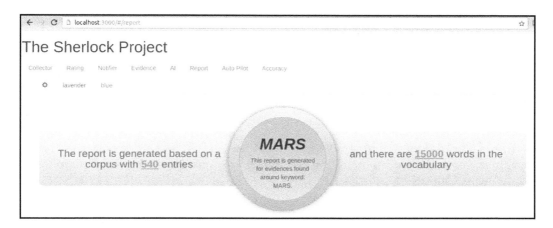

 We have just created a new component here so don't forget to import it inside the application module (`src/app/app.module.ts`) otherwise you will get access error.

Creating the report-corpus component

The component that will be used to render the corpus settings has a different set of input data, but it doesn't matter because the overall structure is the same. Let's start by creating the component itself:

```
// src/app/report/report-corpus.component.ts
import {Component, Input} from '@angular/core';
@Component({
  selector: 'sh-report-corpus',
  templateUrl: './report-corpus.html',
  styleUrls: ['./report-corpus.css']
})
export class ReportCorpusComponent {
```

```
    @Input() corpus: {};
    constructor() {}
}
```

Now we need to set and initialize the `corpus` parameter in the parent as follows:

```
// src/app/report/report.component.ts
// ...
export class ReportComponent implements OnInit {
  private corpus = {
    topFreqs: [{word:'w1', count:10}, {word:'w2', count:9}],
    topIDFs: [{word:'w1', idf:0.4}, {word:'w2', idf:0.3}],
    articleStats: {
      longestArticle: {size: 4765, link: 'http://www.test.com'},
      shortestArticle: {size: 58, link: 'http://www.test.com'},
      averageSize: 759
    }
  }
  // ...
}
```

Again, this is a hard-coded value to begin with. Later we will use the service to set the report values. Now we need to pass that parameter from parent to the child. So modify the parent's view as follows:

```
# src/app/report/report.component.ts
#...
  <div *ngFor="let report of items" id="{{report.$key}}"
    class="tab-pane fade">
    ...
    <sh-report-corpus [corpus]="corpus"></sh-report-corpus>
  </div>
```

Now we can create a view for the child and use the parent's data in it:

```
# src/app/report/report-corpus.component.ts
<div class="row corpus">
  <div class="col-md-3 space">
    <div class="panel panel-default">
      <div class="panel-heading">Top {{corpus.topFreqs.length}}
        Frequent Words</div>
      <table class="table">
        <thead>
        <tr><th>#</th><th>Words</th><th>Counts</th></tr>
        </thead>
        <tbody *ngFor="let w of corpus.topFreqs; let i=index"><tr>
          <th>{{i+1}}</th><td>{{w.word}}</td><td>{{w.count}}</td>
        </tr></tbody>
      </table>
```

```
      </div>
    </div>
    <div class="col-md-3">
      <div class="panel panel-default">
        <div class="panel-heading">Top {{corpus.topIDFs.length}}
          IDFs</div>
        <table class="table">
          <thead>
          <tr><th>#</th><th>Words</th><th>IDFs</th></tr>
          </thead>
          <tbody *ngFor="let w of corpus.topIDFs; let i=index"><tr>
            <th>{{i+1}}</th><td>{{w.word}}</td><td>{{w.idf}}</td>
          </tr></tbody>
        </table>
      </div>
    </div>
    <div class="col-md-1"></div>
    <div class="col-md-4">
      <div *ngIf="corpus.articleStats.length>0">
        <div *ngFor="let s of corpus.articleStats">
          <div class="row" id="talkbubble1">
            <div class="col-md-8">
              <p>The longest article in this corpus with
              {{s.longestArticle.size}} letters is located here:<br>
                <a href="{{s.longestArticle.link}}">
                  {{s.longestArticle.link|slice:0:42}}...</a></p>
            </div>
            <div class="col-md-4 circle">
              <div class="circle-inner">
                <h1>{{s.longestArticle.size}}</h1>
              </div>
            </div>
          </div>
          <div class="row" id="talkbubble2">
            <div class="col-md-8">
              <p>The average article size in the corpus contains
                {{s.averageSize}} letters</p>
            </div>
            <div class="col-md-4 circle">
              <div class="circle-inner"><h1>{{s.averageSize}}</h1>
              </div>
            </div>
          </div>
          <div class="row" id="talkbubble3">
            <div class="col-md-8">
              <p>The Shortest article in this corpus with
                {{s.shortestArticle.size}} letters can be found here:
                <a href="{{s.shortestArticle.link}}">
```

```
                {{s.shortestArticle.link|slice:0:42}}...</a></p>
          </div>
          <div class="col-md-4 circle">
            <div class="circle-inner">
              <h1>{{s.shortestArticle.size}}</h1></div>
          </div>
        </div>
      </div>
    </div>
  </div>
</div>
```

All necessary styles are saved in the CSS file in the code repository:

`https://github.com/Soolan/the-sherlock-project/tree/master/src/app/report/report-corpus.css`

Check out the output and you will see that the page looks like this so far:

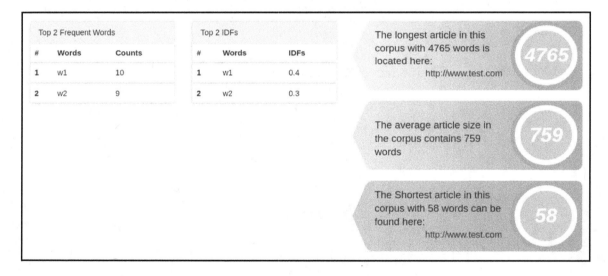

Creating the report-cluster component

The last component that we need in order to render the cluster settings, has more details and as a result needs more graphical elements. In other words, we need to read the network graph data and call a service to render it for us. That means apart from the usual data that we get from the parent we need to read the graph network data from Firebase and render it in the report. But it will be much simpler to compare what we did for evidence service.

Because here we will remove network graph click events. Having said that, we will add the graph to the report after finalizing all other elements, so let's start by creating the component itself:

```
// src/app/report/report-cluster.component.ts
import {Component, Input} from '@angular/core';
@Component({
  selector: 'sh-report-corpus',
  templateUrl: './report-corpus.html',
  styleUrls: ['./report-corpus.css']
})
export class ReportCorpusComponent {
  @Input() corpus: {};
  constructor() {}
}
```

The `corpus` structure is more complex compared to previous input values. It holds many details about graph nodes. So we need to set and initialize the `corpus` parameter in the parent as follows:

```
// src/app/report/report.component.ts
// ...
export class ReportComponent implements OnInit {
  private cluster = {
    // network: this.network,
    root: 'MARS',
    clusters: [{
      name: 'radiation',
      nodes: [{
        word_count: 234, distance: 0.2, link: 'http:www.test.com',
        main_phrases: ['mph1','mph2','mph3','mph4'],
        keyword_phrases: ['kph1','kph2','kph3','kph4']
      },{
        word_count: 434, distance: 0.1, link: 'http:www.test.com',
        main_phrases: ['mph1','mph2','mph3','mph4'],
        keyword_phrases: ['kph1','kph2','kph3','kph4']
      }]
    },{
      name: 'water',
      nodes: [{
        word_count: 657, distance: 0.3, link: 'http:www.test.com',
        main_phrases: ['mph1','mph2','mph3','mph4'],
        keyword_phrases: ['kph1','kph2','kph3','kph4']
      },{
        word_count: 879, distance: 0.2, link: 'http:www.test.com',
        main_phrases: ['mph1','mph2','mph3','mph4'],
        keyword_phrases: ['kph1','kph2','kph3','kph4']
```

```
        }]
      }]};
   // ...
 }
```

Again, this is a hard-coded value to begin with. Later we will use the service to set the report values. Now we need to pass that parameter from parent to the child. So modify the parent's view as follows:

```
# src/app/report/report.component.ts
  #...
    <div *ngFor="let report of items" id="{{report.$key}}"
      class="tab-pane fade">
      ...
      <sh-report-cluster [cluster]="cluster"></sh-report-cluster>
    </div>
```

Now we can create a view for the child and use parent's data in it. The first part of the view belongs to the root node and cluster centers:

```
# src/app/report/report-cluster.component.ts
<div class="row cluster">
  <h1>{{cluster.root}}</h1>
  <ol class="spine">
    <li *ngFor="let c of cluster.clusters">
      <h1>{{c.name}}</h1>
      <div *ngFor="let node of c.nodes; let i=index" class="node">
        <h5>
          <span class="glyphicon glyphicon-ok"
            aria-hidden="true"></span>
          <strong>node {{i+1 }}: </strong>
          Words: {{node.word_count}}, Distance:{{node.distance}},
            URL:{{node.link}}
        </h5>
      </div>
    </li>
  </ol>
</div>
```

We separated the article nodes from others for better view management. We will see how this separation becomes handy during the service implementation.

The `spine` class mentioned in the `<ol>` element is responsible for generating a nice timeline view. We won't show the contents of the CSS file here (it has over 150 lines of the code), but feel free to check out this file here:

```
https://github.com/Soolan/the-sherlock-project/tree/master/src/app/report/r
eport-cluster.css
```

This is how it will look when we check out the browser:

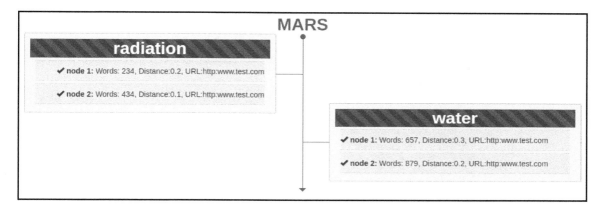

The second part of the template deals with cluster centers, its nodes, and details in each node:

```
<div class="row cluster">
  #...
  <ul class="tree" *ngFor="let c of cluster.clusters">
    <li>
      <h2>{{c.name}}</h2>
      <ul *ngFor="let node of c.nodes; let i=index">
        <li class="node-details col-md-6">
          <h4>
            <span class="glyphicon glyphicon-ok"
              aria-hidden="true"></span>
            <strong>node {{i+1 }}: </strong>
            Article length:{{node.word_count}} | Distance:
            {{node.distance}} | URL:{{node.link}}
          </h4>
          <div class="col-md-6 phrases">
            <h5>These are some phrases in that article which
              contain the word {{cluster.root}}</h5>
            <ul><li *ngFor="let main_phrase of node.main_phrases">
              {{main_phrase}}</li></ul>
          </div>
          <div class="col-md-6 phrases">
```

```
        <h5>These are some phrases in that article which
           contain the word {{c.name}}</h5>
        <ul><li *ngFor="let keyword_phrase of
           node.keyword_phrases"> {{keyword_phrase}}</li></ul>
     </div>
   </li>
  </ul>
 </li>
</ul>
</div>
```

Check out the output and the page should look like this so far:

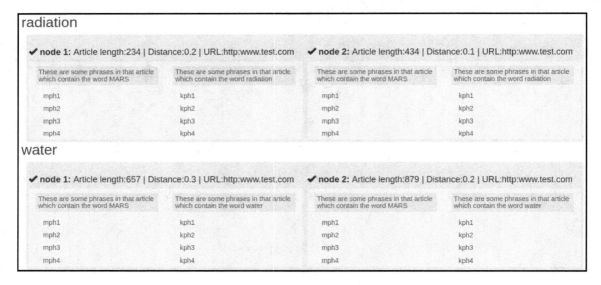

As it shows, now we need a service to extract some extra information–such as phrases with root node and cluster center words–from network graph. The easy part–which was creating child components and feeding their views with hard-coded values–is over. Now it is time to get into the challenging part.

Updating the report component

The objective here is to replace all hard-coded values in the parent component with the real data. That means we have to delegate the task of creating some (not all) data objects for each child component to the Report service. Let's start with the 'general' object. At the moment it looks like this:

```
private general = {
  mainKeyword:'MARS', corpusSize: '540', vocabularySize: '15000'
};
```

We need to check the general setting values for the current template object in Firebase, and if they are true then We can easily read the corpus and vocabulary sizes plus the main keyword from the `Evidence/Corpus/Stats` object. We can read the Stats object via the parent component itself. So update the `report` component as follows:

```
// src/app/report/report.component.ts
//...
export class ReportComponent implements OnInit {
  private stats: FirebaseObjectObservable <any>;
  //...
  constructor(af: AngularFire) {
    this.templates = af.database.list('/Report/templates');
    this.stats = af.database.object('Evidence/Corpus/Stats',
      {preserveSnapshot: true});
  }
}
```

As we know, each report template has been saved inside the items array already. So the next step is to loop through these items and set a report for each one of them:

```
// src/app/report/report.component.ts
//...
export class ReportComponent implements OnInit {
  ngOnInit() {
    this.templates.subscribe(data => {
      this.items = data;
      this.items.forEach(item => this.setReport(item));
    });
  }
}
```

The `setReport()` function has one duty. It should read the Firebase entries and build separate objects for general settings, corpus settings, and cluster settings. Later we will feed these objects to the parent view:

```
// src/app/report/report.component.ts
//...
export class ReportComponent implements OnInit {
  private reports = [];
  //...
  setReport(template) {
    this.reports.push({
      general: this.setGeneral(template),
      corpus:  this.setCorpus(template),
      cluster: this.setCluster(template)
    });
  }
}
```

As we can see, there are three other functions that are in charge of assembling properties for rendering each report. The `setGeneral()` function can be kept inside the Report component because the building blocks of the general object has been initialized inside the parent component already. Having said that, we can implement these functions as follows:

```
// src/app/report/report.component.ts
//...
export class ReportComponent implements OnInit {
  //...
  setGeneral(template) {
    let general = {};
    this.stats.subscribe(snapshot => {
      if (snapshot.exists()) {
        //object exists
        general['mainKeyword'] = snapshot.val().mainKeyword;
        general['corpusSize'] = template.corpusSize?
          snapshot.val().corpusSize:null;
        general['vocabularySize'] = template.vocabularySize?
          snapshot.val().vocabularySize:null;
      }
    });
    return general;
  }

  setCorpus(template) {
    // ToDo: Initialize related values via service
  }

  setCluster(template) {
```

```
        // ToDo: Initialize related values via service
    }
}
```

The main keyword for the current report never changes, so we can read it from the Stats object–generated from the previous chapter–and save it in the `general.mainKeyword` property. But for corpus and vocabulary sizes, first we need to see if they are supposed to be displayed in the current report template. If they are checked in the UI (their Firebase values are `'true'`) then we read their number values from the Stats object and save them in the 'general' property as well. We will deal with `setCorpus()` and the `setCluster()` functions shortly.

Now it is time to get rid of hard coded values in the general variable. Go to the line where we defined the private general variable and remove it altogether. The local variable that we defined inside the `setGeneral()` function will take its place. With these updates, now we have to modify the general selector in the parent view as well. So open the `report.html` and apply the following changes:

```
# src/app/report/report.html
#...
    <div *ngFor="let report of items; let i=index"
      id="{{report.$key}}" class="tab-pane fade">
      <sh-report-general [general]="reports[i].general">
      </sh-report-general>
      #...
```

There are two updates here: first we add a local index variable to use it as an index for the current report element in the reports array. Then we replaced the (hard-coded) general property with the general child of the current report object.

There is one last step before moving on to the next topic. Looking at the view for the general component, there is no logic for dealing with checked/unchecked items. In other words, it doesn't matter if the `corpusSize` or `vocabularySize` is checked or unchecked, they are displayed regardless. So let's add a condition to show them based on the value of selectable items:

```
# src/app/report/report-general.html
<div class="row general">
  <div class="col-md-4 wing move-left">
    <h3 *ngIf="general.corpusSize">
      The report is generated based on a corpus with
      <strong>{{general.corpusSize}}</strong> entries</h3>
  </div>
  <div class="col-md-4 circle">
    <div class="circle-inner">
```

```
        <h1>{{general.mainKeyword}}</h1>
        <p>This report is generated for evidences found around
           '{{general.mainKeyword}}'.</p>
      </div>
    </div>
    <div class="col-md-4 wing move-right">
      <h3 *ngIf="general.vocabularySize">
        and there are <strong>{{general.vocabularySize}}</strong>
        words in the vocabulary    </h3>
    </div>
  </div>
```

As we can see, the *ngIf directive does the trick and the contents of each wing are shown only if they have been checked in the configuration tab.

Implementing the report service for the corpus – part one

The reason that we moved the logic for creating corpus and cluster objects to a new service is because they need in-depth calculations, which involves reading and parsing JSON objects and then selecting only required children from them. Let's start by examining the corpus object:

```
private corpus = {
  topFreqs: [{word: 'w1', count: 10}, {word: 'w2', count: 9}],
  topIDFs: [{word: 'w1', idf: 0.4}, {word: 'w2', idf: 0.3}],
  articleStats: {
    longestArticle: {size: 4765, link: 'http://www.test.com'},
    shortestArticle: {size: 58, link: 'http://www.test.com'},
    averageSize: 759
  }
};
```

This object consists of several complex properties. What they all have in common is the origin where they get their with content from: the corpus.

Create yet another inject-able service and add the following contents to it:

```
// src/app/report/reposrt.service.ts
import {Injectable} from '@angular/core';
import {AngularFire, FirebaseListObservable} from 'angularfire2';

@Injectable()
export class ReportService{
  private IDFs: FirebaseListObservable <any>;
```

```
    private angularFire;
    constructor(af: AngularFire) { this.angularFire = af; }

    setCorpus(template) {
      // ToDo: Initialize related values
    }

    setCluster(template) {
      // ToDo: Initialize related values
    }
  }
```

There are three parts in the corpus section of the report: Top frequent words, Top IDFs, and Article statistics. Let's start by finding top frequent words:

```
// src/app/report/report.service.ts
// ...
export class ReportService{
  //...
  setCorpus(template) {
    let topFreqs = [];
    // calculating topFreqs
    this.angularFire.database.list('Evidence/Corpus/IDFs', {
      query: {
        orderByChild: "doc_with_word",
        limitToLast: parseInt(template.maxFreqWords)
      }}).subscribe(data => {
        data.forEach( d => {
          topFreqs.push({word:d.word, count: d.doc_with_word})
        });
        topFreqs.sort(function(a,b){
          return b['count']-a['count'] });
      });
    };
    return {topFreqs: topFreqs, topIDFs: '', articleStats: ''};
  }
```

Here we did a typical Firebase query from IDFs, sorted the result based on doc_with_word, and limited the result set to the number we have set in the configuration tab for the current report template. Then we looped through the result set and saved them as {word, count} objects in the topFreqs local variable. At the end we sorted them descending based on the word occurrence.

You might ask, why can't we query Firebase inside the `OnInit()` hook? We did that before and it seemed very handy, because by doing that we could save some space in the `setCorpus()` function. Right? The answer is because lifecycle hooks, such as `OnInit()` are available to Directives and Components only. In other words, we cannot use them in injectable services. This is an architectural decision made by the Angular team.

There is something missing here. The question is, why should we go through all this trouble if no value was specified or no boxes were checked in the **Configuration** tab?

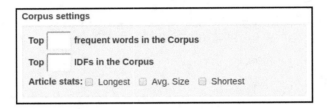

Let's add the control mechanism as follows:

```
// src/app/report/reposrt.service.ts
// ...
export class ReportService{
  //...
  setCorpus(template) {
    //...
    if (limitTopFreq>0) {
      this.angularFire.database.list('Evidence/Corpus/IDFs', {
        //...
      } else {
        topFreqs.push({word:"value is not set", count: "..."})
      }
    return {topFreqs: topFreqs, topIDFs: '', articleStats: ''};
  }
}
```

We simply wrap the query logic around a condition and in case that field is left empty or set to 0 then we push a message to the `topFreqs` array. We will show that message when there is no value.

Here is another question: couldn't we handle that empty array in the view and show a proper message over there? Yes we could, but since we are going to show a loading spinner while the array is still empty, it is better to handle the logic in the service.

Remember, we are dealing with observables here. So while the observable object is fetching the data from Firebase, it is empty and the last thing that we want is to confuse a delayed Firebase response (empty array) with an empty value from the UI. Now let's update the views to reflect these changes.

Updating the views

We want to show a loading spinner while waiting for a Firebase response. So modify the corpus view as follows:

```
# src/app/report/report-corpus.html
<div class="row corpus">
  #...
        <tbody *ngIf="corpus.topFreqs.length==0">
          <tr><td colspan="3"><div class="spinner">
              <div class="bounce1"></div>
              <div class="bounce2"></div>
              <div class="bounce3"></div>
        </div></td></tr>
      </tbody>
```

This is just a simple CSS 3 animation that is controlled by the `*ngIf` directive to show/hide based on the `topFreqs` state. You can find the styling details about the spinner class in the `src/app/report/report-corpus.css` file.

As you can see, the spinner will show up only if the `topFreqs` array is empty. The moment it gets some data from Firebase or the info message from the service it will disappear.

Top 0 Frequent Words			Top 1 Frequent Words			Top 2 Frequent Words		
#	Words	Counts	#	Words	Counts	#	Words	Counts
	● ● ●		1	value is not set	...	1	the	286
						2	of	285
(a) waiting for response			**(b) config tab value is empty or zero**			**(c) response from Firebase**		

Now head to the parent view and modify it as follows:

```
# src/app/report/report.html
  #...
    <div *ngFor="let report of items; let i=index"
        id="{{report.$key}}" class="tab-pane fade">
        <sh-report-general [general]="reports[i].general">
```

```
      </sh-report-general>
      <sh-report-corpus [corpus]="reports[i].corpus">
      </sh-report-corpus>
      <sh-report-cluster [cluster]="cluster"></sh-report-cluster>
    </div>
  #...
```

Again we simply replaced the hard-coded value provided in the private corpus variable with the results that come from the service. That means we have to update the parent component as well. In other words, remove that corpus variable from the component completely and modify the `setCorpus()` function as follows:

```
// src/app/report/report.component.ts
//...
export class ReportComponent implements OnInit {
  //...
  setCorpus(template) {
    return this.reportService.setCorpus(template);
  }
}
```

So far we have managed to implement the first part of corpus reports. It is too soon to see how it looks in the browser. Let's continue with the remaining parts and then test the application.

Optimizing the Firebase performance

At this stage if you look at the browser console, there are some warning messages that complain about indexing the keys:

```
⚠ FIREBASE WARNING: Using an unspecified index. Consider adding ".indexOn":          firebase.js:276
  "doc_with_word" at /Evidence/Corpus/IDFs to your security rules for better performance
⚠ FIREBASE WARNING: Using an unspecified index. Consider adding ".indexOn": "IDF" at  firebase.js:276
  /Evidence/Corpus/IDFs to your security rules for better performance
```

To address this issue, let's add an index to some keys. So open the Firebase console and click on the rules tab. This is where we define configurations for the way Firebase should perform. Add a few .indexOn keys as follows:

```
Unpublished changes    |    PUBLISH    DISCARD    SIMULATOR

 1 ▾    {
 2 ▾      "rules": {
 3          ".read": true, //"auth != null",
 4          ".write": true,
 5 ▾        "Notifier" : {
 6 ▾          "rated-news": {
 7 ▾            ".indexOn": ["rank"]
 8            }
 9          },
10 ▾        "Evidence" : {
11 ▾          "Corpus": {
12 ▾            "IDFs": {
13 ▾              ".indexOn": ["doc_with_word","IDF"]
14              },
15 ▾            "Articles": {
16 ▾              ".indexOn": ["bag_of_words"]
17              }
18            }
19          }
20        }
21      }
```

Now check out the browser console again and you will see that the warnings are gone.

Implementing the report service for the Corpus – part two

Starting from the topIDFs array, we can see that the logic is the same as topFreqs, except that we sort the query based on the IDF field:

```
// src/app/report/report.service.ts
//...
export class ReportService{
  //...
  setCorpus(template) {
    //...
    let topIDFs = [];
    let limitTopIDFs = parseInt(template.maxIDFs);
    // calculating topIDFs
```

```
      if (limitTopIDFs>0) {
        this.angularFire.database.list('Evidence/Corpus/IDFs', {
          query: {
            orderByChild: "IDF",
            limitToFirst:  limitTopIDFs// highest occurrence
          }})
          .subscribe(data => {
            data.forEach( d => {
              topIDFs.push({word:d.word, idf: d.IDF.toFixed(7)});
            });
          });
      } else {
        topIDFs.push({word:"value is not set", count: "..."})
      }
      return {
        topFreqs: topFreqs, topIDFs: topIDFs, articleStats: ''
      };
    }
  }
```

It is worth mentioning that top IDFs here doesn't mean biggest numbers. You might have noticed that instead of `'limitToLast'` we have used `'limitToFirst'`, which brings the smallest numbers first. To understand this logic, we need to remember **IDF** stands for **INVERSE Document Frequency** (*1/some value*).

So the higher that *some value*, the smaller the IDF. For that reason, popular words will have the smallest DIFs. Now let's move on to the last part of the corpus report. Add the following code snippet to the `setCorpus()` function:

```
// src/app/report/report.service.ts
//...
export class ReportService{
  //...
  setCorpus(template) {
    //...
    let stats = [];
    // calculating articleStats
    if ( template.shortestArticle || template.avgArticleSize  ||
        template.longestArticle  )
    this.angularFire.database.list('Evidence/Corpus/Articles')
      .subscribe(data => {
        let sum = 0;
        data.forEach(d => {sum += d.article.length;});
        let shortest = (template.shortestArticle)?
          (data.reduce(function (a, b) {
          return a.article.length > b.article.length ? b : a;
          })):{article:{length:0}, link:'check the box in the
```

```
          config tab'};
      let longest = (template.longestArticle)?
        (data.reduce(function (a, b) {
        return a.article.length > b.article.length ? a : b;
      })):{article:{length:0}, link:'check the box in the
        config tab'};
      stats.push({
        longestArticle: {
          size: longest.article.length, link: longest.link },
        averageSize: template.avgArticleSize?
          Math.round(sum/data.length): 0,
        shortestArticle: {
          size: shortest.article.length, link: shortest.link }
      });
    });
    return {
      topFreqs: topFreqs, topIDFs: topIDFs, articleStats: stats
    };
  }
}
```

We have to calculate the longest, shortest, and average articles based on the checkbox values in the UI. That's why we will initiate the expensive calculations only if at least one of them is checked.

To be more cautious about the performance, even inside the query block, we permit the calculations for longest and shortest articles, only if they are selected in UI. At the end the result is saved in the *stats* variable, assembled as an object–equal to the hard-coded value we set at the beginning of this chapter–and returned by the `setCorpus()` function.

Updating the Corpus view

The parent view stays the same, but we need to update the report-corpus.html and add loading spinners as follows:

```
# src/app/report/report-corpus.html
#...
  <div class="col-md-3">
    #...
      <tbody *ngIf="corpus.topIDFs.length==0">
      <tr><td colspan="3"><div class="spinner">
          <div class="bounce1"></div>
          <div class="bounce2"></div>
          <div class="bounce3"></div>
      </div></td></tr>
      </tbody>
```

```
      #...
    </div>
    <div class="col-md-4">
      <div *ngIf="corpus.articleStats.length==0">
        <p>Depend on the corpus size, calculating article stats
           might takes a few minutes. Please be patient...</p>
        <div class="spinner2" >
          <div class="double-bounce1"></div>
          <div class="double-bounce2"></div>
        </div>
      </div>
      #...
    </div>
  #...
```

Please remember that the styling for the second spinner can be found at report-`corpus.css`. Now we can have a look at the results in the browser:

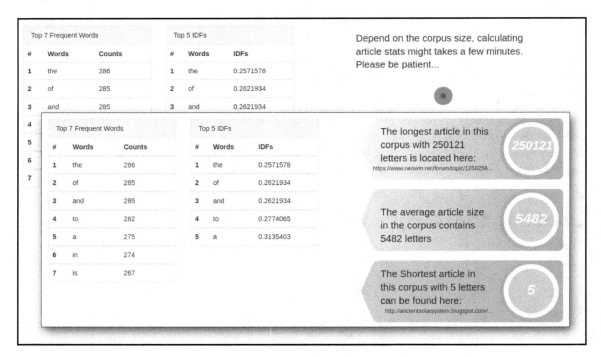

That is interesting. It proves the importance of reports. According to stats the longest article has over a quarter of a million letters! How is that even possible? Did we accidentally download a book! I mean, I'm an author and I know that 250,000 letters is–roughly–equal to a 150 page book. Looking at the article's URL we see the word `forum` in it:

```
https://www.neowin.net/forum/topic/1258256-international-space-station-update
s/?page=41
```

Now that explains. If we open the link we land on page 41 of a long conversation in a forum about 'space stations'.

 Check out the page source and it is over 17000 lines of HTML code. This is insane and explains how those quarter of a million characters ended up in our application.

On the other end, check out the shortest article. It has only 5 letters! What is this? A one-liner joke about aliens? Let's check that link as well:

```
http://ancientsolarsystem.blogspot.co.id/
```

I'm no space expert, but by the look of that page I would say it deserves way more than five letters in our application.

So, what does it mean? That means we manage to welcome a 150 page book to our application and crown it as the champion of the sumo wrestlers – and to make it sound even worse – probably most of it is about people arguing and shouting at each other to defend their own opinion. At the same time we managed to evaluate a good looking article down to five letters. To be specific, a bag of words with only two words in the bag and those two words are: "null" and ".

Are we doomed? No we are not. I'm just exaggerating the dark side of our efforts a little bit to point out two facts:

- The Internet cannot be seen as the source of the truth. It is simply a tool. Nothing more. We can utilize it to our benefits and learn how to work around unwanted results.
- There is no such a thing as a flawless Machine Learning algorithm. While they provide impressive results, they all have weaknesses.

So what is the solution? In the last chapter of this book, Chapter 9, The Accuracy manager, we are going to explore the techniques to evaluate the results, and if there is any dodgy entry there, make the Accuracy manager inform us about it. That is the – rather expensive – cure. So we will also create rules, to prevent unwanted results wasting our precious resources (bandwidth, database space, quota, and so on) on calculating and generating clusters, reports, and so on. As wise men say: an ounce of prevention is worth a pound of cure.

Before moving on to the last part of the report, let's talk about word counts versus IDFs. It seems in both tables we see the same words repeated, so what is the point of having (somehow) duplicate results? Well actually, highly frequent words yield the same IDF level, but if we expand the result set in both tables to, say 150 items, then as we go further down the list we see words with different level of frequency and of course IDF:

Top 150 Frequent Words			Top 150 IDFs		
#	Words	Counts	#	Words	IDFs
Here is the difference between word frequencies and IDFs					
130	scientists	72	130	many	2.2322402
131	last	72	131	take	2.2322402
132	surface	71	132	during	2.2521398
133	during	71	133	see	2.2521398
134	see	71	134	surface	2.2521398
135	well	70	135	should	2.2723176
136	system	70	136	those	2.2723176

Implementing The Report Service For the Clusters

Let's start by analyzing the cluster object in the parent component. This object by far is the most complex part of the report:

```
private cluster = {
    // network: this.network,
    root: 'MARS',
    clusters: [{
      name: 'radiation',
      nodes: [{
```

```
        word_count: 234, distance: 0.2, link: 'http:www.test.com',
        main_phrases: ['mph1','mph2','mph3','mph4'],
        keyword_phrases: ['kph1','kph2','kph3','kph4']
      }]
    }]
  };
```

According to this object, first we need to read the network-graph object from Firebase and then find the root node, cluster centers, and their nodes and save them in this new cluster object. That means we will have a lot of parsing ahead of us.

Open the service and add the last missing piece, the `setCluster()` function, to it. Let's start by reading the nodes and saving them in an array:

```
// src/app/report/report.service.ts
  //...
  setCluster(template) {
    let root ='';
    let centers = [];
    let nodes = [];
    this.angularFire.database
      .list('Evidence/Corpus/network-graph/nodes')
      .subscribe(data => {
        root = data[0].label;
        data.shift(data[0]);
        data.forEach( d => {
          if(d.title[1].indexOf("cluster center") != -1) {
            centers.push(d);
          } else { nodes.push(d); }
        });
      });
```

After getting the result set from the database, the first thing that we did was save the root node in a local variable and remove it from the data array. Then we separated the rest of the items into two groups: Cluster centers and article nodes. Finding the cluster centers is as easy as checking the contents of the title[1] property. If it contains the words "cluster center" (which we saved in the previous chapter) then that node is a cluster center.

Now let's get the edges and assemble the objects we need for the cluster part of the report:

```
// src/app/report/report.service.ts
  //...
  setCluster(template) {
    //...
    let reportNodes = [];
    let reportClusters = [];
    this.angularFire.database
```

```
    .list('Evidence/Corpus/network-graph/edges')
    .subscribe(data => {
      centers.forEach(c => {
        reportNodes = [];
        data.forEach (d => {
          //find edges which has cluster centers in one end
          if (c.id == d.from) {
            //...
```

To find the nodes that belong to a specific cluster center, we implemented a nested loop. The outer side circles through the cluster centers and the inner loop checks all edge entries coming from Firebase. If there is a match between center id and the 'from' property in the current edge, then it means we found a related article.

From that point forward, we used entries saved in the nodes array and data fetched from edges objects to find the required pieces for our final return object:

```
// src/app/report/report.service.ts
  //...
  setCluster(template) {
    //...
              let node = nodes.filter(function(obj){
                return obj.id == d.to;})[0];
              let link = node.title[0];
              let wordCount = node.label.split("\n")[1];
              let distance = d.label;
              let mainPhrases =
                this.getPhrases(node.title[1], root, null);
              let keyPhrases =
                this.getPhrases(node.title[1], c.label, null);
              reportNodes.push({
                word_count:wordCount,distance:distance,link:link,
                main_phrases:mainPhrases,keyword_phrases:keyPhrases
              })
            }
          });
          reportClusters.push({
            name: c.label, nodes: reportNodes
          });
        })
      });
    return { root: root, clusters: reportClusters };
  }
```

Finding the node for the article is easy. We just filter out (the filter function) the array member that shares the same id on the other side of the current edge. Having that node under control, now we can fetch the link (node.title[0]) and number of the words in that article (node.label.split("\n")[1]).

Finding the distance property perhaps is the easiest one. All we need to do is read the 'label' property (d.label) of the current edge (in the network graph from the previous chapter, do you remember that we put distances as the labels on top of each edge? That is how they became handy in this chapter).

Calculating main phrases and key phrases is a little tricky and we need a complete function for them. This function is discussed next. But for now let's wrap up the setCluster() function by pushing the article nodes to each cluster center:

```
reportClusters.push({ name: c.label, nodes: reportNodes });
```

We then return the root node plus all cluster centers as an object from the setCluster() function:

```
return { root: root, clusters: reportClusters };
```

Catching the phrases

Now let's extract related phrases from the contents. What do we mean by related? We are going to find a limited number of phrases that contain the word in the cluster center and we are going to do the same for phrases with the word 'Mars':

```
// src/app/report/report.service.ts
  //...
  getPhrases(id, word, limit) {
    let phrases = [];
    let range = 33; //number of chars on each side of keyword
    this.angularFire.database
      .object('Evidence/Corpus/Articles/'+id+'/article/')
      ._ref.once("value").then(snapshot => {
      let text = snapshot.val();
      let i = text.indexOf(word);
      while(i > -1 && limit-- > 0) {
        (i-range <0)?
          phrases.push(text.slice(0,i+range)):
          (i+range > text.length )?
          phrases.push('...'+text.slice(i-range,text.length)):
          phrases.push('...'+text.slice(i-range,i+range)+'...');
        i = text.indexOf(word, i+word.length);
      }
```

```
        });
      return phrases;
    }
```

The good news is we have the article id, so instead of making an expensive call and getting a bulky response and then again loop through the result set to find what we are looking for; we can land exactly on the destination via the following path:

```
'Evidence/Corpus/Articles/'+id+'/article/'
```

From there we can get the article contents and cut a slice of letters that contain the words we are looking for.

Adding the Conditional Blocks

So far we developed the mechanical part without doing any checks. Let's start by wrapping the database calls into an if block:

```
// src/app/report/report.service.ts
  //...
  setCluster(template) {
    //...
    if (template.rootNode) {
      this.angularFire.database
        .list('Evidence/Corpus/network-graph/nodes')
        .subscribe(data => {... });
      this.angularFire.database
        .list('Evidence/Corpus/network-graph/edges')
        .subscribe(data => {...});
    } else {
      root = 'root node is not selected';
      reportClusters = null;
    }
    return { root: root, clusters: reportClusters };
  }
```

What we are saying here is, let's do all calculations only if the root node in the configuration tab is selected. If not, let's show a message and inform the user about it, and don't bother to render the rest of the view if the value for the 'clusters' property is null:

```
# src/app/report/report-cluster.html
<div class="row cluster">
  <h1>{{cluster.root}}</h1>
  <ol class="spine" *ngIf="cluster.clusters">
    #...
```

The same logic applies to the rest of the checks. Please find the complete code for the service and the related views in the following repository:

```
https://github.com/Soolan/the-sherlock-project/tree/master/src/app/repor
```

Updating the parent

Now that we have the service in place we need to update a few places to reflect the recent changes. Starting with the parent component, update the `setCluster()` function as follows:

```
// src/app/report/report.component.ts
//...
export class ReportComponent implements OnInit {
  //...
  setCluster(template) {
    return this.reportService.setCluster(template);
  }
}
```

While we are here, we need to remove the hard-coded value for the cluster property as well. Next open the parent view and add the indexed cluster report as follows:

```
# src/app/report/report.html
#...
    <div *ngFor="let report of items; let i=index"
      id="{{report.$key}}" class="tab-pane fade">
      <sh-report-general [general]="reports[i].general">
      </sh-report-general>
      <sh-report-corpus [corpus]="reports[i].corpus">
      </sh-report-corpus>
      <sh-report-cluster [cluster]="reports[i].cluster">
      </sh-report-cluster>
    </div>
#...
```

Now all three sections of each report are working together and they depend on the settings inside the configurations tab, they will also render reports with different levels of detail.

Printing the report

Since the beginning of this chapter we had a `printButton` property inside the `ReportConfig` model, but we never used it. We have it inside the configuration UI and if we check the database we can see that there is a valid status for that property, but it does not do anything.

Let's show/hide this button based on its status, create an event listener for it, and print a report page when it is hit. First create a button next to the name of each report template inside the main view:

```
# src/app/report/report.html
#...
<li *ngFor="let report of items">
  <a data-toggle="tab" href="#{{report.$key}}">
    {{report.templateName}}
    <button *ngIf="report.printButton" type="button"
      class="btn btn-default btn-xs"
      (click)="printReport(report.$key)">
      <span class="glyphicon glyphicon-print" aria-hidden="true">
      </span>
    </button>
  </a>
</li>
#...
```

Notice that we show the print button only if it was checked inside that **Configuration** tab:

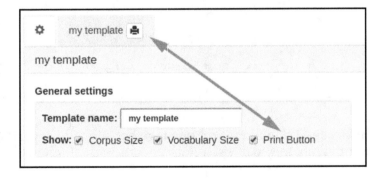

Also pay attention to the report ID associated with each print button. Now in the `report` component, add the `print` function as follows:

```
// src/app/report/report.component.ts
//...
  printReport (id) {
    let print = window.open('', '', '');
    print.document.write('<html><title>Print</title><body>');
    print.document.write(document.getElementById(id).innerHTML);
    print.document.write('</body></html>');
    print.document.close();
    print.print();
    return true;
  }
```

Now if we hit the **Print** button, a tab will open in the browser where all the styles are stripped off and the print properties page will pop up and wait for the **Print** button to be pushed to start printing.

Summary

In this chapter, we learned about how to create parent child interaction mechanisms where the child gets data models provided by the parent and fires back requests to the parent. We saw how to implement components to read the result of previously saved data objects, parse them, and assemble new objects that can be used as building blocks of a report.

We experienced how to optimize the query latency by defining indices in Firebase and we learned how to add various spinners while waiting for an observable object. At the end we saw how simple it is to print a page using pure JavaScript functions.

During the report generation phase we noticed anomalies in the data, and that is why in the next chapter we will focus on how to fix troubled contents and how to prevent them from ending up in our database in the future.

8
The Accuracy Manager Service - Putting It All Together

The job of the accuracy manager is to deal with anomalies found after running the application. For example, from the previous chapter we ended with extreme results. In the report we found out that the longest article is almost as big as a 150 page book and the shortest has only five characters (null characters) in it. So the objective of this chapter can be summarized as follows:

- We need to pin point those issues as soon as they show up (cure)
- We have to make sure that they won't happen again in the future (prevention)

Let's talk about the nature of these two items and expand them a little.

Introducing the anatomy of cure and prevention

The logic behind cure and prevention is very simple and it is all about timing: whatever issue we find AFTER running the application will be considered as a situation that needs a cure. On the other side, the very next time that we use that solution BEFORE the issue arises then we consider it as prevention. So technically what we call a cure here is a note that mentions something is broken and it needs our attention. It simply informs us about it and does not patch it up by itself.

Please keep in mind that there are situations where we cannot find problems until after code execution. For example, we cannot find out if the query result is valid and is within the acceptable range, without letting the Google CSE (Custom Search Engine) do its job. So what happens at that point onward – technically- is a cure, not prevention.

That means we cannot save the query quota before trying something. However, we can save the Firebase quota and database space, by analyzing the URL contents and if there is something wrong we prevent the object from being persisted to the database.

So we need a component that look into the report and analyzes the current code to find if there is any issue in it. Assuming that we have some cure and prevention rules in place, if any of those rules are violated, then we should receive a signal. As we will see, that signal is just a hit counter that increases each time a prevention code is executed.

When a prevention code is executed, it blocks the application from processing the buggy data and that way it saves the system resources. At the same time, it gathers information about reasons why it happened. So later we can investigate them and provide a proper solution for them.

The Accuracy Manager Component and its service is the home for the workflow we mentioned previously.

Why are test frameworks not practical here?

As we can see, the strategy explained previously sounds very much like usual tests. One might say, why can't we use unit tests instead of implementing another component/service for measuring accuracy? The answer is because our intention is not to test the application in order to find flaws. The point is, tests are a way to find flaws in what we EXPECT from a piece of code. Take a look at the following test, for example:

```
it('should test TF-IDF accuracy', () => {
  expect(/* query outcome */).toBe(/* valid */);
});
```

The keywords such as "it", "expect", and "toBe" are the real function names used in testing. If you are interested in learning more about testing try: Jasmin Cookbook (`https://www.packtpub.com/web-development/jasmine-cookbook`).

So this code snippet here says we want 'to test TF-IDF accuracy' and we 'expect that our Custom Search Engine results are valid'. And how possibly can we guarantee that! As you might have guessed, there are so many scenarios that Jasmine tests will lose their efficiency in our application.

The test frameworks are designed based on expectations. The challenge in our application is that we don't know what to expect. Moreover, the nature of this code is dealing with asynchronous requests from various APIs, which makes it even more complicated to implement a linear testing pipeline.

Simply put, we are using some limited Machine Learning flavored asynchronous codes in our application to dive into the unknown and provide some insight. So technically, we don't know what to expect from the unexpected.

Having said that, please keep in mind that putting test codes in place is one of the highly suggested best practices, and it is always advised to follow TDD and BDD approaches during development.

As the name suggests, the main focus of this book is on Angular Services, so we don't spend any time on how to develop tests using Jasmine and how to tune them via Karma (Jasmine and Karma are just examples, you may replace them with your favorite test tools). But by all means do implement the testing suites for the testable part of your code (components, services, directives, pipes, and so on). Here you can find a very robust official article about Angular Tests:

```
https://angular.io/docs/ts/latest/testing/
```

The accuracy manager component

This component controls a view with two main parts: in the Prevention column we have all statistics regarding the current (active) prevention solution. It will contain a description about the prevention mechanism, where it is placed, and how many times it was hit during the last run.

In the cure column we have the option to add feedback about the incident that happened after application execution. In other words, the main difference between prevention and cure is that prevention is a read-only in-memory object that is created during the application run cycle, while cure is a CRUD-able Firebase object (CRUD: Create, Read, Update, and Delete) that we have full control over how it is going to be managed within the component's view. The following screenshot summarizes the business logic for this component:

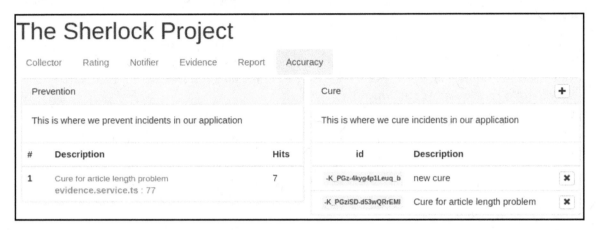

Like a real life problem, in our application cure cannot control the prevention, but prevention may have a chance to delete a specific cure if a condition is met. We will learn about that condition and how prevention will act upon it soon.

With this brief introduction, let's create a new TypeScript class for our new component and add it to the application module and current routes:

```
// src/app/accuracy/accuracy.component.ts
import {Component, OnInit} from '@angular/core';
import {AngularFire, FirebaseListObservabl} from "angularfire2";

@Component({
  selector: 'sh-accuracy',
  templateUrl: './accuracy.html',
  styleUrls: ['./accuracy.css']
})
export class AccuracyComponent implements OnInit {
  private prevents = [];
  private cures: FirebaseListObservable<any>;
  private angularFire;
  constructor(af: AngularFire) {
    this.angularFire = af;
```

```
  }
  ngOnInit() {
    this.angularFire.database
      .list('/Accuracy/prevents')
      .subscribe(data => {
        this.prevents = data
      })
  }
}
```

This component reads the items available in the /Accuracy/prevents object and saves them in the prevents private property for future use. That is how preventions are handled, but the cure is a bit more complex and needs its own service. We will see how to deal with it soon.

Now add this component to the application module:

```
// src/app/app.module.ts
import {AccuracyComponent} from "./accuracy/accuracy.component";
//...
  declarations: [ //...
    AccuracyComponent
  ],
//...
```

And make sure that it is defined inside the application routes as well:

```
// src/app/app.routes.ts
import {AccuracyComponent} from "./accuracy/accuracy.component";
//...
export const rootRouterConfig: Routes = [ //...
  {path: 'accuracy', component: AccuracyComponent},
];
```

Now we need to add a view for this component and make it read cure and prevention properties from the component.

The accuracy manager view

As we mentioned before, the view consists of two tables. In the Prevention table, we loop through the preventions property and assemble a list of preventions that are already in place, their location, and also the number of times that they have been called during the application execution:

```
# src/app/accuracy/accuracy.html
<div class="container">
  <div class="row">
    <div class="col-md-6">
      <div class="panel panel-default">
        <div class="panel-heading">Prevention</div>
        <div class="panel-body">
          <p>This is where we prevent incidents in our application</p>
        </div>
        <!-- Table -->
        <table class="table">
          <thead><tr>
            <th>#</th> <th>Description</th> <th>Hits</th>
          </tr></thead>
          <tbody>
          <tr *ngFor="let p of prevents; let i=index">
            <th scope="row">{{i+1}}</th>
            <td>
              <span class="desc">p.description</span><br>
              <span class="file">p.loc</span>
              <span class="line_no">p.line</span>
            </td>
            <td>p.hits</td>
          </tr>
          </tbody>
        </table>
      </div>
    </div>
  #...
```

As we mentioned before, we will get into how to assemble an array of prevents objects soon. We will use a service to create the prevents array.

The second part of the view involves looping through the cures collected from the Firebase database and assembling table rows accordingly:

```
# src/app/accuracy/accuracy.html
  #...
    <div class="col-md-6">
      <div class="panel panel-default">
```

```
          <div class="panel-heading">
            Cure
            <button type="button" class="btn btn-default btn-xs pull-right"
(click)="newCure()">
                <span class="glyphicon glyphicon-plus" aria-
hidden="true"></span>
            </button>
          </div>
          <div class="panel-body">
            <p>This is where we cure incidents in our application</p>
          </div>
          <!-- Table -->
          <table class="table">
            <thead><tr>
              <th>#</th> <th>Description</th> <th></th>
            </tr></thead>
            <tbody>
            <tr *ngFor="let c of cures; let i=index">
              <th scope="row">{{c.$key}}</th>
              <td contenteditable="true" (keyup.enter)=
                  "editCure(c.$key, $event)"> c.description</td>
              <td>
                <button class="btn btn-default btn-xs pull-right"
                        type="button" (click)="deleteCure(c.$key)">
                  <span class="glyphicon glyphicon-remove"
                  aria-hidden="true"></span>
                </button>
              </td></tr></tbody>
          </table>
        </div>
      </div>
    </div>
</div>
```

As we can see, we have three functions to handle creating, editing, and deleting the cures. So let's edit the Component and add these functions:

```
// src/app/accuracy/accuracy.component.ts
//...
export class AccuracyComponent implements OnInit {
  //...
  newCure() {
    this.cures.push({description:'new cure'})
  }
  editCure(id, event) {
    this.cures.update(id, {description: event.target.outerText}):
  }
  deleteCure(id) {
```

```
    this.cures.remove(id);
  }
}
```

There is nothing new about creating and deleting a cure. In creation, we just push a new object to the database with 'new cure' as its description property and for deleting an object we just pass its ID to the remove() function and let it do its job. But editing a current cure is a little different.

Notice how we used the contenteditable="true" propery inside the <td> tag to be able to do inline editing.

We are using the (keyup.enter) event binder to catch the enter key and pass it on to the editCure() function where it uses the inline text and the cure ID to apply changes in Firebase.

Let's test the application so far and see how it works. As we know, there are two defects found in the reporting component. There is an article with 250k characters and there is another one with five characters.

So we need a cure alert to check the article lengths and see if they are within an acceptable range. Let's add a new entry for this situation by clicking on the plus button:

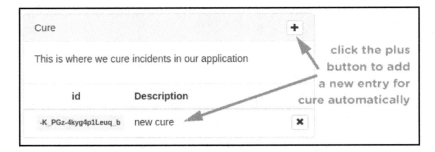

Now we can edit the contents in this entry by clicking on its description column:

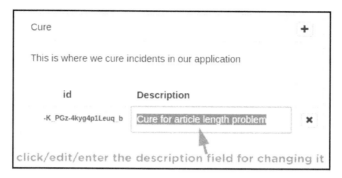

Having the first cure entry in place, now we can get on with implementation and use it in places where it is more needed.

The accuracy service

Implementing the prevention is not as easy as the cures. In other words, we cannot use a Firebase object and hold everything over there. Instead we have to use a service to keep track of implemented cures – called prevention, because when they are in place, their role is to prevent something bad from happening.

Take the current noted cure, for example: it says we want to see if an article is within an acceptable range. So if we implement that mechanism inside the Evidence service and keep an eye on how that service deals with defects, we accomplish two major goals.

First, we have the chance to weed out the problematic articles. This is not a big deal, in fact we could do that by adding a simple condition check in the evidence service and we wouldn't need to implement another service to do that for us.

Second, we can analyze the URL related to that problematic article and find out why we ended up with extra long or extra short content and THAT is what we can't accomplish with a simple condition check. In fact that is how the accuracy manager service becomes handy.

What we are trying to accomplish here is not only preventing an issue, but also having a chance to investigate it.

So the job of accuracy manager is to take a snapshot of the problem and collect all evidences around the situation. Later we will use those facts to find out why that bug happened and how we can fix it.

To begin with, create the last injectable service and add the following code to it:

```
// src/app/accuracy/accuracy.service.ts
import {Injectable} from '@angular/core';
import {preventions} from '../app.module'

@Injectable()
export class AccuracyService {
  private prevents = preventions;
  constructor() {}

  takeSnapshot(id, description, file, line, variables) {
    // ToDo: if id exists increment the hit count and push vars to
    // the var array else add the new id with its properties to
    // the preventions global variable
  }

  getPrevents() {
    return this.prevents;
  }
}
```

This service can be called all over the applications by various components and services. That is why we need a global variable to keep track of prevention calls. So while adding this new service to the list of providers in the application module, let's define the preventions variable over there as well:

```
// src/app/app.module.ts
import {AccuracyService} from "./accuracy/accuracy.service";
// ...
export let preventions = [];

@NgModule({
  //...
  providers   : [ //...
    AccuracyService
  ]
})
//...
```

Next let's implement the `takeSnapshot()` function:

```
// src/app/accuracy/accuracy.service.ts
//...
   takeSnapshot(id, description, file, line, variables) {
     if (preventions.length == 0){
       preventions.push({
         id:id, description:description, file:file,
         line:line, hits:1, variables:[variables]
       })
     } else {
       let p = (preventions.find( item => item.id == id));
       if (p){
         p.hits++;
         p.variables.push(variables);
       } else {
         preventions.push({
           id:id, description:description, file:file,
           line:line, hits:1, variables:[variables]
         });
       }
     }
   }
```

This function takes five input parameters and increases the hit counter if there was a match for a previously applied prevention or creates a new array element for it, in case it was unique.

The `find()` function returns an array element in case there is a match for the ID or returns an 'undefined' value if a match is not found.

As we will see during the implementation, we will use the current Firebase IDs for the Cures object as the input ID for this function. That way we can establish a direct connection between each pending cure and the implemented prevention.

The 'file', 'line', and 'description' parameters should be self explanatory. We are just going to use them to point out where the prevention was called. Perhaps the most important input parameter here is the 'variables'. This parameter is an array of key/value objects, in which keys are holding the variable names and in which values are used for saving their values at the moment when an incident happened. By looping through the 'variables' parameter and analyzing its elements we learn more about the cause of each incident so we can provide a solution for it.

Implementing the first prevention

Based on the current cure note, we need to look into our Evidence service code and put the prevention mechanism over there. As the cure description suggests, we need to prevent any article that is too short or too long from being persisted to the Firebase.

So let's add another global constant to the application module and define what we mean by article length boundaries:

```
// src/app/app.module.ts
//...
export const articleRange = {min: 100, max: 10000};
//...
```

Now import this new constant and the Accuracy service to the Evidence service and set up the news constructor and private variables for it:

```
// src/app/evidence/evidence.service.ts
import {articleRange} from "../app.module";
import {AccuracyService} from "../accuracy/accuracy.service";
//...
@Injectable()
export class EvidenceService {
  //...
  private accuracy;
  constructor( //...
    as: AccuracyService) {
    //...
    this.accuracy = as;
  }
  //...
}
```

Now let's find out where an article is processed and added to the corpus. As we can see, the wordAnalyzer() function is behind all of the processing. The moment it finds that the article private variable has a value it blindly goes through the process of evaluating words and adds them to the corpus. Let's tweak the previous logic as follows:

```
// src/app/evidence/evidence.service.ts
//...
  wordAnalyzer(url) {
    return this.getArticle(this.getYahooQueryUrl(url))
      .subscribe( data => {
        this.resetCounters();
        this.findKey(data, 'content');
        if (this.article.length < articleRange.min ||
          this.article.length > articleRange.max) {
```

```
            this.accuracy.takeSnapshot(
                '-K_PGziSD-d53wQRrEM1',
                'Cure for article length problem',
                'evidence.service.ts', 77,
                [{url: url}, {data: data}]
            )
        }
        else {
            this.evaluateWords( // normalizeWords
                this.countInstances(
                    this.extractWords(this.article)
                )
            ).then(data => {
                this.corpus.push(
                    {article:this.article,link:url,bag_of_words:data});
            })
        }
    });
    }
//...
```

As we see here, the heavy calculations stop the very moment that length of article falls outside of the acceptable range. At the same time we take a snapshot of the situation and pass the current value of local variables to the Accuracy service to find out what just happened.

 The question here is, why do we have too many hard-coded values as parameters of the takeSnapshot() function? We have no other choice for the cure id and description. But why are we not using JavaScript's Error object? As we know this object has properties such as lineNumber and fileName, which have exactly what we are looking for.
Please don't do that, according to official documents:
https://developer.mozilla.org/en-US/docs/Web/JavaScript/Reference/Global_Objects/Error/lineNumber

These properties are non-standard and won't work for everyone. Besides they might be removed in the future.

Running the code with the prevention mechanism

Looking at the Evidence code, we see that the `wordAnalyzer()` function is called in two places. Inside the Evidence view, when we click on a suggested link or enter a URL for investigation, that click actually triggers the `onSelect()` function inside the Component, which ultimately calls the `wordAnalyzer()` only once:

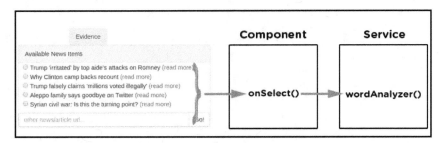

The Component call causes one entry to be saved in the corpus. But inside the service there is another reference to the `wordAnalyzer()` function. Around line 273, the `fetchLink()` function calls `wordAnalyzer()` several times (for multiple time spans for each keyword). That means we are facing multiple calls and we will spend a lot of processing power on that. So if our prevention mechanism does its job properly, we can save a noticeable amount of processing time.

So let's nominate main keyword (Mars) and a few other keywords (water, radiation, transport) and see how the application handles the request.

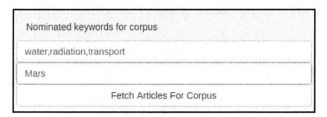

The first thing to notice is the speed. If you remember from the Evidence chapter, usually it takes a few minutes to process all links for the given time spans. Now everything is processed almost within a minute. That means that there should be a couple of preventions that save the processing time. Let's have a look at the Accuracy page and see what we have there:

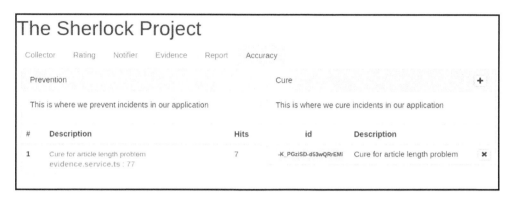

It says that our prevention mechanism was hit seven times and that there is a snapshot of the variables saved in the preventions global variable.

Please note that you might get different results depending on the keywords you have set in the Evidence page. But the point is that the prevention mechanism should be hit a few times.

We can continue on developing the view for Accuracy manager and showing the contents of each snapshot in the view. But to keep things simple, let's check out the variables in the console by adding a log command at the end of takeSnapshot().

It turns out that the first prevention hit was made by a link pointing to the Accor Hotel website and it seems that there is an array of 62 paragraphs (<p> elements) as the contents of that link. No wonder the contents exceeded the boundary that we have defined inside the application module. Simply by visiting the prevented link we will see that it was hit by our application, just because the word *Mars* was part of the hotel name:

And later it was detected by our prevention mechanism just because there was a long list of guest comments on that page, complaining or praising the hotel services.

On the other hand, we can investigate the articles with null contents and see why they ended that way. For example, the findKey() function in the Evidence service is in charge of extracting contents from each link:

```
// src/app/evidence/evidence.service.ts
//...
@Injectable()
export class EvidenceService {
  //...
  findKey(object, string) {
    for (var key in object) {
      if (object[key] && typeof(object[key]) == "object") {
        this.findKey(object[key], string);
      } else if (
        key == string ||
        typeof (key) == "string" &&
        key != 'class' &&
        key != 'id' &&
        key != 'href'
      ) {
        this.article += object[key]+' ';
      }
    }
  }
  //...
}
```

This `findKey()` is a recursive function that parses the big JSON object returned by the query and looks for 'content' properties.

This function drills down to the JSON structure until there is no lower level and only then if the type of the bottom key is string and it is not one of 'class', 'id', or 'href' values, then it is considered as the contents that we are interested in. So if a link returns empty contents, that means we either hit an empty page or we need to add more logic to include more DOM elements with valid contents.

Now that we know how the prevention mechanism works, we can nominate more cure options for various pages and implement the related prevention blocks whenever they are needed. We can think about scenarios where we expect something but it is not happening. For example, the number of results returned by our Google Custom Search Engine can be another good scenario. In other words, if we make 500 queries, then we might expect at least 400 valid responses (these numbers are just examples and we can fine tune them to get optimum results).

So if the number of responses is below 400 then there might be an issue with the code that blocks the expected results and we can put a prevention mechanism in front of those issues.

Summary

In this chapter, we learned about how to add cure and prevention codes inside the application and save the programming resources by halting undesired situations.

We saw how to use global variables exported from the application module in order to store local variables and analyze their contents on demand.

We implemented a snapshot collector function to investigate the reasons of an incident and work on solutions based on the given situation. We saw how that snapshot function revealed the URLs pointing to an irrelevant website (Accor Hotels) with irrelevant contents (hotel guest comments).

With those basic principals now we can expand the prevention mechanisms to all concepts provided in this book. For example we can use them for content extraction, number of valid HTTP requests and so on.

We used the Sherlock Project as a platform to study Angular Services and how we can manage data flow with them. Now it is your turn to take the current project to the next level, by adding all bells and whistles that you can imagine to it.

Index